Breaking the Bronze Ceiling

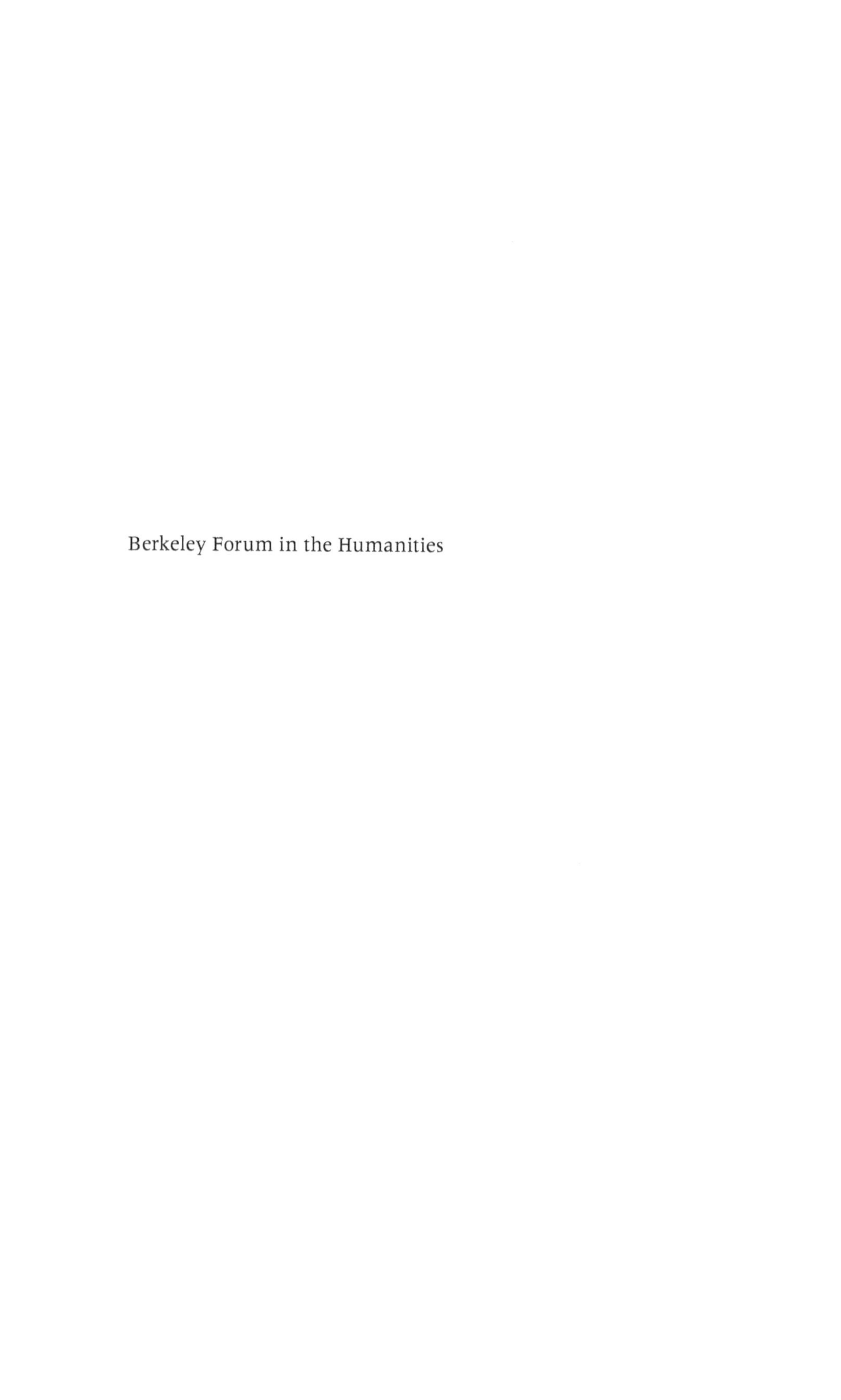

Berkeley Forum in the Humanities

Breaking the Bronze Ceiling

Women, Memory, and Public Space

Edited by Valentina Rozas-Krause
and Andrew M. Shanken

Townsend Center for the Humanities
University of California, Berkeley

Fordham University Press
New York

Library of Congress Cataloging-in-Publication Data is available.

Printed in the United States of America

25 24 23   5 4 3 2 1

First edition

Contents

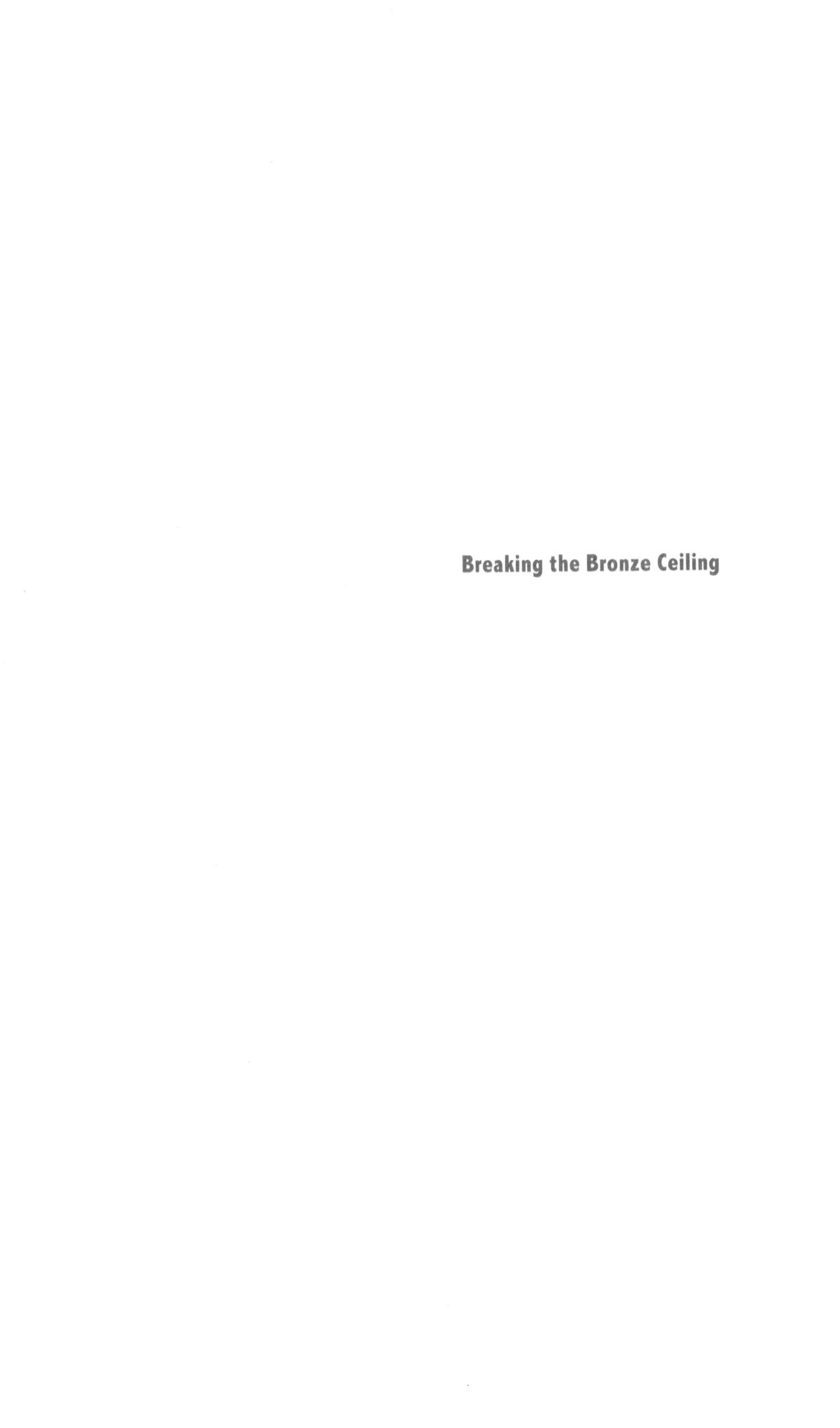

Breaking the Bronze Ceiling

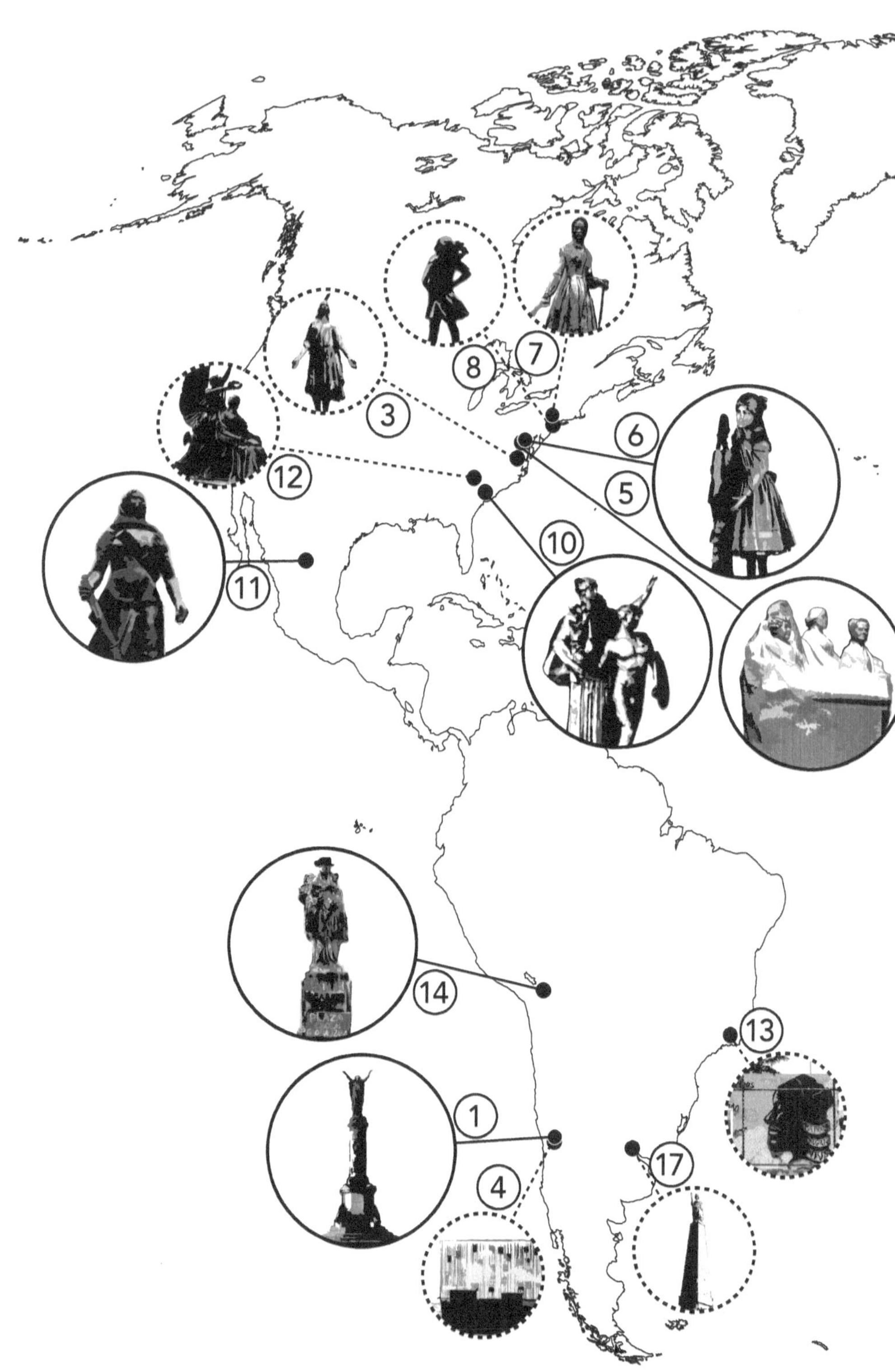

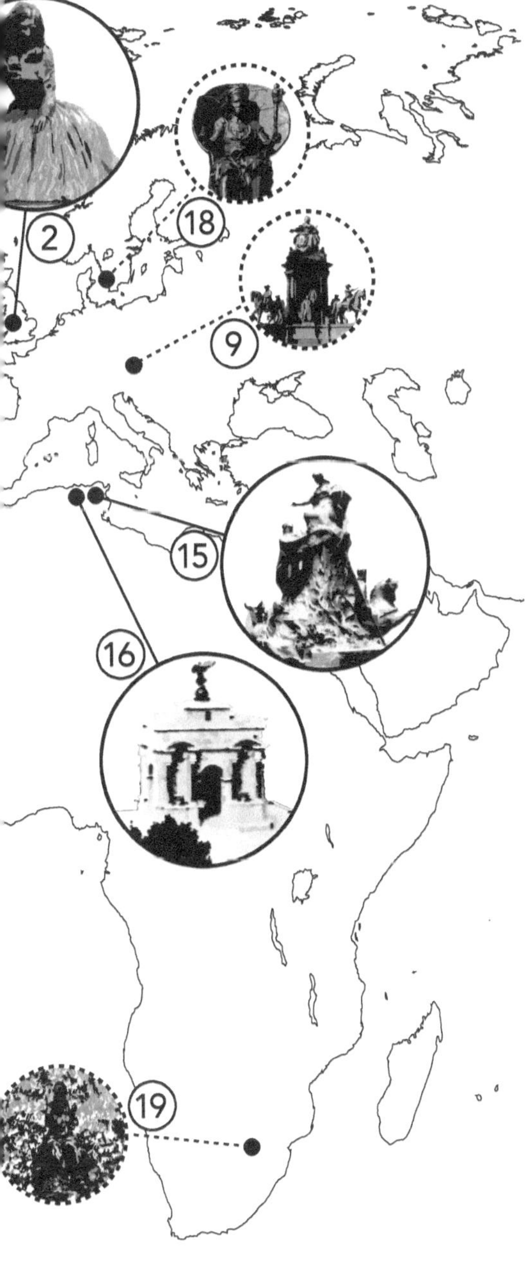

1. La Dolorosa—Santiago, Chile
2. George Elliot Statue—Nuneaton, United Kingdom
3. Pocahontas Memorial Statue—Williamsburg, Virginia
4. Monument to the Women Victims of Political Repression—Santiago, Chile
5. Portrait Monument—Washington, District of Columbia
6. Helen Keller—Washington, District of Columbia
7. Sojourner Truth Statue—Highland, New York
8. The Fearless Girl—New York, New York
9. Monument to the Empress Maria-Theresia—Vienna, Austria
10. Confederate Defenders of Charleston—Charleston, South Carolina
11. La Adelita—Torreón, Coahuila
12. Monument to the South Carolina Women of the Confederacy—Columbia, South Carolina
13. Memorial to the Black Mothers of the Periphery Fighting against State Terrorism—Rio de Janeiro, Brazil
14. Plaza Chola Globalizada—La Paz, Bolivia
15. Model for monument "to the glory of France and the Protectorate"—Tunis, Tunisia
16. Mont Sidi M'Cid—Constantine, Algeria
17. Plaza de Mayo—Buenos Aires, Argentina
18. I am Queen Mary—Copenhagen, Denmark
19. Patience on a Monument—Johannesburg, South Africa

Map by Amelia Hansen

Valentina Rozas-Krause and Andrew M. Shanken

Introduction

TO SAY THAT women are underrepresented in the memorial landscape is a gross understatement. According to a recent audit of monuments in the United States performed by Monument Lab, of the "top 50 individuals recorded in US monuments," only 6 percent represent women. Abraham Lincoln is the most monumentalized figure, with 193 statues, while only three individual women—Joan of Arc, Harriet Tubman, and Sacagawea—make the list. In total, these three women account for 67 statues in the country, which is barely more than the disgraced Robert E. Lee, who at the time of the audit (2021) was still the subject of 59 monuments.[1] The situation outside of the United States is no better. A recent survey of 16 cities in Chile discovered that only 4.7 percent of the monuments there are dedicated to women.[2] In the United Kingdom, a paltry 2.7 percent of statues are to non-royal or historical women.[3] In response, memory activists and cities around the world are grappling with the striking gender disparity of their commemorative infrastructure by adding monuments to women. But much of the new work has invited brutal criticism. The Mary Wollstonecraft statue in London (Maggi Hambling, 2020) was called a "shambolic mess" and "ejaculatory" and likened to a Rolls Royce hood ornament.[4] Critic Jerry Saltz called the *Medusa with the Head of Perseus* in New York City (Luciano Garbati, 2020) an "ooh-la-la monstrosity" and condemned her "shaved pudenda." She is "dead, optically inert, intellectually barren."[5] Clearly something is going wrong, not just with the statues but also with how we talk about them. The issue goes beyond age-old dilemmas of how to depict women's bodies. A plan for a Maya Angelou monument in San Francisco would have circumvented these issues by biting a portrait of her face into a nine-foot-tall bronze "book" and thrusting it mid-sidewalk next to the public library.[6] The project was scuttled originally because its non-figurative elements displeased a female city supervisor. Although it was finally approved, women cannot win and neither can their memorials.

As cities have endeavored to add statues of women, their efforts, however noble, have been forced. Part of this is a failure to match new forms of commemoration with a vivid artistic language. Cities have turned to bronze and other traditional materials, mostly in emulation of male statuary. The prevailing way to figure a woman in public space is through realism, a mode marginalized by modernism generations ago and kept alive most actively in conservative art practice or kitsch. Artists are seldom taught to model human form in bronze in leading art schools or to think out how to represent women realistically. The result is that the figures themselves are unconvincing, old-fashioned, maudlin, or hackneyed. Precious few engage in any meaningful way with contemporary art practice. Many are widely panned as art. The obvious response to this criticism of the quality of memorials to women is that cities are filled to the brim with appalling statues to men, but it has never stopped them from being made. It has also not stopped them from being appreciated by the wider public, even as they are sometimes condemned by elites.[7] We hope the chapters and cases in this volume open up the possibility of taking memorials seriously, no matter their aesthetic merit. In fact, it is a vital part of the story that statues to women are often created not by elites for elites but by common people for common people. In fact, this idea is foundational to several of the chapters and cases. Some of the most sentimental and tired commemorative work has garnered a fierce international following of women.

Almost as a compensatory reaction to the dilemmas of representation, female figures are channeled into a narrow range of possibilities. They are passive and often rendered in tortured poses. Artists try to hide their backsides, clothe them generously, surround them with domestic objects, or distract them with some activity. Every one of the statues in the *Boston Women's Memorial* (Meredith Bergmann, 2003)

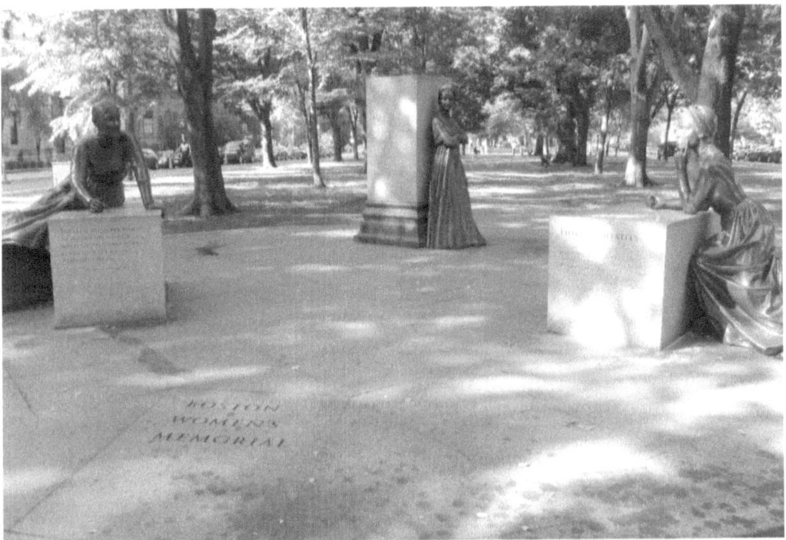

Figure 1. *Boston Women's Memorial*, Meredith Bergmann, 2003. Bob Linsdell, photographer.

suffers from this problem (figure 1). Phillis Wheatley kneels strangely at a horizontal granite block, chin on fist, with feather poised as if at her desk, the long folds of her dress protecting her modesty. Her companion, Lucy Stone, has lifted herself partly onto another horizontal block, twisting her body while her feet dangle improbably on another smaller block, as she tries to write. Anyone who has ever written for more than two minutes knows the painful cost of this pose. The third woman, Abigail Adams, stands oddly with her back against a vertical granite block. Who knows why. This is realism in the service of three totally unrealistic poses.

To insist on representing women in this literal way dramatically limits aesthetic possibilities. Yet representation is only part of the problem. The Boston memorial is conceptually undercooked: having chosen figuration, the monument had to communicate in other ways. Hence the granite blocks, which speak for the laconic women. The bronze needed help. In fact, it is unclear what work the statues are doing. In monuments, feminism seems to be fifty years behind contemporary thought and even farther behind artistic practice. In Boston, the fact of the monument aligns with First Wave Feminism, while aesthetically the statues date back to the statuemania of the nineteenth century. A quick comparison to Adelaide Johnson's marble *Portrait Monument to Lucretia Mott, Elizabeth Cady Stanton and Susan B. Anthony*, begun in 1886 (and discussed by Lauren Kroiz in chapter 3), shows just how little ideas have advanced. It is not at all clear what sort of commemorative forms Fourth Wave Feminism might generate, if any. The very premise of the statue is now troubling. Understandably, suffrage memorials proliferated around the centenary of the Nineteenth Amendment in 2020. Suffrage quickly became an uncontroversial subject matter for commemoration and this made it too easy. After all, who is against women voting! With self-congratulatory memorials like these, the work has already been done: they cannot challenge, unnerve, or press for structural change in a society where women remain unequal. In breaking the bronze ceiling, suffrage memorials may inadvertently obscure the persistence of the glass ceiling, among other inequalities women face.

This book is an attempt to begin to sort out how we arrived at this current state of affairs. Its contributions range across cultures, geographies, and time periods to explore dilemmas of gender and representation in light of materiality, urban agendas and national traditions, activism, and a range of other issues, all pivoting around cultural memory. It takes on the politics of who gets memorialized and where, while plumbing traditions of public statuary, from Marians and Virgins to handmaidens and helpers, Victories, Liberties, and other allegorical figures that can be found throughout the world. Simultaneously, it raises questions about the relationship between allegorical women and historical women in memorials. Taking the cultural landscape in its broadest form, it considers the gross motor movements of memory—the monuments—alongside subtler or more ephemeral gestures such as commemorative practices, toponyms, plaques, performance, and protests. Finally, it illuminates the historical role of women as memory activists (see chapter 5 by Nathaniel Robert Walker and Dell Upton's case, which explore the work of the women of the Confederacy), while turning a critical eye to the terms of debate. These issues are urgent. As the glut of statues to great men is being reconsidered, moved, or taken down, a parade of great women are poised to replace them. The majority of the chapters elaborate on papers delivered in sessions we chaired at the Society of Architectural Historians conference in 2020 and the College Art Association conference in 2021. Interspersed between these chapters are shorter essays (cases) about specific monuments and memorials.

"Breaking the Bronze Ceiling" refers to the feminist term that became increasingly popular in the mid-1980s after the *Wall Street*

Journal published the "The Glass Ceiling: Why Women Can't Seem to Break the Invisible Barrier That Blocks Them from the Top Jobs."[8] Unlike the glass ceiling, the bronze ceiling is blatantly visible, as the recent monument audits demonstrate. It is not surprising, however, that feminists have eschewed monumental machismo. The relentless struggle for voting, reproductive rights, and workplace equality, paralleled by a consistent rise of violence and discrimination against women and those who identify with them, has pushed the subject of this book to the back burner. Only recently have the astonishing statistics of female representation made headlines, most prominently as the anti-racism movement of 2020 began to bring down a wide array of public monuments as a way of dismantling the legacies of slavery, colonialism, and misogyny.

The book borrows "Breaking the Bronze Ceiling" from a Kentucky-based campaign to build a monument in Lexington to celebrate the 100th anniversary of the passage of the Nineteenth Amendment.[9] The resulting suffragette monument unveiled in Lexington (Barbara Grygutis, 2020) is not made out of bronze but aluminum, and this brings home the fact that bronze is a metaphor for permanence and prestige. It is aspirational for something that women have often been denied. For example, the *Women's Rights Pioneers Monument* (Meredith Bergmann, 2020) on the mall in Central Park, New York City, also unveiled for the centenary of women's suffrage, is bronze and depicts Sojourner Truth, Elizabeth Cady Stanton, and Susan B. Anthony gathered around a coffee table (figure 2). The logic was to make it fit in this monumental axis of the nineteenth-century park, which prescribed figurative bronze as its medium.[10] It belongs to a type, the bronzed photograph, but while early photography shares a commemorative link with sculpture, it is an improbable and awkward subject, especially for a bronze in a park. Even in the nineteenth century, Mariana Griswold Van Rensselaer, a leading American architecture critic of the period, had discredited such artifice as "sadly out of place."[11] While we admire the efforts of women-led monument groups working on the ground to close the monumental gap, this book aims to take a step back from conceiving monumental inequality as a bronze ceiling.

Borrowing the concept of "breaking the bronze ceiling," then, pays homage to the various feminists, activists, and artists who have used it before, while playing with the double meaning of "breaking." The monumental tradition is broken. It painfully reveals how women have been neglected, ignored, oppressed, mistreated, and underestimated. To think in terms of bronze ties female representation to the tired yet

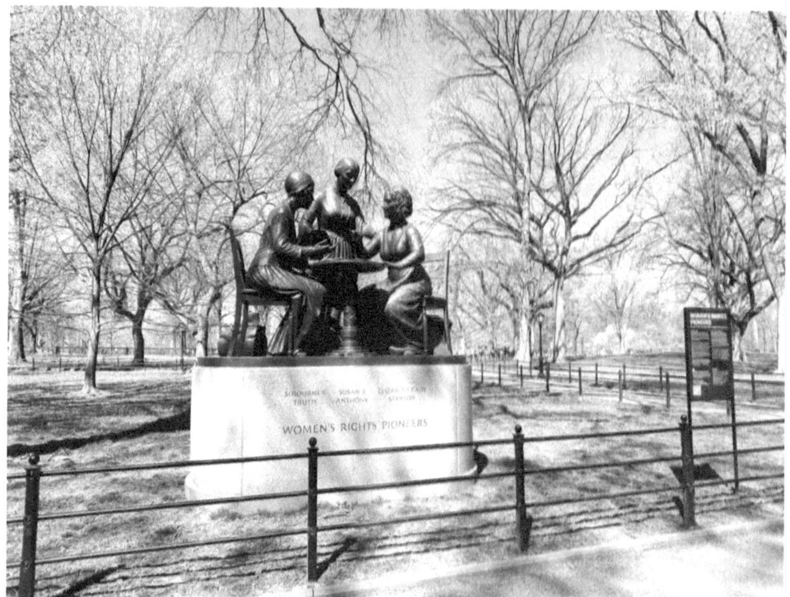

Figure 2. *Women's Rights Pioneers Monument*, Meredith Bergmann, 2020, Central Park, New York City. Jonathan Etkin, photographer.

dominant tradition of monuments to "dead white men," imposing a limiting condition that makes women's contributions intelligible by reference to men and whiteness. In order to fix this inequality, it is necessary to think beyond the bronze ceiling, to encourage women to forge their own commemorative languages, regardless of their male counterparts, and possibly to think beyond commemoration.

Monuments to women are often countermonuments to male monuments, rejoinders in the dominant memorial landscape. They carry a dialectical burden with male representation. By contrast, monuments to men rarely have to contemplate or compete with monuments to women. Rather than evening the score, breaking the bronze ceiling should mean moving beyond this burden. One might think that powerful women could be memorialized on their own terms, yet when figures of powerful women appear in public spaces, they are frequently not historical women (excepting monarchs; see Mechtild Widrich's case), or they are only nominally women. The *Fearless Girl* on Wall Street in New York City is a poignant example (see Marita Sturken's case). Why is a little bronze girl staring down the charging bull of capitalism? The trope of the naive moxie of innocents becomes a charming gesture, a laugh. We all know the bull wins. In a similar mode, why is Helen Keller represented as a child, instead of as a grown woman, socialist, and political activist in the mostly male National Statuary Hall, as Sierra Rooney explores in chapter 4? Even a historical figure like Joan of Arc raises intriguing issues. Formidable, armored, and mounted on a horse, as so many powerful men have been commemorated, the "Maid of Orléans" is ambiguously feminine. She is masculinized, canonized, aestheticized, and frozen between childhood and womanhood. She is the Fearless Girl graduated to virginal adolescence. The historical Joan, moreover, has morphed into a mythic figure with none of the qualities to remind us that monument and monster share an etymological root in the Latin *monere*. She scares no one, warns of nothing, and is reduced to civic ornament, thus fulfilling another exhausted womanly role. Some of the chapters and cases in this book explore the veiled bonds that tether female representation to its male counterpart or to masculine cultures of war, politics, and colonization, narrowing its existence, while others explore possibilities beyond this binary.

Like bronze, gender requires a similar hesitation. Even as this book has taken shape, concepts of gender have been shifting, reminding us that we need to avoid fixing it biologically or assigning universal meaning to it. In other words, breaking the bronze ceiling might open up wider questions about gender in memory studies and make common cause with other underrepresented people, as Amanda Su explores in chapter 2. With this in mind, our understanding of gender is intentionally flexible and non-binary.

Part of the problem is subject matter. Pietàs, mothers and handmaidens, victims and virgins, innocents and allegories are all common, but female heroes, warriors, moral giants, and titans of culture are rare. Even to state it this way, however, goes straight to the absurdity of the problem. The range of acceptable topics and types of monuments to women confines the field from the start. At the same time, the standard types of monuments to men create unhelpful and sometimes comical false equivalencies. Honorable or heroic death eludes women, who are memorialized in death most often as victims. Likewise, there is no easy equivalent to the numerous traditions of male heroism in memorials and monuments. Notable exceptions can be found in African monuments, particularly in representations of female Benin warriors.

Each of the monumental types presents its own dilemma. Pietàs are arguably the *Urmodel* for women's commemorative work, with Käthe

Kollwitz's example in the Neue Wache in Berlin being one of the most well-known (figure 3). These passive figures, usually seated, suggest that women are mourners or vessels of memory but not active agents or memorable themselves (see Daniel Herwitz's case). Pietàs, moreover, pair passivity with pathos, fixing women in stereotypical realms of emotion. Through Michelangelo's *Pietà* (1499), a sculpture of Mary holding Christ after the Crucifixion, this standard type is linked to mothers and virgins. It is not surprising then that women are also commonly represented as mothers, whether symbolic or literal. The French Revolutionary Marianne, for instance, is an allegory of nation, but as Richard Sennett has argued, this was a complicated image: a Greco-Roman goddess but with a body that "tended to the fuller domestic form of a young mother" and overtly evoking the Virgin. This virginal mother's bare breasts were "an image of revolutionary nourishment" and purity, behind which revolutionary violence could hide (see Fernando Luis Martínez Nespral's case).[12] When this figure was transposed to the French colonies in North Africa, the meaning was further complicated, as Daniel E. Coslett argues in chapter 7. The many statues of pioneer mothers with their children that dot the western United States celebrate stoic endurance. It is hard to imagine comparable monuments to men. Pioneer men abound, of course, but they break land, subdue natives, and gaze boldly into the future, rifles in hand. The occasional pioneer woman who takes up arms, as one at the Kansas State Capital does (Robert Merrill Gage, 1937), sits with a baby in one arm and an older son sheltered by her other arm (figure 4). Stalwart and dignified, nonetheless she is a pietà with a gun who begs the question: what happened to her man? Both Marianne and most pioneer women are abstractions or types, not real women.

Following from the Kansas example, women are commonly figured as handmaidens, helpers, and caregivers. The *Vietnam Women's Memorial* in Washington, D.C. (Glenna Goodacre, 1993), turns the handmaiden into a pietà. It picks up on a common war memorial type popularized by World War I: fallen men held by women, again riffing on Michelangelo's sculpture. Here the action is done and the women are left to clean up the mess. It is striking how this type appears across cultures. As Tania Gutiérrez-Monroy's chapter 6 reveals, in Mexico women warriors who actively fought in the Revolution were remembered as handmaidens, the domestics who fed the men and kept camp. In a completely different context, memorials to brick gatherers in post–World War II Germany are represented as helpers or urban housekeepers, cleaning up the rubble that the men made in war. Even

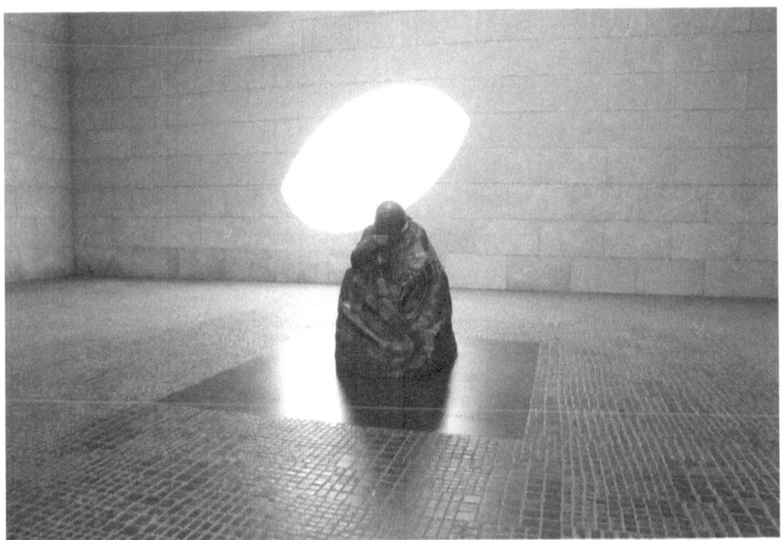

Figure 3. Käthe Kollwitz, *Mother with Her Dead Son* (1937–38), placed inside the Neue Wache in Berlin, 1993. Fred Romero, photographer.

Harriet Tubman, who is often depicted more actively, is a helper, and this might be part of the secret to her appeal.

Another common trope is woman-as-victim. Here a powerless woman is tossed in the mighty storms of world events. Even monuments to women who played active, if not violent, roles in history fall back on this type. The *Monument to the Partisan Woman* in Venice (Leoncillo Leoncilli, sculptor, 1955, in a setting designed by Carlo Scarpa) exemplifies the type (figure 5). In contrast to monuments to male partisans in Italy, who surge or fall heroically, the Venice *partigiana* is but a pathetic dead body washed up on the shore. Her defenseless body was not enough to protect her: the original polychromatic ceramic sculpture was brutalized in 1961 and only a stump remained.[13] More recently, the restored *Partisan* was embroiled in scandal when a half-nude tourist swam in the harbor, climbed on top of the *Partisan*, and imitated her pose.[14] To be sure, monuments of all kinds are desecrated, but statues of women endure strikingly different forms of mistreatment. Forms of representation activate modes of reception and iconoclasm.

Of course, Virgins are a type unto themselves, one that blends easily with other forms of statuary. Mary's miracle is that she is simul-

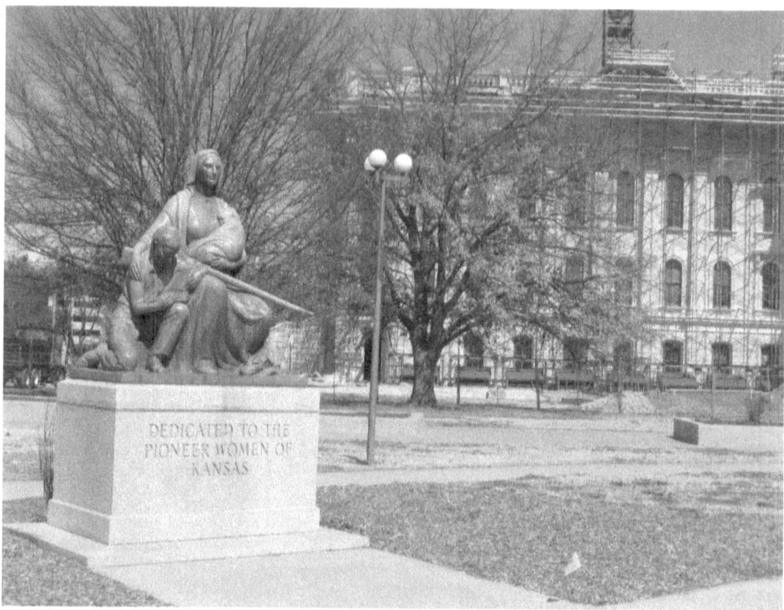

Figure 4. Pioneer women memorial, Robert Merrill Gage, 1937, Kansas State Capitol. Laura Perkins Cox, photographer.

taneously virgin and vessel, innocent and handmaiden, human and quasi-divine, victim and survivor, historical and allegorical. Anything can be mapped onto Mary, as Pía Montealegre's contribution vividly demonstrates (chapter 1). Having one foot in history and another in mythology, Mary reveals how allegories are often reserved for powerful women, who tend not to be represented directly as real women. Men have employed allegorical women, moreover, to speak about their grand historical doings, making them ciphers (see chapter 8 by Susan Slyomovics). Allegories of Peace and Liberty, for instance, soften or veil war, revolution, and conquest. Yet allegories of women pull in two directions. They idealize women, creating a distance from reality that opens up the possibility of depicting powerful women, but then they are often nude, making them vulnerable and open to the gaze. As in Hollywood, women lose their clothes in memorials far more often than men do. While in some times and places, nudity is not necessarily lascivious or even sexual, the hand-shined surfaces of sculpted breasts attest to their sexualization. Poor Juliet in Verona—child, innocent, victim, virgin—has posed with her gropers, male and female, for decades. Even when they are dressed, female statues are

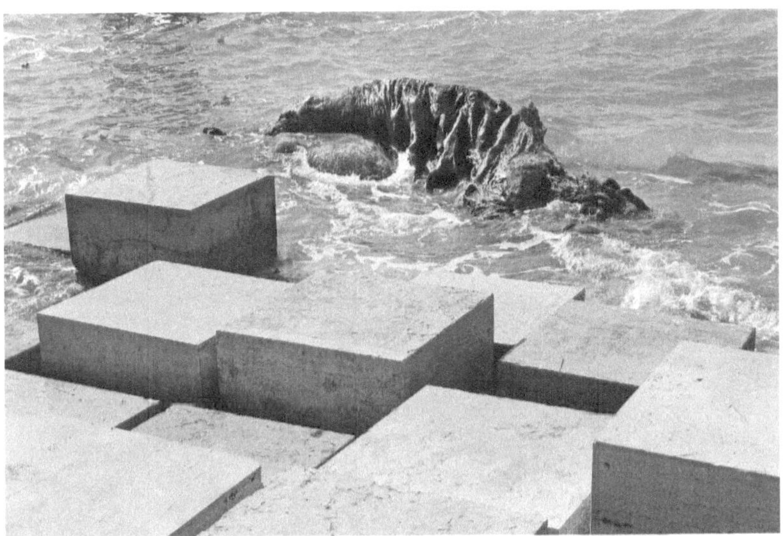

Figure 5. *Monument to the Partisan Woman* in Venice. Leoncillo Leoncilli, sculptor, 1955, in a setting designed by architect Carlo Scarpa. Jean-Pierre Dalbéra, photographer.

often clothed again by visitors, suggesting how vulnerable they appear to passersby (see Ana María León's case).

Monuments are also dedicated to minor female civic leaders, an overlooked type of commemorative work. These are usually modest statues erected as countermonuments to more prominent monuments to men nearby. They appear almost always as a form of urban ornament. Inoffensive, even trivial, they follow all the rules of urban decorum. The Lillian Feinstein monument in Providence, Rhode Island, competes with a monumental equestrian statue of General Ambrose Burnside and stands directly across from a more intimate statue of Major Henry Harrison Young, both Civil War heroes (figure 6). Where Young's achievement is extensively explained in a plaque, Feinstein is but a name and a face in bas-relief, with no mention in online sites dedicated to the park and Providence memorials. In form and placement, monuments like this are incidental and thus forgettable, which means they work against their very commemorative purpose. And, returning to a theme above, these minor civic leaders convey the quiet message that women are marginal, adjunct, less memorable. This is a paradox, perhaps, that the very project of breaking the bronze ceiling brings out.

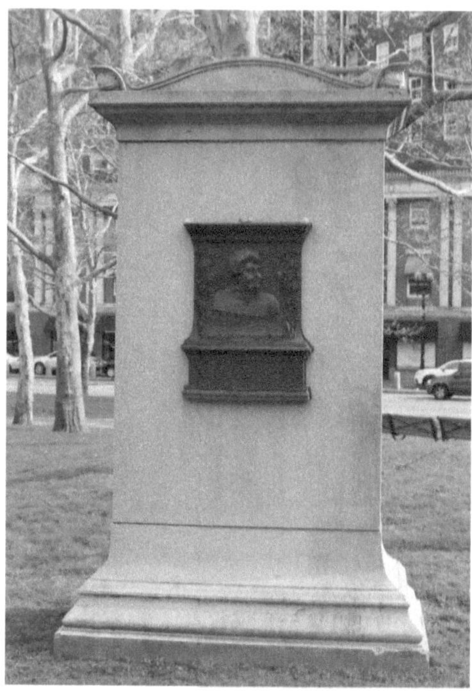

Figure 6. Feinstein memorial, Providence,
RI. Andrew M. Shanken, photographer.

Yet another type has become popular in recent years: the monument to all women. A generic catchall of a commemorative strategy, it presumes to even the memorial scorecard and to bring attention to women as a group, while scuttling the problem of choosing real historical figures or issues. Imagine a monument to all men and the absurdity of a monument to all women becomes obvious. It betrays in its very being the problem it does not solve. It reinforces the false idea of women as minorities, mashes all women into one steadfastly depoliticized commemorative site.

These various types raise an obvious objection, namely that allegorical women and historical figures are clearly different, as are monuments and memorials, statues in pantheons such as the Statue Hall in the U.S. Congress and public art that features female figures. These distinctions remain important and we believe they are explored with sensitivity in the chapters and cases in this book. At the same time, we see merit in considering them all in one place because all of these forms of female representation blur. Monuments frequently take on commemorative value and memorials are monumentalized. Historical figures succumb to allegory and allegory is filtered through history. As Rosalind Krauss has observed, moreover, in its traditional role "sculpture is a commemorative representation," lending even the most political or campy statue of a woman a commemorative aura or meaning, however dim.[15] When representations of women appear in public, whether they are called memorials, monuments, or statues, and whether they appear in allegorical or historical form, a host of related issues arise about bodies, gender roles, art, materiality, and the public sphere itself. The contributions to this volume begin to explore the topic across cultures and time periods, in part to inquire into the varying, if not volatile, meaning of these issues.

We also hope that this volume opens up serious questions about the entire project of "breaking the bronze ceiling." For instance, it is not difficult to imagine a world in which every other statue one encounters memorializes a woman but still fails to make a more equitable world, or even a more equitable commemorative landscape. Why would we expect people to treat statues of women better than they treat women? Even if they did—even if commemorative objects mediated as intended and allowed healthy revisions of gender—what would that mean? The historical examples in this volume cross-check present-day assumptions. They demonstrate evocatively, sometimes shockingly, the ways in which memorials to women have been ill-conceived, malformed, misunderstood, mistreated, and made to reinforce the very stereotypes people so often hope they challenge. Amanda Su's chapter analyzes a monument to George Eliot, whose defining gesture as a writer destabilized gender norms. While Eliot wears a bronze dress and sits passively at the crossroads of her hometown, her womanhood was defended perversely by men who feared she would be canceled.

Other more general assumptions cloud the picture of what memorials are capable of doing. The desire to break the bronze ceiling is predicated on the belief that the myriad statues of men around the world are potent and create a gender imbalance. This may be so, but going back to the mid-nineteenth century, when the statuemania of the period began to populate cities with statues of men, critics were unsparing. Thomas Carlyle, one of the most astute writers of the period and a celebrator of "great men," was particularly savage. The new statues "stand there, poor wretches, gradually rusting in the sooty rain; black and dismal." They "sanction and consecrate artistic botching" and "pretentious futility. . . . No soul looks upon them approvingly or even indifferently without damage, all the deadlier the less he knows of it." He counseled that they be "melted into warming-pans."[16] Critics across Europe and the United States echoed Carlyle, frequently calling for a moratorium on new statues or demanding that public spaces be cleared. Throughout the long nineteenth century, they were physically assaulted, moved, or iconoclastically destroyed and used as political caricature. Edgar Degas proposed walling off "green spaces in order to protect them from new monuments."[17] Waves of statuephobia followed surges of statuemania.[18] Abuse and neglect are more the norm than the exception. In short, statues to men were ill-conceived, malformed, misunderstood, mistreated, and made to reinforce stereotypes about men (and their power) that undermined the intentions of their creators, noble or otherwise. What will save the iconoclastic urge to break the bronze ceiling from being anything more than another attack on monuments, a contemporary form of *damnatio memoriae*?

With few moments of respite, these questions of representation, as well as the waves of statuemania and statuephobia, have remained pressing issues. Recent attacks on statues to "dead white men" have challenged memorials in ways that Carlyle could not have imagined. Many monuments to men have become anonymous. Admittedly, even anonymous monuments can uphold a generic image of patriarchal power or vicious colonialism. Larger-than-life men on pedestals lord over public spaces as they gesture forcefully, pontificate, and tell us that great men are immortal. In the words of William Godwin, they are erected to "paralyze the hand of oblivion."[19] The scarcity of monuments to women implies that oblivion is their lot, that they have been omitted from greatness and are doomed to obscurity. Even Godwin, husband and father to two women who would be memorialized (Mary Wollstonecraft and Mary Shelley, respectively), only proposed monuments to great men. It is easy to sympathize with the instinct to thin out the "dead white men." Yet the impotence and anonymity of commemorative statues were abundantly clear from the start. Mariana Griswold Van Rensselaer found a graceful way around Carlyle's objections: "If a work of art is agreeable to look upon," she wrote, "we may be glad to possess it even if it commemorates a well-meaning nobody."[20] In other words, memorials to men arrived in post-Revolutionary Europe and America as contentious, even if overt considerations of masculinity were rare.

Matters of race complicate these issues still further. A large number of new monuments to women depict white women, which perpetuates the historical entanglement between the suffragette movement and whiteness, as explored by Lauren Kroiz in chapter 3. The late and remedial inclusion of Sojourner Truth to the Central Park suffragette monument reflects a much larger problem: women of color are marginalized for both their gender and their race. Even when Black and Brown women are included in monuments, this is often as an instrument to placate critics and cover the bronze with a veneer of diversity. In other words, to break the bronze ceiling uncritically risks further perpetuating the racism it superficially addresses in the name of feminism.

This unhappy *longue durée* of modern memorials, oscillating between moments of enthusiasm, exhaustion, and iconoclasm, makes us question the cultural form itself. Should we join with those nineteenth-century critics, admit that we are asking impossible things of memorials, and call for a moratorium on them? Perhaps the question is not how to break the bronze ceiling but rather how to move beyond the monument entirely. With such a bleak view, what is the value then of taking on the subject at all? As the chapters and cases in this collection reveal, memorials to women (or those that employ female figures) have been treated differently from those to men. It is not so much a question of underrepresentation but of representation: of women, the commemorative objects themselves, and the public response to them.

Notes

1. Monument Lab, National Monument Audit, 2021, https://monumentlab.com/audit.

2. Consejo de Monumentos de Chile, *Estudio de Monumentos Públicos a Mujeres en capitales regionales de Chile*, March 2021, https://www.monumentos.gob.cl/publicaciones/articulos/1er-estudio-monumentos-publicos-mujeres-capitales-regionales.

3. Caroline Criado-Perez, "I Sorted the UK's Statues by Gender—a Mere 2.7 Per Cent Are of Historical, Non-Royal Women," *New Statesman* (March 26, 2016).

4. Jerry Saltz, "The Mary Wollstonecraft Monument in London Is Bad Kitsch Feminism," *Curbed*, November 10, 2020, https://www.curbed.com/2020/11/mary-wollstonecraft-statue-london-feminism.html.

5. Jerry Saltz, "The Ooh-La-La Fake Feminism of That Big Naked Medusa Statue by the Courthouses," *Curbed*, October 13, 2020, https://www.curbed.com/2020/10/medusa-statue-nyc-jerry-saltz.html.

6. See https://www.sfartscommission.org/content/dr-maya-angelou-monument.

7. Michele H. Bogart, *Public Sculpture and the Civic Ideal in New York City, 1890–1930* (Chicago: University of Chicago Press, 1989).

8. Carol Hymowitz and Timothy D. Schellhardt, "The Glass Ceiling: Why Women Can't Seem to Break the Invisible Barrier That Blocks Them from the Top Jobs," *Wall Street Journal*, March 24, 1986.

9. The "Breaking the Bronze Ceiling" campaign concluded with the inauguration of a suffragette monument designed by Barbara Grygutis in August 2020. See https://breakingthebronzeceiling.com/; https://www.kentucky.com/news/local/counties/fayette-county/article237305234.html.

10. The creation of the Central Park monument was spearheaded by the organization Monumental Women; see https://monumentalwomen.org/about/.

11. Mariana Griswold Van Rensselaer, *Art Out-of-Doors: Hints on Good Taste in Gardening* (1893; New York: Charles Scribner's Sons, 1925), 221.

12. Richard Sennett, *Flesh and Stone: The Body and the City in Western Civilization* (New York: W. W. Norton, 1994), 285–88.

13. Renata Codello and Joanna Dezio, "Carlo Scarpa's *Monument to the Partisan Woman*," *Future Anterior* 6, no. 1 (Summer 2009): 38–48.

14. Julia Buckley, "Tourist Thrown out of Venice for Sunbathing Topless on War Memorial," CNN, January 25, 2022, https://www.cnn.com/travel/article/tourist-nude-venice-war-memorial/index.html.

15. Rosalind Krauss, "Sculpture in the Expanded Field," *October* (Spring 1979): 13.

16. Thomas Carlyle, *Latter-Day Pamphlets* (1851; London: Chapman and Hall, 1888), 223–24.

17. Degas's idea is mentioned in Sergiusz Michalski, *Public Monuments: Art in Political Bondage, 1870–1997* (London: Reaktion Books, 1998), 45, but the source is not cited.

18. For statuemania, see ibid., especially 17, 29, 31, 34, 44, 49–54.

19. William Godwin, *Essay on Sepulchres* (London: Printed for W. Miller, 1809), 99.

20. Griswold Van Rensselaer, *Art Out-of-Doors*, 206.

PART I

Patronized Women

Pía Montealegre

1. Innocence and Guilt: Memorializing a Gender Tragedy in Nineteenth-Century Santiago de Chile

A Gender Tragedy

OPPOSITE THE OLDEST cemetery in the Chilean capital, Santiago, lies a monument dedicated to the greatest gender tragedy in the city's history, and one that rocked much of the Western world at the time. The monument stands in the middle of a large traffic circle used frequently as a venue for concerts and celebrations. Few people are aware of the events commemorated by the structure, and its bronze inscriptions make scant reference to the tragedy that gave rise to it. Instead, the dedication honors the foundation of the First Fire Brigade of Santiago, an institution that, had it existed at the time of the disaster, would have made erection of the monument unnecessary. Few realize that below the column rests a crypt with the charred remains of 2,000 women, devotees of the Virgin Mary, who died at Mass on December 8, 1863.

At 8 p.m. on that Tuesday evening was to be held the liturgy of the Immaculate Conception—the closing ceremony of the Month of Mary, at the Church of the Society, the most attended house of prayer in the capital, located a block away from the Plaza Mayor. Originally named

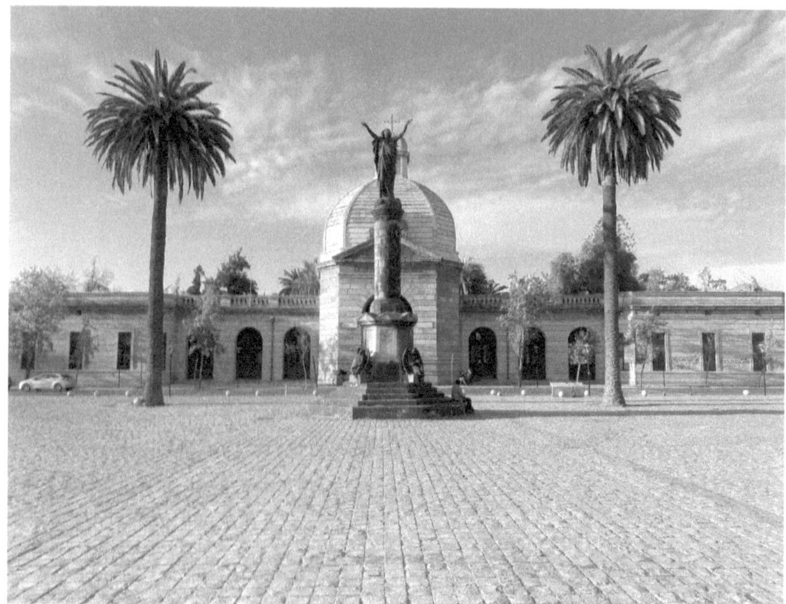

Figure 1. Monument known as *La Dolorosa*, 2021. Photograph by Raúl Rojas.

after the Society of Jesus, it had been in the hands of the archdiocese since the expulsion of the Jesuits in 1767. In the early afternoon, the doors were opened and a crowd formed in the square outside, pushing and shoving to ensure their place at one of the best-loved ceremonies at that time. Presbyter Ugarte had made a special invitation to the sisterhood of the Daughters of Mary, a women's association with a considerable following, which was celebrating its anniversary. Earlier in the day, fabric and paper decorations had been hung and myriad candles and lamps lit in the chandeliers, on the altars, and along the walls of the building. According to the chronicles, with a little over an hour remaining before the ceremony was due to begin, a lamp placed on a crescent of fabric near the altar issued a sudden gout of flame. This was a relatively common event in those days and people were unconvinced of the need for immediate flight, rooted by reluctance to give up their coveted vantage points in the congregation. Onlookers remained confident that the fire would be brought under control even as it leapt from ornament to ornament, rapidly reaching the wooden structure of the roof.

A large number of testimonies and historiographical works have documented the series of events that conspired to render this accident a tragedy of such monumental proportions.[1] Limited visibility from within

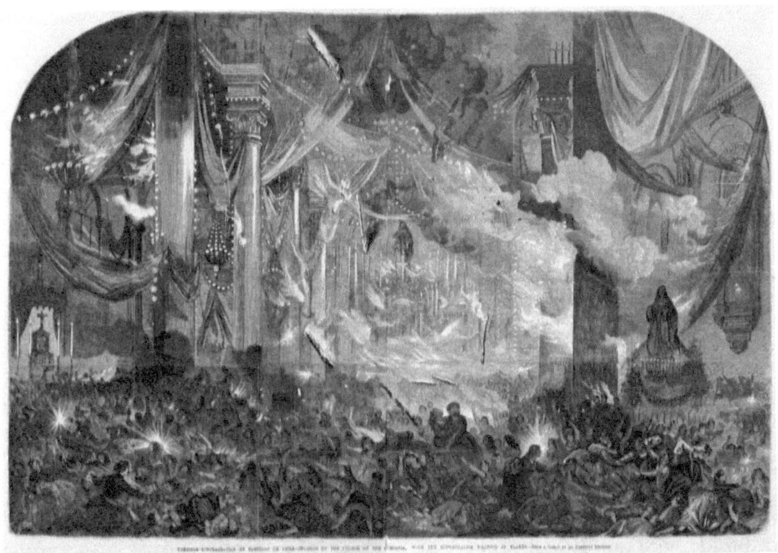

Figure 2. Interior of the church during the fire. *Frank Leslie's Illustrated Newspaper* (New York, February 6, 1864).

the enormous crowd meant that the severity of the threat was not fully appreciated until it was already beyond control. The vast stock of fuel in the form of candles, lamps, and garlands intensified the blaze, triggering a stampede. This did not present a problem for the men in attendance, as they were seated in the sanctuary, an area behind the high altar linked to the sacristy and an exterior patio through which they were able to escape. The women, on the other hand, would customarily sit and kneel on rugs scattered across the floor, occupying the nave from wall to wall. Pews were not used and, as such, there was neither order to the space nor room for free movement. It is likely that the crowd closest to the focus of the blaze began to stumble over those on the floor in their haste to flee, preventing the latter from getting to their feet. Located two-thirds of the way down the space between the altar and the main entrance were two small side doors that opened into the street on one side and a small patio on the other. Some testimonies report that these were closed on the day in question and that all of the doors of the church opened inward. The majority of the congregation were unable to escape; bodies struggled ineffectually, jostling and becoming tangled together. The bells began to toll and the city gathered to witness the disaster. With no fire brigade, the resources available with which to combat the fire were pitiful. Any-

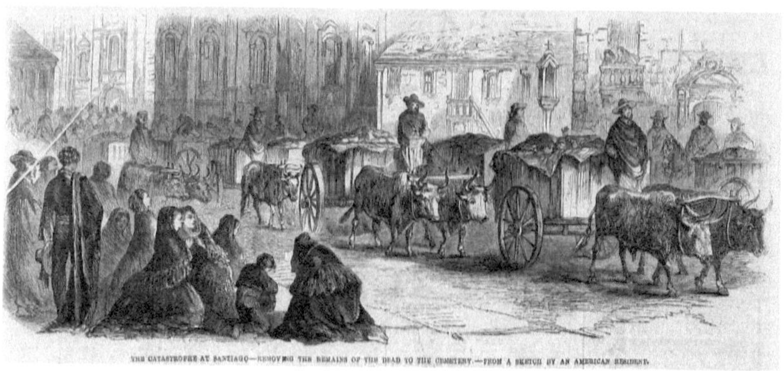

Figure 3. The transportation of bodies to the cemetery. *Frank Leslie's Illustrated Newspaper* (New York, February 6, 1864).

one attempting to rescue members of the human knot found themselves trapped by scrabbling hands and arms, and over the heads and tangle of bodies in the doorway, blazing timbers could be seen raining down upon the multitude. In little under an hour, the roof structure collapsed in flames, creating what has been described as a human oven. The impotent citizenry could only testify to—or at least imagine—the horror of the event, and an account coalesced and spread of the women as they burned alive in attitudes of desperation and supplicancy. The fruitless attempts at rescue ceased at 8 p.m. following the collapse of the bell tower.

The inconsistency of statistical records from the time makes it difficult to reliably establish the number of fatalities. However, media reports, the collective imaginary, and, ultimately, tradition speak of over 2,000, of whom only a score were men, and, of these, many were small children. In a city of barely 100,000 inhabitants, this equated to the death of one in twenty-five women—some 4 percent of the female population. Chile's centralism meant that the country's upper class were concentrated in Santiago, and the endogamy characteristic of the elite connected them in one way or another. As such, the fire affected them all as it would an extended family. However, although the press lamented the loss of "the most select of our society," a third of the victims were servants and another third were of modest standing.[2] It was said that one could see a house bearing signs of mourning on every block and that some households had been lost entirely. Everyone had a cousin, sister, or aunt who had passed away or was fatally wounded. The numbers of the tragedy were repeated as a mantra in the various media: 20,000 lamps lit in the church, 2,000 women dead, 150 carts that spent four days transporting the bodies to a mass grave dug by 200 men. Children would later remember the images of that sinister procession and the stiff arms protruding from between the corpses, still jerking aloft as if to shake off death.

The news broke in the Chilean press the following day and the newspapers strove to outdo one another with sordid and dramatic narrations of the events. Many articles denounced the distortion of what had happened, revealing the political extent of the tragedy and the desire of different parties to establish their own truth, with the honor and memory of the women thrown in for good measure. The fire also experienced a moment of international fame, hitting the U.S. press a month later and reaching Paris in early February.[3] Foreign newspapers repeated and exaggerated the accounts published in the Chilean press, often twisting the events but nevertheless reproducing the image of the struggling multitude that blocked the entrance as liquid fire rained down from the heavens. The death toll was recited in a similar way, becoming iconic and memorable, and even used to measure other calamities, including certain gender-related issues, such as: "the number of deaths from crinoline in three years in London, it is stated, equals the loss of life by the Santiago fire."[4]

Many interwoven discourses sought to instrumentalize the interpretation of the tragedy. It symbolized a conflict that undeniably transcended the boundaries of Chilean society: the struggle between Church and State, between liberals and conservatives, or between regalists and ultramontanists.[5] Regarding the latter, the fire provided an abundance of material upon which the Protestant Anglo-Saxon world feasted, using headlines such as "A dreadful massacre and Jesuit barbarity."[6] Building upon these reproaches of Catholicism, a series of mythical fables emerged, such as claims that the priests had handed out indulgences instead of saving the victims. One of the more questionable events was the rescue of a set of objects of dubious value through the sacristy, a task that justified the barring of this potential escape route. One anti-clerical newspaper claimed that prayer cards were handed out during the ceremony as a "Memento of the last communion of the Daughters of Mary," insinuating that the word "last" referred not to the previous communion but to a premeditated collective massacre.[7] A lengthy criminal investigation was launched, followed by a trial, but the process failed to unearth the evidence needed to prove any culpability. At the same time, questions were raised about the safety standards maintained at massive events, along with the regulations applied to public buildings, which eventually came to include churches. In the immediate wake of the fire and motivated by concerns regarding the capacity to respond to such a catastrophe, a group of elite men founded the First Fire Brigade of Santiago. While all of these responses were unquestionably beneficial, what cannot be overlooked is the discourse woven between the many fragments of the upheaval—a discourse that looked unfavorably upon women. In the various press articles, such voices were heard time and again, amplified and reverberating in a chorus of condemnation.

Victims of Their Own Making

THE FORMULATION OF a story about women is not the same as using gender as an analytical category, notes Joan Scott.[8] What is crucial is to identify the evident asymmetry within the story in order to understand how the constructions of gender are replicated within historical processes. In the same way, the account of the events—the writing of which began the day after the tragedy by a masculine, patriarchal, and chauvinistic society—not only gave rise to the memorialization process but fixed and reinforced the subaltern position of gender within the culture. Women, in their inferiority, were at the same time both victims of and responsible for their own tragedy. The female stereotype forged in the nineteenth century is easily identifiable: a rigid model structured around conservative values and bourgeois customs, with European culture as its only point of reference. However, Amelia Valcárcel observes its construction as a twin discourse, mixing in a single breath both gallant praise and damning judgment, which the author terms "romantic misogyny."[9] On one hand, the masculine liberal elite would extol the feminine qualities of innocence, beauty, and piety, while on the other branding women as sanctimonious and fanatical, superficial, slaves to fashion, and even promiscuous. In all recognition there was an opportunity for reproach, and opinion swung between interpretations of women as passive objects and victims of circumstance, and as culpable subjects capable of twisting will and reason.

Catholic devotion was an attribute used to characterize Chilean women up and down the social classes. Although the majority of associations were exclusively masculine, men were not generally thought of in connection with Catholic ceremonies and rites, whether because of liberal fashions or popular rebellion.[10] Women's religiousness was viewed with disdain by male society, winning them a variety of epithets: the *beatas*, equivalent to blessed, the name applied to the first category in the Catholic hierarchy of holiness, or the *mojigatas*, equivalent to prudish, a skeptical reference to religious scruples. Marian devotion, a favorite among women, was viewed with apprehension by the purist factions of Catholicism, who rejected adoration of the Mother over the Son. Practices of this kind were considered fanaticism and, as such, typical of the weak—a common form of ignorance shown toward the lower classes and women. There was concern over a supposed distortion of faith and this was magnified by the discovery, among the charred wreckage, of cilices: metallic accessories for personal pietistic torture. During the funeral rites, the archbishop of Santiago referred to the women as Christian martyrs, models of virtue for their families and communities, noting that the torture implements redeemed them in the eyes of God despite their vain aristocracy: "how astonishing to see, hidden beneath all the finery, such great mortification!" He framed their deaths as a supreme, almost apocalyptic moment of resigned submission and salvation, going so far as to say that the women knew, as they left their homes, that they would be called by that divine destiny. Driven by the power of their devotion, "they would have stepped up to the gallows to die for their God. Their desire called for martyrdom."[11] Thus, even from a religious perspective, indeed from a discourse that sought to empathize with them, the women were portrayed as invoking their own sacrifice.

In parallel to this, there was doubt as to the profoundness of female faith, with suggestions that they attended rituals out of mere "curiosity."[12] Women were believed to be impressionable, to allow themselves to be manipulated by priests, and to be tricked by lights and phantasmagoria. Their forms of celebration were referred to as "these terrible manias intent on sweeping up our feminine society," a description that insinuated a lack of intellectual autonomy on the part of their gender.[13] The irrational sensitivity attributed to women had also driven them to their deaths. In an attempt at scientific objectivity, one doctor explained that "the woman, owing to the inherent weakness of her organization and her greater impressionability, is more susceptible to such commotions."[14] As one journalist more eloquently put it, the rate of the fire would have allowed them time to escape "had they been men"; however, they acted affectively: in the midst of the flames, the women embraced one another, collided, and prayed.[15] "If the events had involved men, none would have perished," insisted the commentator.[16]

In many of the accounts, the women who lost their lives in the tragedy were exalted as aesthetic objects; the "brightest ornaments" of society had been lost.[17] However, at the same time, and in the same vein of aesthetics, women were held responsible for bringing frivolity to the whole culture, and these lavish liturgies were just another example of that contaminating ostentation. While some voices claimed that women allowed themselves to be dictated to, others said that, with the endorsement of the chaplain, these devotees had taken the helm in deciding the form of the celebrations, generous in decoration, lighting, and music. It may be that some churches had become spaces of feminine realization, creativity, and power. The Society was home to an organ, which would be joined by musicians contracted by the sisterhood, and hymns sometimes overlapped with profane songs.[18] The influential liberal politician Benjamín Vicuña Mackenna—who, a decade later, would become governor of Santiago—was a regular voice in the press covering the event, and there he expressed his regret that churches had become "dance salons in which the senses are lavished with festoons of flowers, lights, songs, incense, and everything else, while the soul rids itself of the austere severity of its meditations."[19]

As was occurring in capitals around the world during the nineteenth century, the customs of the bourgeois salons spread to the public domain and, in Santiago, contrasted strongly with colonial sobriety. The new cosmopolitan consumer culture found expression in forms of amusement, carriages, and women's clothing in particular. One respected personage of the time likened the long dresses worn by women to "a filthy street-sweeping broom," a particularly absurd luxury in the rudimentary reality of the city with its unpaved streets and generous complement of dust clouds and mud.[20] Church was an occasion for women to wear their best outfits, leading to accusations that they attended Mass for the sole purpose of showing them off. Fashion dictated the wearing of corsets and crinolines, and it was said that, if unable to obtain these, the women of Santiago would make their own using "bent whips."[21] In an attempt to assign a punishment for such wayward absurdity, many articles proposed that the women had, in the midst of the fire, fallen victim to their own clothing: "Thanks to those dresses and crinolines, fortresses of women began to form within the church as they became tangled together and so set light to one another."[22] The archbishop did not pass up the opportunity to describe the example of a group of corpses that had become strung together by their steel crinolines. As such, "it was almost impossible to separate one body from another in order to bury them," thus heaping further condemnation upon the already wretched women.[23] For the women believers, assurance of a Christian burial that would not hinder the resurrection of the flesh was a major concern, and the description offered by the monsignor must thus have caused them distress. The well-respected doctor who reported on the fire indicated that the burns resulting from the blazing dresses would have been "worse than those occasioned by hot water or boiling

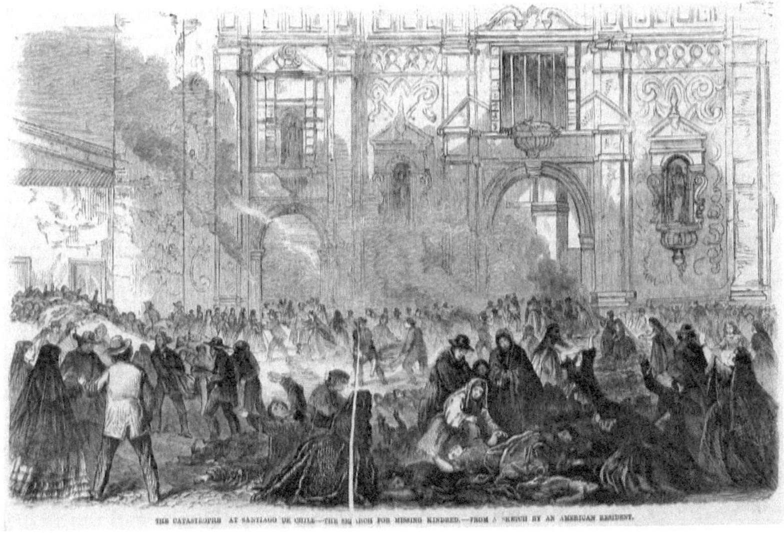

Figure 4. The outside of the church during the fire. *Frank Leslie's Illustrated Newspaper* (New York, February 6, 1864).

oil."[24] One newspaper ventured to summarize the fate of the women in two forms: "entangled in their crinolines or fainting through fright."[25] To the whimsical dresses were added another garment vilified by men: the manto, a black cape fastened at the neck that covered the wearer from head to toe, worn when attending church. Typical of Chilean women, the manto had been inherited from the Spanish, who in turn had likely adapted it from the Muslim chador. Men saw them as a device to conceal a lack of cleanliness, or sexualized them, enjoying their insinuation of the feminine form. The erotic image was completed by the custom of sitting on the floor in churches: "Use of the rug requires a degree of abandon, a pose of somewhat intimate trust and, let us speak plainly, a certain crossing of the legs. . . whose secret is one of the most formidable weapons in the arsenal of enchantment possessed by the Chilean woman."[26] Chaste or voluptuous, the conclusion was that the women had perished in "that dreadful knot of crinolines, mantones, skirts, and rugs."[27]

Marta Lamas proposes that the female gender, as a functional symbolic construction of masculine ideals, should embody purity and innocence.[28] Following the postulates of Rousseau, and as observed by Valcárcel, women were assigned virtue as a natural quality. This implied a condition in which a woman had no "right to evil." She was obliged to remain distant from vice, violence, and, incidentally, reason and politics.[29] Women thus were seen as cultural guarantors of values such as peace, mildness, and stability. In accordance with this argument, accounts of the fire reveal an inclination to portray women as devoted mothers or angelic virgins, even in the imagined descriptions of the climax of the tragedy: "mothers embracing their daughters and hiding, amidst the multitude, their flaming hair. Daughters who looked upon their saved mothers with the resignation of the martyr."[30] Or corpses transformed into statues of "women kneeling in attitudes of supplicancy and children embracing them around the neck."[31] Simultaneously, it was proposed that this same chastity and virtue had led them to their deaths. The archbishop explained that, in the midst of the fire and having been forced to extricate themselves from their clothing, many women were unwilling to leave the church for fear of being seen naked: true "martyrs of purity."[32] The story was told of one mythical young woman who, upon finding herself in her undergarments, sought to cover herself with her plaits, but as these were burnt, "she then crossed her arms and returned to the flames."[33] As can be seen from the testimonies, a small number of women did have the temerity to remove their clothing and seek a way out of the building. Once outside, they were received by a crowd who swiftly procured the means of saving their modesty. Although they had just escaped from an oven on a hot summer's night, the people covered their scorched skin with cloaks and blankets.

The discussion revealed the annoyance caused by churches and their ceremonies, in particular because they were spaces beyond the control of the patriarchy. It was said that forms of feminine piety caused disorder in the household because they bred disobedience— "domestic anarchy."[34] Religious celebrations featured strongly in urban public life. The Hijas de María held evening prayers every Wednesday, and during the Month of Mary these activities took place on a daily basis. For the closing ceremonies, women arrived at the church at four o'clock in the afternoon in order to make preparations and did not return home until night. Men remained alone in their houses, "discontent and irritated," suspicious of the motives and true destination of the outing.[35] The home was synonymous with the spirit, virtue, austerity: outside lay banality, vice, ostentation. The word "promiscuity" appeared in many articles that questioned priestly control over female consciences or insinuated furtive trysts under the pretext of attending Mass. But this annoyance laid bare another form of promiscuity that was even more intolerable to the elite: that of social classes. Despite charging an annual membership fee of one peso, the Hijas de María was a particularly inclusive association. Women would attend services with their servants, and these used such outings as an opportunity to meet with relatives and suitors. Women also conspired among themselves, heedless of class or age, in order to attend the nocturnal ceremonies: servants would make excuses on behalf of their mistresses and vice versa, feigning visits to other houses or claiming that they were indisposed, then escaping with their manto hidden beneath their crinolines.[36] The church became a place of freedom. Its heterogeneity projected it as a modern public space and the antithesis of the stifling patrician salon in which young people were monitored constantly. As such, the complicity and faithfulness of feminine networks were called into question. Concepts such as the "stake"—at which witches had once been burned—and the "horrors of hell" began to shape a discourse that positioned women as responsible for the tragedy. Whether for their devotion, superficiality, chastity, promiscuity, fanaticism, disobedience, solidarity, or foolishness, they had all met with a common destiny. Men, and even priests, were, by contrast, always associated with reason, truth, wisdom, and heroism.

The Incarnation of Guilt

Wounded with His every wound,
steep my soul till it hath swooned,
in His very Blood away;
Be to me, O Virgin, nigh,
lest in flames I burn and die,
in His awful Judgment Day.
    —Stabat Mater dolorosa, attrib. Innocent III
    Translation by Edward Caswall, *Lyra Catholica* (1849)

ON DECEMBER 11, with the victims recently buried, the archbishop expressed his intention to conduct the funeral rites in the ruins left by the fire. The lack of sensitivity in making the relatives return to the site of the catastrophe horrified the anticlerical press, which interpreted, furthermore, an intention on the part of the Church to rebuild the edifice. The Society had already been reconstructed three times in the wake of two earthquakes and a fire, disasters whose impact was not even remotely comparable to the human conscquences of December 8. Since its original construction, the church had been associated with a fateful feminine mythology: the first Jesuit chapel, although not built on the same site, boasted as a relic the head of one of the 11,000 virgins martyred at Cologne alongside Saint Ursula.[37] The building, cursed by the Jesuits following their expulsion, had served as an authentic "apparatus of torment," and that fateful mark was one of the arguments raised by the public in support of its demolition.[38] The land was owned by the state and, in accordance with canon law of the time, the damage occasioned by the fire to the walls of the church dictated that the building should be condemned.[39] The motion united voices from across the political spectrum, and on December 14 some 2,000 citizens, dressed in mourning, congregated before the ruins, some armed with the intention of marching as far as the government palace. The demonstration could only be pacified with a reading of the presidential decree of demolition.

The creation of a memorial was proposed as a strategy to wrest the space from the Church and put it to secular use, and it was thought that such an installation should take a form quite unlike that of the site of the tragedy. Proponents settled on the planting of a garden that would cleanse the memory of the calamity through its natural rebirth and represent the innocence of the victims: "This site does not require more altars. . . . Let us create a garden,. . . let the plants regrow, as do souls throughout eternity," urged one poet in the press.[40] In the center was imagined a piece in white marble—perhaps, as one anonymous relative suggested, a sculpture of a kneeling angel. On December 15, the office of the governor decreed that a monument would indeed be created, calling for engineers and architects to put forward proposals. Management and funding for the work was supplied by over 150 men of the elite with various political leanings. One option, created in France and presented in the form of drawings, showed a chapel complete with altar and sacristy, sheltered beneath the figure of Our Lady of Sorrows. It included a special space to hold one hundred bodies and an underground crypt in which the remains of the other victims could be laid to rest. It would serve as both a tomb and a place of piety, with the celebration of two daily funeral Masses.[41] In contrast, the archdiocese put forward the erection of a funereal monument at the mass grave in the cemetery, a proposal that failed to capture the public interest.

While the material demolition was fast, the symbolic demolition took several months to complete. On July 8, 1864, perpetual commemoration of the fire was decreed, but the site remained empty and eventually fell into use as an urban livestock pen.[42] The process slowed as the events faded from memory and exactly one year after the tragedy, Presbyter Ugarte once again led a crowded liturgy to close the Month of Mary in the church of Saint Augustine. During the ceremony, the recently formed fire brigade carried out their precautionary exercises in the opposite square.[43] Despite the initial urgency, work on the memorial took ten years to be completed. Benjamín Vicuña Mackenna, who by then had become the governor in charge of the urban modernization of Santiago, led the reactivation of the initiative and incorporated it into his government program. In October 1872, he called upon the public to contribute to the work, indicating that it should be "a commemorative monument, in no way funereal," to be situated on what he considered a "site of immolation."[44] He reported that he had already initiated the process, commissioning a range of allegorical sculptures from Europe, and that through this initiative he was echoing the requests made a decade earlier by society and the relatives. However, in a number of ways, the governor's plan ran counter to the voices that he invoked. Although the ensemble included a crypt—which ultimately was not executed—the allegorical and ornamental characteristics of Vicuña Mackenna's proposal failed to reflect the degree of piety demanded by the relatives. For the governor, the piece held urbanistic value and was part of an extensive complement of statues that would adorn the city. Seeking a democratic process, he asked the interested parties to choose the model of the memorial from among the options commissioned. However, according to Vicuña Mackenna himself, "almost all of the attendees" pushed for the memorial to take the form of an "outdoor chapel," that is, a place of prayer, liturgy, and pilgrimage.[45] The Congress, whose splendid and republican building had become the host of the memorial site, opposed a religious program. A section of liberal and anticlerical public opinion took up this idea, which Vicuña Mackenna also echoed. Once all dissident opinions had been rejected, the decision was taken to move forward with the statue favored by the governor. This option did not include the crypt requested by the relatives, thus disposing of the funereal function that went so strongly against both the hygienist logic of restricting the interment of bodies to cemeteries and the secular notion of monuments. As the governor himself noted, the list of financial contributors to the monument included very few relatives and women.[46]

The sculptural ensemble was designed by Albert-Ernest Carrier-Belleuse, a prolific French sculptor who produced monumental statues on commission, along with decorative pieces. His figures were characterized by movement, dramatic poses, and a high level of detail. The sculptor enjoyed considerable fame and, at the time the monument was commissioned, was in the process of creating lamps for the Opéra Garnier. Although many people—both then and today—saw the central figure as an anonymous woman, it is in fact a representation of

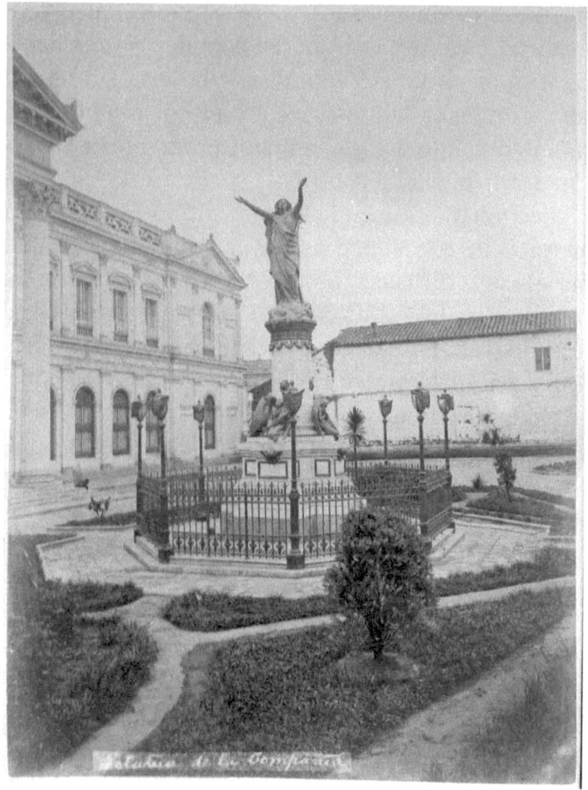

Figure 5. Photograph of *La Dolorosa* on the Society plot, c. 1890, National History Museum, Santiago.

the Immaculate Conception standing upon a celestial sphere. It was given the name of *La Dolorosa* in reference to the maternal sufferings of the Virgin Mary. She is accompanied by four angels, childlike and grieving figures who hold in their hands three symbols of the passion, or *Arma Christi*: the hammer and nails, the crown of thorns, and the crucifix. The fourth angel bears a palm frond—representation of the victory of spirit over flesh and symbol of the Christian martyrs. The central figure, with her arms and gaze raised to heaven, is far from passive and resigned, appearing to project her misfortune imploringly to the higher spheres. The close-fitting sleeves and folded drapery give the piece a more voluptuous aspect than those of the more traditional and hieratic representations of Mary, in which her body remains concealed. The dark color of the bronze and the half-covered head of the

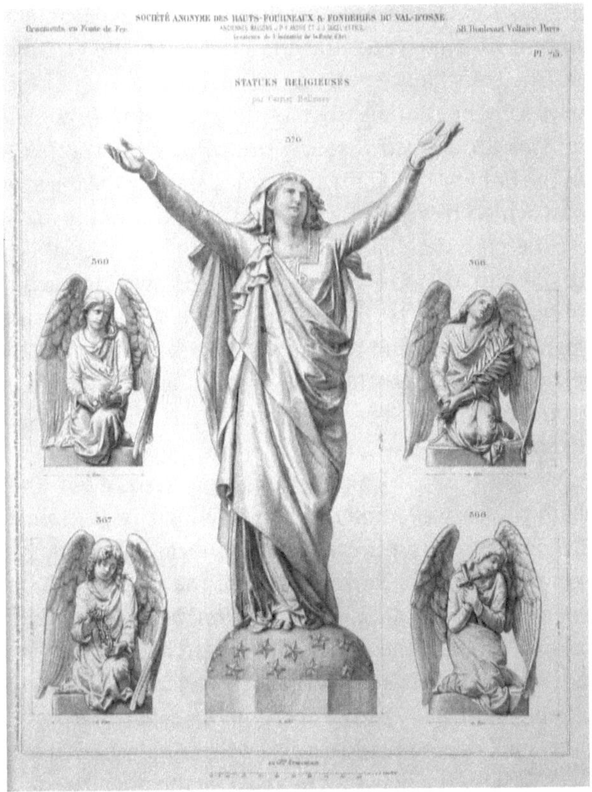

Figure 6. The *La Dolorosa* ensemble in the Val D'Osne
foundry catalogue, c. 1900.

Virgin are reminiscent of the image of the manto. At first sight, the
allegory could easily be misread, and the figure was even described in
one Catholic newspaper as a Virgin in flames.[47]

The monument was inaugurated with fasti on December 8, 1873. The
perimeter of the square was hung with enormous curtains and the piece
itself covered by a black veil with white stars, which was removed with the
arrival of the president of the republic. This dramatic moment, very much
to the approval of the governor, was accompanied by cannon shots fired
from Santa Lucía hill and peals rang out from all the churches of Santiago every fifteen minutes throughout the day. According to the French
newspaper *L'Illustration*, at the end of the ceremony, practically all of the
musicians available in the capital took part in a rendition of Rossini's "Stabat Mater."[48] *Stabat Mater dolorosa*, translated literally as "The sorrowful

mother was standing," is the opening phrase of the medieval hymn attributed to Innocent III, which recounts the suffering of the Virgin at the foot of the cross. The coincidence extends beyond the figure represented and the musical piece. The Marian trope of the sorrowful Virgin is a plea for redemption: sins are purged through the pain of the mother, and thus "burning in the flames" of Judgment Day is avoided. One guest priest gave an address in which he carefully differentiated the victims according to two groups: the true Catholics on one side, and on the other a significant number of vain, curious, distracted, and negligent women motivated to attend the church only by the desire for diversion—although all, ultimately, daughters of God and pardoned through Providence. He implied that, to the former, God gave the strength to escape, and to the latter, the repentance to die in peace. The disaster was thus offered as "horrific torture in atonement for their own failings," the monument and its ceremonies surrounded by allusions to sin, guilt, immolation, martyrdom, and fire.[49]

Beyond anticlerical and impious interpretations, *La Dolorosa* must have been disturbing for its personification of an unbearable memory. It was an overly patent portrayal of a tormented feminine body; the flame-backed silhouette of a woman burning in desperation, as had been the fate of so many witnessed through the doors of the church. It was the pose of the charred corpses, with their heads raised and their arms aloft, which had been described scientifically by the doctor in his report.[50] It was the bodily gesture interpreted during the funerals by the archbishop as a final exaltation of God. Besides the déjà vu provoked by the pose, besides its macabre aesthetic, *La Dolorosa* came to stir up a more profound, shocking, and unpardonable guilt: the brutal incarnation of romantic virtue. The idealized youthful, beautiful, healthy feminine body had been renamed in the fire as an indistinguishable "hideous mass,"[51] forming "a dense forest of charred skulls."[52] Hair ablaze, faces disfigured, once delicious extremities dismembered by attempts at rescue or lying discarded in the street. One article told of how, from the uncovered carts in which the remains were being transported to the cemetery, "fell to the ground a calf, delicately clad."[53] As the doctor observes, exposure to different types of fire had produced a variety—describable in culinary terms—of "charred, roasted, and cooked bodies."[54] Transformed into black statues, they retained their horrific features and poses, carbonized for eternity. These feminine bodies had produced the stench of burnt flesh and the pall of putrefaction that hung over the city for several days. The damsels had been transformed into "nauseating particles"[55] carried by the wind, or "were part of the mud that was removed from the church in buckets."[56] The duality of a body idealized by a romantic culture, now brutally rendered flesh, was a

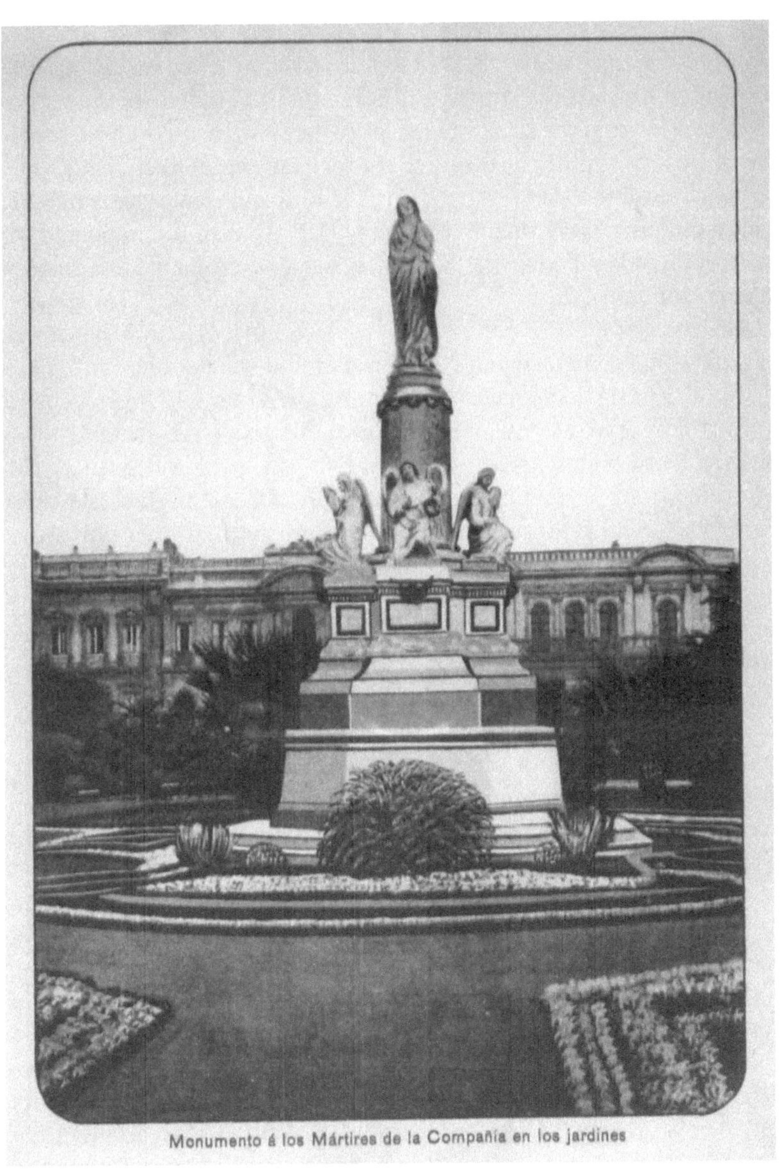

Figure 7. Retouched photograph of the second monument, from Jorge Walton S., *Album de Santiago y vistas de Chile* (Santiago: Sociedad imprenta y litografía Barcelona, 1915).

frequently conjured image that contrasted beauty with horror: the jux-taposition of those bodies masked by the hygienist and cosmetic moder-nity of the nineteenth century transformed into filth. Furthermore, the accounts classified the male and female bodies into their positions, situat-ing the women within the oven and the men outside: mothers, daughters, servants burning alive; brothers, fathers, husbands, and lovers making vain attempts to save them. *La Dolorosa* thus recalled the impotence of male flesh and embodied the women as spoil—twin shame in a tragedy of feminine culpability.

The monument did not remain in place for long. *La Dolorosa* was moved to the cemetery and before the end of the decade, the Italian sculptor Ignazio Jacometti was working on a new figure to replace it.[57] It had been commissioned by Carmen Lucía Ossa, daughter of a distinguished oligarchic and conservative family who, beginning the day after the fire, fought for the erection of a memorial, and most likely was among those marginalized from the first one. This time, a Virgin Mary in white marble and covered by her veil prayed with hands together at her breast, her gaze barely raised to heaven. Accom-panied again by four angels, the figure represents the other extreme of this twin construction of the feminine gender, and in her pious, passive, and resigned attitude, she contrasts with the defiant figure of *La Dolorosa*. Although documents have not been found to confirm this entirely, this version of Mary, despite her apparent conventionality, portrays an act of contempt for women: an incipient yet persistent—and ultimately triumphant—agency promoted by Catholic women who eventually decided the form and memorialization of their own tragedy and challenged the imposition of an instrumentalized image.

The controversial statue was included in a renovation project of the cemetery. A crypt was constructed at its base to which, around the year 1890, the bodies of the 2,000 victims were brought from the mass grave. Temporarily dispossessed of her four original angels, the bronze Vir-gin Mary finally provided a tomb for the bodies of the women. How-ever, their rest endured only until 1928, when firefighter Alberto Ried launched a project to move the sculpture to a plaza located outside the cemetery. Intent on using the monument to celebrate the fire brigade, and completely ignorant of its function as a mausoleum, he discovered the women's remains partway through the operation. He decided to move them without ceremony—in his own words, in sacks and hand carts—to a purpose-built vault in the statue's base. The city, and indeed the country as a whole, was passing through a period of political authoritarianism at the time, which explains the autonomy with which Ried operated and,

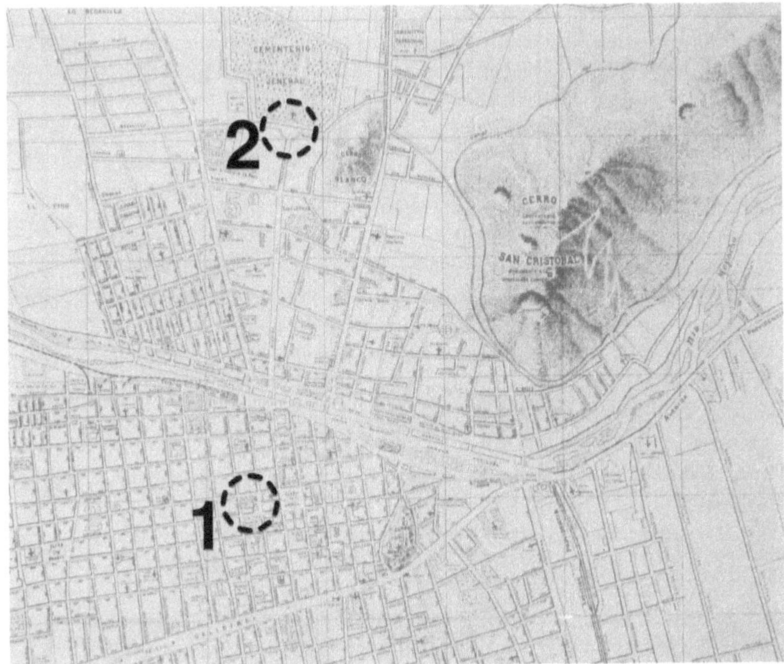

Figure 8. Fragment of a map of Santiago by Nicanor Boloña, 1910, National Library of Chile. At number 1, site of the Church of the Society and location of the second memorial. At number 2, current location of *La Dolorosa*, opposite the General Cemetery. Notations by the author.

at the same time, the complete lack of awareness on the part of the public regarding such a disgraceful exhumation. The place was never blessed or even marked as a tomb.[58] The commemorative plaques record only the founding of the all-male First Fire Brigade of Santiago. Today, the bodies of those devout women who lost their lives in a gender tragedy of unparalleled proportions lie ignored and forgotten in the middle of a traffic circle, their resting place daubed with profane practices.[59]

Notes

1. The most prominent accounts of the period are provided by the anonymous text *Resumen histórico del gran incendio de la Compañía* (Valparaíso: Librería Española de Nicasio Ezquerra, 1863); the version written by Benjamín Vicuña Mackenna, *Relación del incendio de la Compañía acaecido el 8 de diciembre de 1863* (Santiago: Imprenta del Ferrocarril, 1864); the image of the church summarized in the texts of Mariano Casanova, *Historia del Templo de la Compañía de Santiago de Chile y de su Incendio Acaecido el 8 de Diciembre de 1863* (Valparaíso: Imprenta del

Mercurio, 1871) and *El incendio de la Iglesia de la Compañía: Acaecido en Santiago de Chile el 8 de diciembre de 1863* (Bruselas: H. Goemaere, 1865), and one written later by Daniel Riquelme, *Episodios chilenos: El incendio de la Compañía, el 8 de diciembre de 1863* (Santiago: Imprenta Cervantes, 1893). The most recommendable contemporary works include Alfredo Palacios, *Del Infierno al Cielo: Imágenes y testimonios del incendio de la iglesia de la Compañía de Jesús ocurrido el 8 de diciembre de 1863* (Valparaíso: Ediciones Universitarias de Valparaíso, 2014), and Sol Serrano, *¿Qué hacer con Dios en la República? Política y secularización en Chile (1845–1885)* (Santiago: Fondo de Cultura Económica, 2008).

2. "*El Bien Público*" newspaper, in Vicuña Mackenna, *Relación del incendio*, 39.

3. The newspaper *La Patria* issued a "Steamer edition" for distribution abroad, Valparaíso, December 16, 1863.

4. "The News Condenser," *Moore's Rural New-Yorker* 15, no. 17 (April 23, 1864): 138.

5. Serrano, *¿Qué hacer con Dios* addresses this issue.

6. *Weekly Ottumwa Courier*, February 18, 1864, Ottumwa, Iowa. Although the Jesuits had returned to Chile, the order had no links to the church at the time of the disaster.

7. El Ferrocarril in *Resumen histórico del gran incendio* . . . (Historical account of the great fire . . .), 32.

8. Joan W. Scott, "Gender: A Useful Category of Historical Analysis," *American Historical Review* 91, no. 5 (1986): 1053–75, https://doi.org/10.2307/1864376; Joan W. Scott, "Gender: Still a Useful Category of Analysis?" *Diogenes* 57, no. 1 (February 1, 2010): 7–14, https://doi.org/10.1177/0392192110369316.

9. Amelia Valcárcel, *La política de las mujeres* (Madrid: Ed. Cátedra, 1997).

10. Serrano, *¿Qué hacer con Dios*.

11. Funeral prayer by Archbishop Casanova from *Resumen histórico del gran incendio*, 27–29.

12. Recaredo S. Tornero, *Chile ilustrado: Guía descriptiva del territorio de Chile, de las capitales de Provincia, de los puertos principales* (Valparaiso: Libr. i ajencias del Mercurio, 1872), 457.

13. El Mercurio, in Vicuña Mackenna, *Relación del incendio*, 12.

14. Francisco Javier Tocornal, "Relación médica de lo sucedido en el Templo de la Compañía el 8 de diciembre de 1863," *Anales de la Universidad de Chile* 25 (October 1864): 557, https://doi.org/10.5354/0717-8883.2012.20145.

15. El Mercurio, in Vicuña Mackenna, *Relación del incendio*, 13.

16. El Mercurio in *Resumen histórico del gran incendio*, 34.

17. *New York Herald*, January 18, 1864.

18. Serrano, *¿Qué hacer con Dios*.

19. Benjamín Vicuña Mackenna, *Miscelánea*, vol. 1 (Santiago de Chile: Imprenta de la Librería del Mercurio, 1872), 338.

20. Vicente Pérez Rosales, *Recuerdos del pasado: 1814–1860* (Santiago: Imprenta Gutenberg, 1886), 8.

21. Riquelme, *Episodios chilenos*, 55.

22. *Resumen histórico del gran incendio*, 34.

23. Casanova, *Historia del Templo de la Compañía*, 47.

24. Tocornal, "Relación médica," 557.

25. *New York Herald*, January 18, 1864.

26. Tornero, *Chile ilustrado*, 458.

27. El Mercurio in *Resumen histórico del gran incendio*, 34.

28. Marta Lamas, "Usos, dificultades y posibilidades de la categoría género," *Papeles de Población* 5, no. 21 (September 1999): 147–78.

29. Amelia Valcárcel, *Sexo y filosofía: Sobre mujer y poder* (Barcelona: Anthropos, 1994).

30. El Ferrocarril in *Resumen histórico del gran incendio*, 10.

31. Ibid., 13.

32. Funeral prayer by Archbishop Casanova from ibid., 28.

33. Riquelme, *Episodios chilenos*, 79.

34. La Patria, in Vicuña Mackenna, *Relación del incendio*, 35.

35. Ibid., 34.

36. Riquelme, *Episodios chilenos*.

37. According to the medieval legend, Saint Ursula and her 11,000 virginal handmaidens were beaded by a horde of Huns during a Christian pilgrimage across Europe. The large number of victims, very convenient for a future repartition of relics around the world, had its origins in the mistranslation of a document. In fact, the slayed virgins were eleven.

38. Vicuña Mackenna, *Relación del incendio*, 6.

39. Justo Donoso, *Instituciones de Derecho Canónico Americano*, Libro III, capítulo XVI: "Lugares sagrados" (Paris: Librería de Rosa y Bouret, 1858), 79–100.

40. Guillermo Matta for the *Voz de Chile* in Vicuña Mackenna, *Relación del incendio*, 44.

41. Francisco Javier Rosales, *A mis conciudadanos* (Paris: Imprenta Walder, 1864).

42. Vicuña Mackenna, *Un año en la Intendencia de Santiago: Lo que es la Capital i lo que debiera ser*, Documentos, vol. 2 (Santiago: Imprenta de la Librería del Mercurio, 1873).

43. Riquelme, *Episodios chilenos*.

44. Vicuña Mackenna, *Un año en la Intendencia de Santiago*, 2:326.

45. Ibid., 1:150.

46. Vicuña Mackenna, *Obras completas*, vol. 12, *Discursos Parlamentarios* (Santiago: Universidad de Chile, 1939); Vicuña Mackenna, *Un año en la Intendencia de Santiago*.

47. Article describing the outline of the piece and published in the Catholic newspaper *El Independiente* on September 14, 1872, cited in Palacios, *Del Infierno al Cielo*.

48. *L'Illustration, Journal Universel* (Paris, April 11, 1874), 235.

49. José Ignacio Eyzaguirre, *Discurso pronunciado en la inauguración del monumento conmemorativo del incendio de la Compañía* (Santiago: Imprenta Andrés Bello, 1873), 16.

50. Tocornal, "Relación médica."

51. Vicuña Mackenna, *Relación del incendio*, 7.

52. El Mercurio in ibid., 13.

53. Riquelme, *Episodios chilenos*, 134.

54. Tocornal, "Relación médica," 558.

55. La Patria in *Relación del incendio*, 19.

56. Riquelme, *Episodios chilenos*, 136.

57. Francesco Jacometti, *Vita di Ignazio Jacometti: Scultore* (Nuova tip. nell'Orfanotrofio di S. Maria degli Angeli, 1892).

58. Alberto Ried Silva, *El llamado del fuego* (Santiago: Ediciones de Librería Renacimiento, 1966).

59. Translation and proofreading by Pedro Veloso and Paul Salter, sponsored by the Translation Stimulus Grant Program, Directorate of Research and Creation of the Faculty of Architecture and Urbanism, Universidad de Chile.

Amanda Su

2. George Eliot at Nuneaton and Trans Monumentality

ON JUNE 14, 2020, in the wake of protests against the death of George Floyd, and a series of statues of white men being pulled down and defaced on both sides of the Atlantic, a group of men took it upon themselves to protect the statue of Victorian writer George Eliot, in Eliot's hometown of Nuneaton, England. They stood just yards away from a group of rival protesters organized by the Black Lives Matter (BLM) chapter of the Nuneaton and Bedworth area. The image circulated widely online: the men, thronged around the base of the Eliot statue, hands thrust belligerently in their pockets, one of them wearing a camouflage jacket, legs spread wide in a protective stance (figure 1). Their air of obstinate masculinity stands in sharp contrast to the figure they are guarding, who is a vision of demure femininity—eyes lowered, veiled hair, one of her delicately articulated hands resting on her voluminous skirt. The cascade of derision that ensued on Twitter zeroed in on the ignorance of the men and the incompatibility of their ideals with those of the writer they were guarding. Though the men claimed to be protecting their history, they appeared to have no idea about what they were protecting. Eliot had been a supporter of the Union cause during the American Civil War and a supporter of

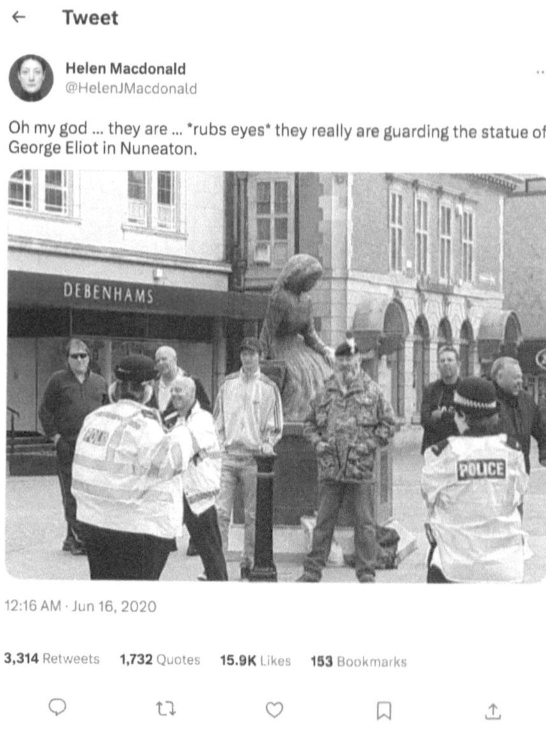

Figure 1. Twitter thread mocking the George Eliot statue defenders. Screenshot by the author.

Irish home rule, and little in Eliot's biography suggests that the writer could be linked to British slave trader Edward Colston, or to Winston Churchill, whose statues in Bristol and Westminster were pulled down and defaced days prior. Neither had Eliot's statue been named in a list of statues of slavers that BLM supporters published online a week earlier. The self-seriousness of the white statue defenders only exacerbated, in the eyes of the Twitter hive, the ridiculousness of their endeavor.

Yet there may be more in this unlikely tableau than meets the eye. The affective nostalgia that subtended this mistaken alliance invites a parsing of how and why a group of white male protestors chose to corral around the statue of an ostensible woman, and what gendered and racialized imaginaries coalesced around this encounter. By "ostensible woman," I refer to the premise that underlies Grace Lavery's idea of trans realism, wherein Lavery writes that Eliot, assigned the name Mary Ann Evans at birth, was "a figure for whom the term *masculine pseudonym* has never proven persuasive."[1] She compellingly discredits the common conception that Eliot wrote under a masculine pen name in order to boost book sales as mistaken, citing dozens of women writers who wrote under their own names and to great success (including the Brontë sisters). Instead, Lavery argues that Eliot was committed to being read and thought of as a man; was gleeful when assumed to be a man and mildly concerned when not. This project was borne out in Eliot's aesthetic practice as well: Eliot's mode of "trans realism" operates as an ethical injunction in which "realism will only have been accomplished when readers have learned not merely to respect, but to desire, the dysphorically sexed bodies of others."[2]

Lavery invites us to consider that one of the greatest novelists of the British nineteenth century inhabited a transgender identity in life and advocated for the same in letters. The claim has enormous ramifications for the ongoing reception of Eliot's letters—if not also Eliot's statue—as well as for the status of contemporary literary feminism in the UK, which in recent years has been plagued with accusations of transphobia and transmisogyny. This has been demonstrated not only by author J. K. Rowling's highly publicized stance against trans identity but also by multiple incidents regarding the UK's foremost literary prize for women, the Women's Prize. In 2019, Akwaeke Emezi became the first non-binary trans writer to be nominated for the prize and subsequently withdrew their work from consideration when asked by the prize for information on their sex as defined "by law."[3] In 2020, the prize celebrated its twenty-fifth year by releasing twenty-five novels "previously published under a male pseudonym, published for the first time with the female author's name on the jacket," including an edition of Middlemarch under the name Mary Ann Evans.[4] In 2021, after trans novelist Torrey Peters was nominated for the same prize, she became the target of an open letter by the Wild Woman Writing Club, which was signed by a number of readers and writers employing the names of famous dead British women writers as pseudonyms "because of the threat of harassment by trans extremists." Topping the list were the names Aphra Behn and Mary Ann Evans.[5]

As evidenced by these occasions, Eliot's gender identity has rendered the writer into something of a lightning rod for gender critical, or trans-exclusionary, feminists in the UK. The male defenders at Eliot's statue unintentionally roped Eliot's legacy into the realm of far-right protest culture as well. The two movements are not as disparate as they might initially seem; contemporary scholars have increasingly honed in on the affiliations between gender-critical feminists and the far right. In the UK, intense anti-trans media coverage runs the entire gamut from leftist and progressive to right-leaning and mainstream, with the proliferation and cross-pollination of far-right and gender-critical feminist hate groups serving as a major site in which the UK transphobic movement acquires a mass platform and following.[6] The otherwise disparate argumentations of gender-critical feminists and religious or far-right actors converge on a traditional alignment of sex/gender and serve to promote migratist and racist ideologies in both.[7] As Alyosxa Tudor explains, the construction of trans people in general and trans women in particular as sexual predators shares rhetorical and ideological overlaps with racist projections of Black and Brown men:

> The strategy of accusing trans people of sexual violence echoes a discourse that externalizes sexual violence as taking place somewhere else, outside the West, or that is ascribed to migrants, Black and Brown persons, or Muslims—all of whom are constructed as the eternal migrants who can never belong in the Western nation-state. With this ascription, sexual violence gets displaced to an elsewhere; and the imagined "here," in this case white heterosexuality (or some forms of homonormative sexuality) built on sex/gender alignment, becomes the pure place free of sexual violence that needs borders in order to be protected from the phantasmatic outside.[8]

Some critics have identified the collusion between gender-critical feminists (who self-identify as liberal or leftist) and right-wing conservatives as bizarre, referring to them as "strange bedfellows" or as an "unholy alliance."[9] But other scholars have also suggested that their alignment is not as aberrant as it may appear and that the genealogy of liberal feminism—also colloquially referred to as "white feminism"—is consistent with systemic racism and transphobia alike. Serena Bassi and Greta LaFleur, for example, argue that contemporary trans panics are "genealogically coherent with multiple conservative moral panics and resilient fascist tropes but also with the *longue durée* of liberal, bourgeois, white feminist exclusions perpetrated along racial and class lines."[10] Bassi and LaFleur locate these exclusions within the non-universal promises offered by liberal feminism in the movement's inaugurating push for women's suffrage, as well as in more recent critiques of liberal feminism and its alignment with colonial and neocolonial logics by Black women of color and Third World feminists. As Maria Lugones argues regarding the coloniality of gender, "biological dimorphism [serves] Eurocentered global capitalist domination/exploitation."[11]

In this chapter, I suggest that the protest at the Eliot statue in summer 2020 provides a way to examine the growing affiliations between gender-critical and far-right groups, as well as the ways in which these affinities play out in contemporary memorial culture. Situating the protest at the Eliot statue at the intersection of these movements allows us to further exfoliate the uncanny political alliances that are building between the two. These convergences are not so much serendipitous as they are predetermined. In Nuneaton, a former mining town, the discontents of the white working class were metabolized into a battle over the sexes, following decades of financial devastation in the wake of Thatcherite reforms. This stance was undergirded by the valorization of the most reactionary features of their former social reproductive system: the exclusion of non-white labor and the relegation of women to roles of unwaged household labor. I argue that the formal elements of the Eliot statue, which lodge it within a binary sex/gender system, lent itself to a protest that read on the surface as an anti-BLM protest but that doubled as a protest against the disappearance of this prior social order. A close reading of the protest at the Eliot statue thus provides a perspective on ongoing struggles over memorials that does not elide the issue of class in its consideration of race or gender. The final section of this chapter explores the tensions between a politics of representation and a politics of redistribution in the contemporary landscape of memorialization, as situated within the struggle to erect statues to women and transgender people.

The George Eliot Statue at Nuneaton

GEORGE ELIOT'S STATUTE at Nuneaton was erected in 1986 after a sustained, decades-long effort on behalf of the George Eliot Fellowship (figure 2). The society was founded in 1930 by a local newspaper editor, A. F. Cross, who had, for twenty-five years prior to the founding, been campaigning for a statue to honor Eliot in Nuneaton. The idea for the society came about as a means of amassing a critical mass of supporters for the proposed statue; however, dogged by insufficient membership and funds and the subsequent world war, during which

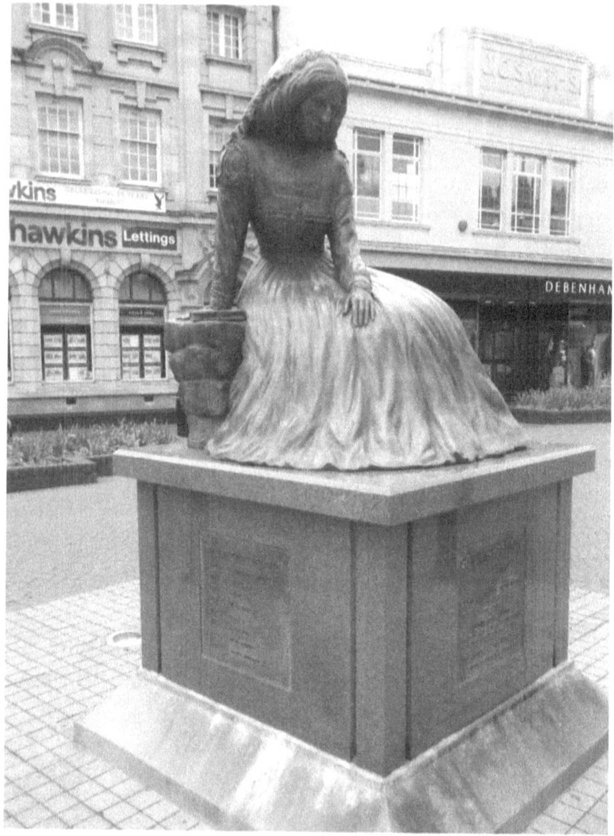

Figure 2. The George Eliot statue, created by John
Letts. The sign advertising "Lettings" in the background
creates a punctum with the sculptor's name. Photograph
by ell brown, distributed under a CC BY-SA 2.0 license.

Nuneaton was heavily bombed, the society languished as did its hopes
of erecting a memorial. In 1984, the Nuneaton Borough Council,
which was in the process of pedestrianizing the town center, suggested
to the society that they were interested in incorporating a statue,
though the society was to be responsible for soliciting the appropriate
funds and organizing its installment. The statue was finally unveiled
in Newdegate Square on March 22, 1986.

Originally an Anglo-Saxon settlement known as "Etone" or
"Eaton," translating to "settlement by the water" in reference to its
location on a convergence of ancient routes on the River Anker,

Nuneaton became one of the earliest market towns established in North Warwickshire in the mid-twelfth century.[12] The town's two major industries in the nineteenth century consisted of a silk ribbon weaving industry (which was wiped out by an 1860 treaty that removed duties on imported silks) and a rapidly burgeoning coal industry. Though coal had been mined in Nuneaton in small amounts since the thirteenth century, improved mining techniques as well as railroad logistics greatly enhanced its position in the coal industry. In 1862 a railroad line was established between Birmingham and Nuneaton that opened up access to coal and clay and their derivative products, brick and tile. A third of the male workers in Nuneaton were employed in the coal industry by the first decade of the twentieth century.[13] As was common with industrial boomtowns associated with coal mining, Nuneaton lacked a sense of a real civic center. Civic buildings (which typically serve as a town center focus) were occasioned by rapid civic and population expansion, such that they were created and replaced on an ad hoc basis whenever plots and resources permitted, and thereby scattered through the town. A straggling set of dormitories was erected in order to accommodate influxes of coal workers. A master plan laid out by the Borough Council under architect Frederick Gibberd in 1947 attempted to correct for the lack of a town center, calling for a western loop road that would develop into an almost complete town center ring road commonly seen in highway designs from the 1930s to 1970s. A conservationist appraisal of Nuneaton architecture and infrastructure commissioned by the local government in 2009 critiqued the ring road for "disrupting the intricate medieval pattern of streets, cutting them off from their approach roads and isolating the center from its surroundings."[14] It was at almost precisely the center of the ring road, at the center of the town itself, in the midst of what is now a commercial shopping area, that the Eliot statue was placed (figure 3).

The placement of the statue in the heart of town extended beyond the geographical. The statue served as the centerpiece of Nuneaton's transition from coal mining to the tourism industry, as situated on Eliot's own monumental legacy. Eliot was born there and based the fictional town of Milby from the story collection *Scenes of Clerical Life* on the town itself. The coal industry, which expanded rapidly in the latter half of the nineteenth century, peaked in the early twentieth century and plummeted in the 1950s and 1960s, with oil shipped from the Middle East replacing coal as the major source of fuel for multiple industries. The last coal mine in Nuneaton closed in 1968.

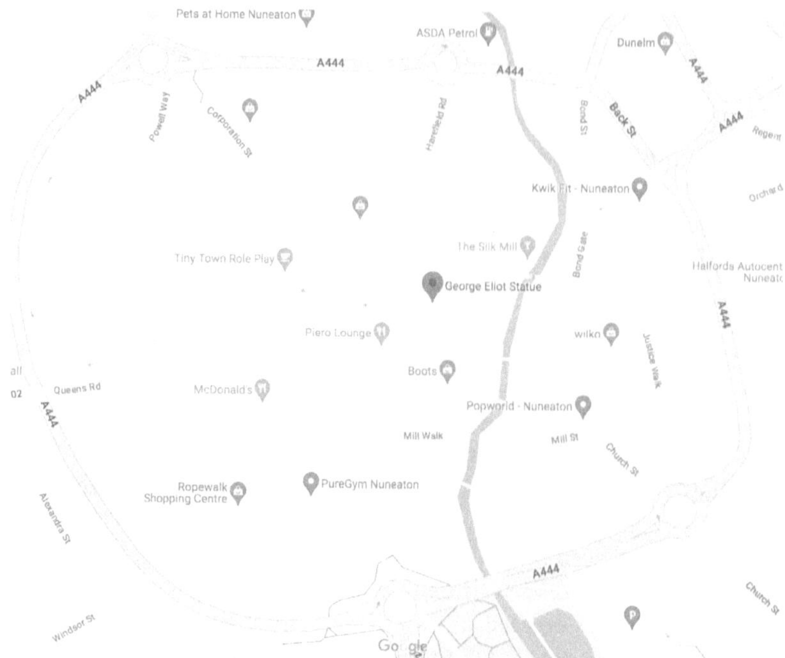

Figure 3. Google Maps rendering of the statue's location at the heart of town. Screenshot by the author.

The notes of the George Eliot Fellowship indicate its members had been attempting to persuade the town leadership to transition to a tourist economy for some time amid the long economic downturn, with recorded efforts stemming from 1953 at the earliest, including a joint effort between the society and the town council on a "George Eliot Trail" that was instituted in 1978. According to Kathleen Adams in a written history of the society, Eliot served as "the peg on which to hang" the town's transition to a tourist economy, given that "pilgrims come from all over the world to the George Eliot Country."[15] Eliot's legacy continues to shore up the town's tourism prospects. In a 2016 report written by a tourism consultation agency as commissioned by the Nuneaton and Bedworth Borough Council, Eliot's name appears forty times in a fifty-eight-page report. One of the key recommendations was to develop a signature and recurring "George Eliot event" that would solidify the town's otherwise "unclear brand."[16]

The Eliot statue was made by a local sculptor named John Letts. Letts had previously sculpted a bust of Eliot for the local hospital, also named for Eliot. In a document that the society filed under the name "John Letts, the Gifted Warwickshire Sculptor," Letts describes his relationship to the subject of the statue: "Some four years have elapsed since my first brief encounter with Mary Ann Evans—or 'Ann' as I had called her at that time. It had been a strange, emotional experience with moments of deep passion and quiet companionship. But, it was not to last. The affair ended as it began, with a suddenness that was, in itself, an awakening."[17] It appears that the "first brief encounter" that Letts describes was the occasion of sculpting the bust of Eliot for the local hospital. "It was a surprise, therefore," Letts writes, "when I discovered that a few of her close 'friends', knowing of our fondness for each other (it would seem that 'Ann' had conveyed her feelings on this matter to them) arranged that 'Ann' and I should renew our acquaintance."[18] The rather baroque quality of this narration suggests an attempt at mimicking the stylistics of Victorian prose, with the parentheticals bracketing the name "Ann" serving as simultaneous formality (the acknowledgment of Eliot's nom de plume) as well as indiscretion (the institution of a coquettish pet name for a distinguished author). Partway through the piece, as Letts begins to materialize the statue, the parentheticals bracketing the name "Ann" drop off, and he refers to Eliot without it: "The first sight of Ann brought back all the old feelings that I had taken so long trying to forget. It was then the end of May, and I knew that Ann would be leaving me again in the following October" (i.e., when the statue departed for the bronze casters).[19] After the space of some pages, over which Letts continues to dilate on the feelings that he had for his subject, he indulges in a revision of Eliot's birth name, "Mary Ann" to "My Ann." The relationship between Eliot and Letts is thoroughly that of Galatea and Pygmalion; the subject of the sculpture solipsized by the desire of the sculptor. Even the seeming chasteness of the prose vibrates in tandem with a certain libidinal excess premised on the frisson of unattainability. Nowhere does Letts describe Eliot's status as a writer in the piece nor any reference to Eliot's writerly corpus; in fact, the name "George Eliot" never even makes an appearance, as though even the mention of the masculine name would interrupt his erotic attachment to his own work. The time capsule inserted beneath the statue at time of installation included a photograph of Letts, as though to discreetly stare up Eliot's skirts for eternity (figure 4a).

Eliot posed for only one photographic portrait, in 1858 (figure 4b). Representations of Eliot's visual likeness are slim, which contributed to an obsessive interest in honing in on the exact contours of Eliot's

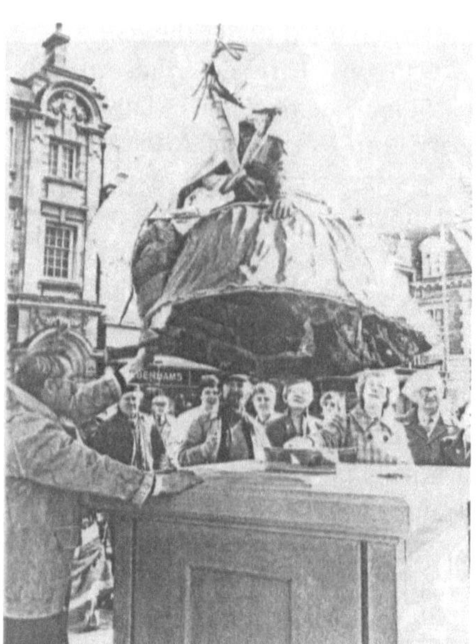

Figure 4a. Installation of John Letts's George Eliot statue, March 1986. Courtesy of *Coventry Telegraph*.

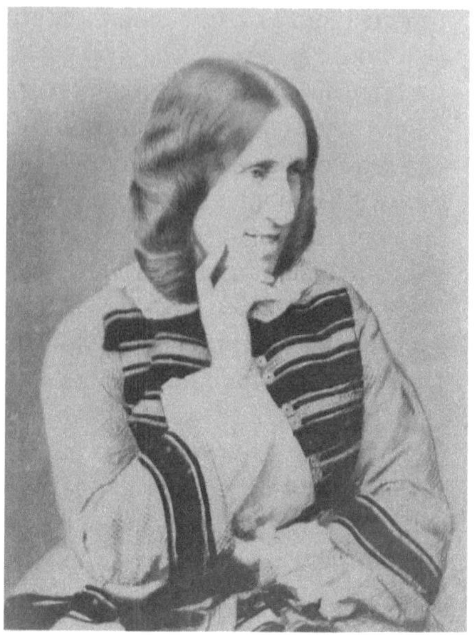

Figure 4b. Eliot's sole photographic portrait. Photograph by John Mayall, 1858. © National Portrait Gallery, London.

physiognomy even in recent years. For example, in 2013 the actress and writer Lena Dunham tweeted a revelation that Eliot was "ugly AND horny!" which occasioned a *New Yorker* article by Rebecca Mead in 2013 that compiled an array of biographers and contemporaries on the subject of Eliot's "ugly beauty."[20] In 2017, the *Guardian* ran an article by Eliot scholar Kathryn Hughes that claimed that a new chalk pastel portrait of the young Eliot had emerged, in which the sitter is "revealed as an individual, not a type. Her long face, big nose and flinty grey eyes are the opposite of the generic dolliness that passed for beauty in the early Victorian period."[21] Eliot's lack of beauty was also a preoccupation of the George Eliot Fellowship. Kathleen Adams mentions the discovery in 1981 of a "most attractive portrait of a young Victorian woman" thought to either be Eliot or Eliot's older sister, Chrissey Evans—the society attributed it to the latter on the basis of the sitter's attractiveness.[22] In a short essay on the occasion of the unveiling of the statue, Adams writes, "Jonathan pulled the cord, the green veil dropped away, and a gasp of delight arose from the large crowd. She was beautiful! I hasten to add that John Letts has not made her face beautiful, for that would not have been correct, but neither has he made an undoubtedly plain woman grotesque."[23]

The lack of substantial visual depictions of Eliot gave John Letts a wide range of latitude in terms of sculpting Eliot "in the round" (as the statue is described in the society's papers—the innocuousness of this technical term acquiring a rather different valence within the context of Letts's prose). The statue depicts a woman sitting on a low stone bench, her eyes downcast, seemingly lost in contemplation. A closed book rests beside one of her hands. She wears a dress with a wide yoke extending to the mid-chest, the simplicity of the design relieved by rows of rounded embellishments marching along the edges of the yoke, at the collar, and as buttons down the bodice. Letts took inspiration from George Eliot's one photographic portrait: the hair curls around the face in a soft oval, the ridges on the nose are dominant, as are those on the brow. The idiosyncrasy of the figure's facial features—too pronounced to be thought of as prototypically Victorian à la George Elgar Hicks's 1863 triptych *Women's Mission*—fulfills the parameters of what Margaret Bozenna Goscilo calls the Pre-Raphaelite type, "with her rich, rippling hair, her striking but not traditionally pretty face, and her exophthalmic or prominent eyes."[24] Her posture is peculiar. The figure is sitting down, but also possibly on the verge of rising, pushing herself up by the hand resting on the bench. The figure torques excessively at the tightly corseted waist in a way that appears anatomically difficult, if not impossible, reminiscent of what Julie F. Codell refers to as another of the prevailing traits of Pre-Raphaelite paintings: "the gestures and body language. . . are to a marked degree intentionally transitional and mundane. . . . Many postures seem so uncomfortable that they could not be sustained for long."[25] The formal qualities of Letts's statue affiliate it with one of the primary works of Pre-Raphaelite art, William Holman Hunt's *The Awakening Conscience* (1853–54) in which a woman is depicted in an ambiguous mode, either sitting down or rising from a man's lap (figure 5). Eliot knew of Hunt's work, having described him in 1856 as "one of the greatest painters of the pre-eminently realistic school."[26] Eliot's own interest in Pre-Raphaelite philosophies of art subtended the development of several of her primary characters in *Middlemarch*, "making the development of a Pre-Raphaelite sensibility an integral part of Dorothea Brooke's growth in spiritual awareness—what Eliot calls her 'awakening consciousness.'"[27] In what appears to be an echo of both Pre-Raphaelite and Eliot's own concepts of "awakening," Letts

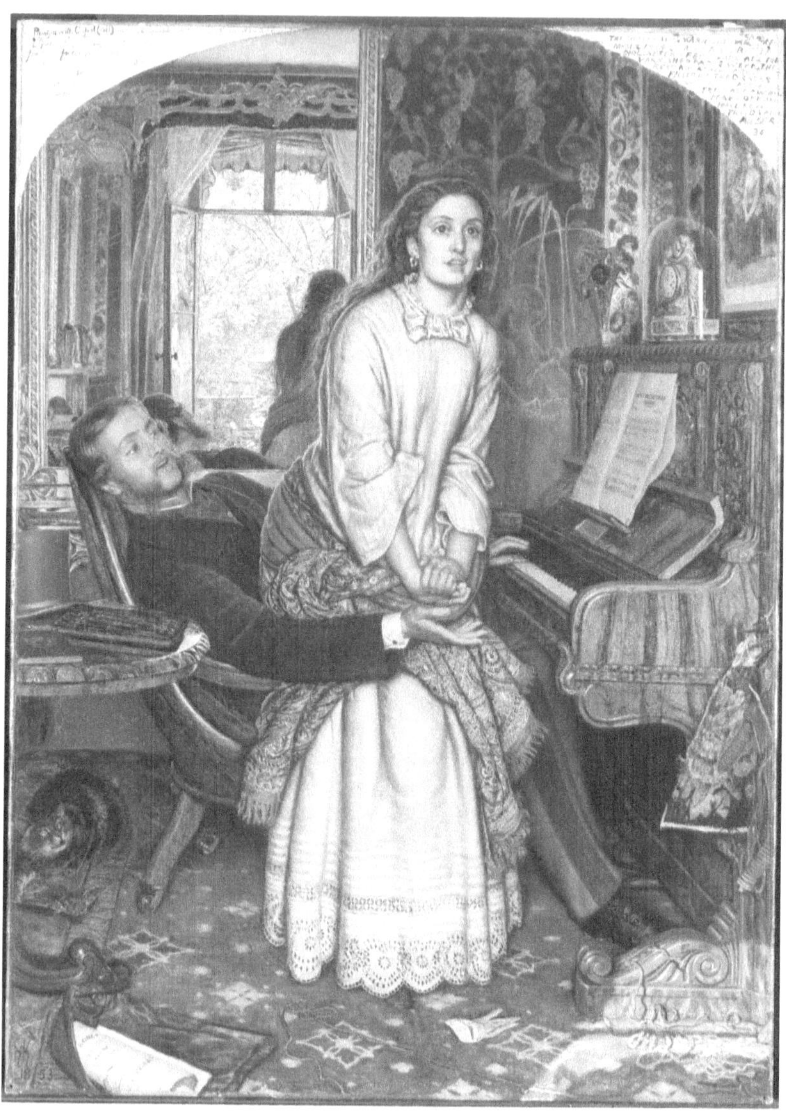

Figure 5. *The Awakening Conscience*, exhibited 1854, William Holman Hunt. Presented by Sir Colin and Lady Anderson through the Friends of the Tate Gallery 1976. Photo: Tate Gallery.

writes, "the affair ended as it began, with a suddenness that was, in itself, an awakening."[28]

John Ruskin's analysis of Hunt's *Awakening* brings to the fore the latent social and sexual implications embedded within Letts's evocation of Hunt. The painting had served as a par excellence example for Ruskin on the merits of the Pre-Raphaelite movement: "Examine the whole range of the walls of the Academy," Ruskin writes. "There will not be found one [painting] powerful as this to meet full in the front the moral evil of the age in which it is painted."[29] According to Elizabeth Prettejohn, Ruskin's analysis of this painting is "locked into a moral system. . . in which sexual immorality entails doom."[30] This moral system included, for Ruskin, the idea that the sexes are complementary opposites:

> Each has what the other has not; each completes the other. They are in nothing alike, and the happiness and the perfection of both depends on each asking and receiving from the other what the other only can give.
>
> Now their separate characters are briefly these. The man's power is active, progressive, defensive. He is eminently the doer, the creator, the discoverer, the defender. His intellect is for speculation and invention; his energy for adventure, for war, and for conquest. . . . But the woman's power is for rule, not for battle and her intellect is not for invention or recreation, but sweet ordering, arrangement, and decision. She sees the qualities of things, their claims, and their places. Her great function is praise; she enters into no contest, but infallibly adjudges the crown of contest. By her office and place, she is protected from all danger and temptation. The man, in his rough work in the open world, must encounter all peril and trial—to him therefore must be the failure, the offence, the inevitable error; often he must be wounded or subdued, often misled, and always hardened.[31]

Kate Millet surmises that Ruskin's argument rests on the "threadbare tactic of justifying social and temperamental differences by biological ones," wherein the doctrine of "Nature" that Ruskin and his followers advocated for in their writings on aesthetics serves also as an argument for separate spheres based on sexual difference.[32] But also note Ruskin's use of the terms "defensive" and "defender," the only time he employs repetition in this excerpt. The role of man, according to Ruskin, is to defend women from the greater world so that they can go about their "sweet ordering, arrangement, and decision" within the confines of the home. If Letts's statue of Eliot extracts the woman from *The Awakening*, divesting her of her male complement, then the male statue defenders can be envisioned as stepping back in to repopulate the referenced painting. They unwittingly re-create a new scene, arrogating a male-and-female presence at the heart of town. But what are they enacting? Letts's statue of Eliot, in its portrayal of a sweetly generic, tightly corseted Victorian woman (notwithstanding the idiosyncrasy of the facial features), plays precisely into what Michel Foucault critiques as the reductive, commonplace imaginary of the Victorian era as one of rigid and repressive sexual mores: that is, utterly regardless of Eliot's personal opinions or writings on social issues, the statue comes to symbolize a conservative sexual and gendered ethos with implications for how one envisions larger economic and societal roles. In other words, it became the focal point of a moral panic. As Stuart Hall reminds, moral panics often coincide with economic downturns and income inequality and are sometimes engineered by politicians as a mode of public distraction during crises of inflation and profitability.[33] An understanding of the moral panic that undergirded the protest at the Eliot statue requires a deeper understanding of the history of the devastation of the coal mines not only in Nuneaton but across the country, and the impact that deindustrialization wreaked upon local economies and preexisting gendered social arrangements.

The Demise of Coal Mining and Gendered Social Arrangements

COAL MINING FORMED the primary driver of British industrial capitalism in the early postwar period, feeding into the railway system, steel production, engineering, shipyards, and the chemical industry. The nationalism of coal mining in 1947 was undergirded by hopes that sustained, long-term employment would follow.[34] These hopes were further bolstered by an enthusiastic state-sponsored orchestration of newsreels that featured heroic depictions of the miner, documenting industrial accidents, tragedies, and triumphs. These newsreels, shown in local cinemas in and around the coal fields, entwined ideas of masculinity with nationalized coal mining labor, deepening a sociocultural understanding of the division of labor between men and women and furthering a resistance to foreign labor.[35] As Andreas Malm and the Zetkin Collective write, the work of "those white men who extract black fuel. . . is imbued with an authenticity few other categories of workers can approximate: they haul up the inner body of the nation."[36] The history of fossil fuels has proven "infinitely more congenial to the imaginaries of nationalism. It can be apprehended as our coal, our oil, our gas. . . . Nations blessed with fossil fuels have felt the stock within them, as an ultra-deep material inheritance to which the mystique of nationalism easily sticks."[37]

In the 1960s, the replacement of coal by oil shipped from the Middle East as the major source of fuel for transportation, industrial, and domestic use had cataclysmic effects on the domestic coal industry as well as on prior gendered social arrangements that enabled the industry. In 1983, Thatcher appointed Ian McGregor, who had played a major role in the privatization of Britain's formerly nationalized steel industry, to head the National Coal Board. The goal was to privatize the coal industry accordingly. McGregor's call to close unprofitable pits and dramatically reduce the workforce led to a sustained and massive strike on behalf of the miners. Thatcher's government unleashed an arsenal of strike-breaking tactics: secret stockpiles of coal and coke sequestered in advance in strategic sites around the country, agreements with non-unionized haulage firms to break pickets and distribute coal to processing plants, changes in legislation targeting strike benefits, and the weaponization of police brutality. A year later, the strike finally ground to a halt and the pit closures began in earnest. The mythology of the heroic mine worker vanished, only to be replaced by newer, shinier icons. The "offshoring" of labor under Thatcher was accompanied by steep cuts in the top rates of taxation and the loosening of stock market controls in 1986—the same year that the George Eliot statue was erected—which enabled foreign capital to pour into London. "The yuppie in the black suit, the Cockney futures trader, the 'phone number' bonus, the Porsche and the Cotswold manor became icons of Thatcher's Britain, cruelly contrasted with the unemployed miner and docker."[38] In 1994, the coal industry was finally privatized, with a scant fifteen mines remaining open. Over a hundred and fifty mines had closed in the mere span of a decade. Working-class hopes of new jobs to be created by the Labour Party under Tony Blair's tenure as prime minister starting in 1997 were also dashed. Rather than breaking with the precedents set by the former Conservative government, New Labour under the consecutive governments of Blair and Gordon Brown further divested from the welfare state, embracing globalization and new markets.

The working class's rejection of the state's embrace of financialization over industrialization, and the replacement of an economy based on the production of material goods by one that was based on foreign assets, took its most pronounced shape in the form of Brexit. The core support for the Leave vote was concentrated in the south and the east, but the working-class vote in North England and in South Wales—former coal mining areas—tipped the balance.[39] The voting pattern seen in those areas was borne out in the Nuneaton and Bedworth counting area as well, with two-thirds of voters backing Leave. In the wake of Brexit, commentators claimed that working-class individuals voted against themselves due to their intellectual inability to understand their own economic interests.[40] However, Luke Telford and Jonathan Wistow make the argument that voters also based their choice in a "localized experience of neoliberalism's slow-motion social dislocation linked to the deindustrialization of the area" and the failure of the Labour Party to represent working-class interests.[41] Their argument resonates with that of Raymond Williams, regarding the massive yearlong strike that occurred thirty-odd years earlier: that theirs was a revolt against "the logic of a new nomad capitalism, which exploits actual places and people and then (as it suits it) moves on. . . . Back in the shadow of their operations, from the inner cities to the abandoned mining villages, real men and women know that they are facing an alien order of paper and money, which seems all-powerful."[42]

Yet the virulent anti-immigrant racism that characterized large swathes of the Leave campaign in 2016 is undeniable and threatens to overwhelm the characterization of Brexit as a substantive critique of neoliberal establishment. Leaders of the Leave campaign deliberately stoked the fears of economically disenfranchised voters by collapsing the question of free labor movement within the EU with incendiary rhetoric describing a flood of foreign refugees.[43] To this point, the work of Moishe Postone articulates how the free-floating, migratory nature of capital can become tethered to the migration of racialized bodies. Postone argues that the "specific characteristics of the power attributed to the Jews by modern anti-Semitism—abstractness, intangibility, universality, mobility"—are all characteristics of Marx's value dimension of social form.[44] According to Postone, Jews were perceived not only as the representatives of capital but also the "personifications of the intangible, destructive, immensely powerful, and international domination of capital as an alienated social form," such that the "overcoming of capitalism" and its destructive effects became associated with the "overcoming of the Jews."[45] To a similar point, Michelle Hale Williams has theorized immigration as the "funnel issue" of the far right, the issue through which all other issues pass on their way toward resolution. Under this framework, unemployment, rampant crime, segregation, poverty, and social decay—which might otherwise be attributed to the deleterious effects of neoliberal capitalism—would all be resolved via the cessation of immigration.[46]

Read in this light, the anti-BLM protest at the Eliot statue was not random but instead decades in the making: an instance of systemic, socioeconomic devastation finding an outlet in the form of anti-Black and anti-immigrant vitriol. But it also calls our attention to the specifically gendered nature of this nostalgia. The coal miners' strike during the early years of Thatcher did not merely protect the livelihoods of male coal miners against the threat of foreign labor; it protected and consolidated the uncompensated forms of female household labor that made it possible. The intense domestic labor that women performed incorporated them into a "coal mining regime of production" in which their labor not only was disguised as "unproductive" but also went toward reinforcing the power of men within the family, local communities, and the labor movement.[47] As Florence Sutcliffe-Braithwaite and Natalie Thomlinson describe in their study of gender, trade unionism, and community activism in the 1984–85 strike, the wives of striking coal miners were often called on to disavow the political nature of their support for the strike—for to be political was to be unwomanly—and also to perform models of domestic femininity in order to authenticate their working-class identities.[48] The escalation of mine closures led to an expansion of employment opportunities for women in the welfare state, with jobs in local authority administration, and public sector education, and health care. At the same time, male unemployment soared, and former coal mine workers were hounded by chronic ill health and injuries caused by hazardous working conditions.[49] Neither was it easy for them to find employment in other manufacturing industries: one of the first actions taken by the Thatcher government that took power in 1979 was to remove capital export controls and allow companies to employ cheaper labor outside of the UK, gouging employment levels in domestic factories. The protest at the Eliot statue demonstrates how a segment of the British working class ends up valorizing the most reactionary features of its former social reproductive system: the exclusion of non-white labor and the relegation of women to roles of unwaged household labor. In the words of Bernard Hare, on the dramatic transformation of this social order:

I wasn't born into the underclass—it didn't exist when I was born—but my whole family sort of plopped into it after the Miners' Strike in 1984–85. Before that we felt that we were part of something, a community, a great nation with a great history. After that, we knew that we were redundant, rubbish, nothing. . . . Our communities crumbled, people lost hope and felt betrayed.[50]

That a protest against a loss of this scale should coalesce around a statue appears intuitive. Statues are the manifestations of complex histories of thought and affect and action—one might say, "tradition"—solidified through its rendering in stone or bronze. They are reassuringly "concrete" as opposed to abstracted.[51] So too does it appear intuitive that the statue defenders would have arrayed themselves around the figure of a Victorian woman, standing in as shorthand for the binary sex/gender system of the sort theorized by Ruskin, with men and women each in their separate spheres. As Klaus Theweleit writes regarding fascist fantasies and the process of industrialization, wherein labor and its commodities become continually abstracted, a desire for the concrete manifests in the form of desire for the symbolic body of femininity: "Streams were channeled— into factories and chancellories. Streams of sweat became streams of money. . . . The body of woman [serves as] a territory of desire in place of the body of the earth."[52]

The protest that happened at the George Eliot statue was an instance of sociopolitical and economic discontent disarticulated from its sources, oscillating without an object, latching instead onto a feminine emblem of a better, bygone past. It illustrates how systemic economic disenfranchisement can manifest in an enforcement of a constructed form of femininity understood to exclude Black and transgendered bodies as such. It is crucial to understand the social and symbolic mechanisms that engender these affiliations and antagonisms, because the same concepts that undergird this ideological framework have been mobilized in other places. Gender-critical thinkers have latched onto the supposed antagonism between the working class and transgender issues, wherein gender theory and trans rights are made out to be "an elite fixation of [the] upper- and upper-middle class."[53] For example, in an article titled "Will Left's Gender Agenda Fall Flat with Minorities and Working Americans?" posted by the Heritage Foundation (a right-wing think tank that lobbies against feminism, LGBTQ rights, and immigration), a writer queries, "How many Chinese immigrants know what 'queer trans femme' means? How keen is the average plumber, UPS driver, housekeeper, construction worker, or landscaper to make sure high school males who identify as female get to shower with the girls?" Self-proclaimed leftist feminists have also leveraged the language of the left in their transphobic crusades. In 2019, a group of radical feminists appeared at a panel hosted by the Heritage Foundation called "The Inequality of the Equality Act: Concerns from the Left."[54] Melinda Cooper's theory of how neoliberalism and neoconservatism often accompany each other helps illuminate the rhetoric of scarcity that these so-called "leftist feminists" draw on to discourage public spending on transgender populations. According to Cooper, as neoliberal policymakers cut spending on health, education, and welfare, they simultaneously identified the patriarchal nuclear family as a wholesale alternative to the welfare state, which would step in to provide the functions of care and social reproduction that the state had divested from. Reactionary moralisms go hand in hand with neoliberal states.[55]

Memorials function, in part, as not only the commemorative but also the distributive politics of the state made visible. In the following section, I situate the contemporary bid to install more monuments to women and gender-nonconforming people within a history of monuments that were coextensive with a state project of racial and distributive exclusions.

Transgender Rights and the Struggle to Erect Memorials

IN NOVEMBER 2020, the newly erected statue of Mary Wollstonecraft in London was covered by a gender-critical feminist group in a T-shirt that read, in words that serve as the calling card of this particular group, "Women, noun, adult human female."[56] Their targeting of the Wollstonecraft statue was no accident: the statue depicted her in the nude, with both primary and secondary sexual characteristics prominently on display, marking her as a "biological woman" in the parlance of this group. Wollstonecraft's reputation as an early liberal feminist thinker was likely also an effort on behalf of this group to allege that their version of feminism is the natural culmination of over a century's worth of feminist thought—a statement with which Bassi and LaFleur, who argue that contemporary trans panics are coextensive with liberal feminism, would likely agree.

Bassi and LaFleur's critique of liberal feminism, rooted in its historical entwinements with white supremacy, casts skepticism on the project of erecting more memorials to cis and trans women as a means of protecting their rights. The contemporary space of memorial politics bears out liberal feminism's preoccupation with the politics of representation, with memorials to women increasingly erected across the globe. In 2019, New York City mayor Bill de Blasio unveiled plans for a $10 million initiative to build seven memorials honoring women across the five boroughs, including monuments to honor gay liberation pioneers and Black transgender activists Marsha P. Johnson and Sylvia Rivera near Stonewall Inn. The statues to Johnson and Rivera were touted as one of the world's first monuments to transgender people.[57] At the end of de Blasio's term in January 2022, plagued by insufficient funding and persistent delays caused by the pandemic, none of the promised statutes had materialized. Frustrated by the years of inaction, in August 2021, transgender artist and activist Jesse Pallota installed a statue of Johnson in Christopher Park across from the Stonewall Inn without the city's approval, submitting a First Amendment permit through the National Park Service to protect the statue.

Yet, as Reina Gosset, Eric A. Stanley, and Johanna Burton argue, representation can serve as a "trap door" in which modes of visual allocation outstrip means of resource allocation. De Blasio's plan to "break the bronze ceiling" by incorporating statues of transgender activists alongside cis women activists is not innocent of what Lisa Duggan has termed a "rhetorical commitment to diversity, and to a narrow, formal, *nonredistributive* form of 'equality' politics."[58] Gosset and colleagues caution that while representation is a "door into making new futures possible," at the same time, "when produced within the cosmology of racial capitalism, the promise of 'positive representation' ultimately gives little support of protection to many, if not most, trans and gender non-conforming people, particularly those who are low-income and/or of color—the very people whose lives and labor constitute the ground for the figuration of this moment of visibility."[59] They remind that when the hypervisibility of transgender people—in movies, TV, fashion—is unaccompanied by structural resources and protections for transgender life—for example, access to hormone therapy and gender-affirmative surgeries, single-use gender-neutral bathrooms, and the right to change one's legal gender—such visibility may only serve to increase acts of rhetorical, institutional, and physical violence against transgender people.

Though the forms of representation offered within the auspices of a public or civic memorial are not entirely coincident with the forms of social and media representation critiqued by Gosset and colleagues, their caution still holds. Monuments and memorials signal an ostensible commitment on behalf of the government to the protection of the community that the memorial purports to celebrate, though this commitment is one that any given designated community across the political spectrum can easily protest as hollow or inadequate (one only need think of the glut of veteran memorials across the United States and veteran communities' extensive complaints of institutional neglect). The space of memorialization is one wherein the politics of the visible consistently and often disappointingly brush up against the politics of distributive justice. The erection and maintenance of monuments, though expensive, still pales in comparison to the potential scale of renewable annual spending on transgender health and wellness. Johnson and Rivera's permanent, municipally approved statue in Greenwich Village was estimated to cost $750,000 in 2019, whereas transgender advocates have suggested that the New York State Department of Health set aside $6 million dedicated to transgender and nonbinary causes in their 2024 budget.[60] One might recall that Johnson and Rivera's legacy rests directly on their early championing of transgender youth who were neglected by governmental and private gay organizations alike. Johnson and Rivera's Street Transvestite Action Revolutionaries (STAR) was a collective home for street youth and transgender youth that also doubled as the first trans sex worker labor organization in the United States. Its first manifestation was in the form of a parked trailer in Greenwich Village that was not owned by either Johnson or Rivera: one morning, they arrived with food for the sleeping youth and discovered to their horror that it was being driven away by a trucker.[61] The contemporary struggle to erect statues to these particular transgender activists instantiates the tensions between the ethos that they embodied in the form of direct action (wherein actors appropriate the means necessary to attain their goals without any recourse to hierarchical bureaucratic processes) and those of indirect action (wherein actors vie for influence through various channels of legislation, elections, or corporate campaigns), with the realm of memorial politics falling squarely into the latter.

Johnson and Rivera's respective figurations at the intersection of Black and trans identities also provoke a paradox in the project of attempting to assimilate them into the state memorial apparatus. Trans studies scholar Marquis Bey argues that the terms "Black" and "trans*" are ontological markers that seek to name "the anoriginal lawlessness" that characterizes these "fugitive identificatory demarcations."[62] Thinking alongside Black studies scholars Fred Moten and Stefano Harney, Bey writes that Blackness is a "no/place, a spaceless space that renders governability ungovernable," whereas "trans* denotes the ubiquity, the transitivity, the fundamentality of the primordial force of unfixing openness."[63] "Blackness" and "trans*-ness" designate the refusal of fixity and the disruption of systematicity and are "unresponsive to the governance that it calls and the governments that it rouses."[64] Bey's formulation of their intersection suggests that Pallota's fugitive statue of Johnson in Christopher Park may have been the most fitting tribute to Johnson's own fugitivity, insofar as "Blackness" and "trans*-ness"—as well as Johnson's own personal ethics of care—are radical projects that will not align themselves with the state to meet the vouchsafe of either memory or distribution.

Finally, it is worth noting that the history of memorialization in the United States itself is deeply entrenched within racist ideologies that also insist on the cisgender female body; that the politics of the visible as pertaining to the question of women in memorials have never been separate from the politics of race and systems of racialized distribution. The equation of protecting statues with protecting history is one that stems back to the enormous push by the Daughters of the Confederacy at the end of the nineteenth century to commemorate the Confederate generation and to promote a new form of Southern nationalism that was inseparable from the project of white supremacy. According to Karen L. Cox, women were given a special role in this tradition, with biblical metaphors invoking Mary and Martha applied to their honoring of the Confederate dead.[65] One of the linchpins of their movement, alongside the revision of history books and educational curriculum, was the dogged erection of statues honoring the Lost Cause, in which the bodies of women—not even necessarily those of soldiers—proliferated. According to Lost Cause ideology, women were defenders of the home, and many statues depicted Confederate women as Penelope awaiting the return of Odysseus.[66] The Confederate Memorial at Arlington National Cemetery, also erected by the Daughters, prominently features a woman in Grecian robes who symbolizes the South, as well as the stalwart figure of Minerva supporting the body of a fallen woman, who also represents the South. This visual discourse in allegorical female bodies partly originated in Britain. As Rebecca Senior argues, female figures such as "Winged Victory" grew popular during the most aggressive phase of British imperial expansion as a means of sanitizing its imperial project, and the same figures were conscripted for Confederate memorials over a century later.[67] This visual history goes to show that the use of cisgendered female bodies in transatlantic memorial culture is inextricable from the forms of social and sexual reproductions that racist regimes have sought to extract from them.

So where does that leave us with regard to the statue of George Eliot at Nuneaton? Should we consider it a statue to a gender-transgressive icon, in a memorial landscape otherwise devoid of them? The material history of the statue, the circumstances of its design and execution, and certainly some of the ways that it has lent itself to the agendas of local actors (as demonstrated in the anti-BLM protest) seem to suggest that it does not stand as a memorial to transgender life so much as it stands as a testament to the ways in which transgressively gendered bodies are misread and misrepresented. It also suggests that to reckon with the bodies of women in memorialization—especially those of white women—is also to reckon with the ongoing nexuses of certain racist and feminist agendas. The protest that occurred at the Eliot statue shows how intuitive and flexible the practice of co-opting a female figure in bronze can be, even when the historical figure in question arguably had nothing to do with it. It is not surprising that the Eliot statue, embedded within a transatlantic visual and material culture that allies emblems of femininity with the prerogatives of the racist state, was appropriated in the way that it was. But the material history of Nuneaton itself, the social and economic impoverishment of the miners and their families due to deindustrialization and unregulated global markets, also points to the widespread, nongendered devastation that neoliberal policies leave in their wake. It should enable a more clear-eyed understanding of neoliberalism's penchant for masking its failures of distribution with a politics of racial and gendered diversity that does not extend beyond the realm of the visual. The erection of more memorials to women and gender-nonconforming bodies in society, as laudable and crucial as this effort may be, should not fail to continue to beg the question of whose living and breathing bodies we are committed to protecting.

Notes

Warm thanks to Andrew M. Shanken and Valentina Rozas-Krause for supporting this article and for thinking with me through its various stakes. The members of the Graduate Post45 Symposium at Northwestern University and the English Department's Graduate Student Publication Workshop at UC Berkeley offered invaluable feedback and suggestions for revisions. I also thank John Burton of the George Eliot Society for his help in locating materials.

1. Grace Lavery, "Trans Realism, Psychoanalytic Practice, and the Rhetoric of Technique," *Critical Inquiry* 46, no. 4 (Summer 2020): 722.

2. Ibid.

3. Alison Flood, "Akwaeke Emezi Shuns Women's Prize over Request for Details of Sex as Defined 'by Law,'" *The Guardian*, October 5, 2020, https://www.theguardian.com/books/2020/oct/05/akwaeke-emezi-shuns-womens-prize-request-for-details-of-sex-as-defined-by-law#:~:text=Akwaeke%20Emezi%2C%20who%20became%20the,as%20defined%20%E2%80%9Cby%20law%E2%80%9D.

4. Laura Hampson, "New Women's Prize Project Sees Female Authors Replace Male Pseudonyms," *London Evening Standard*, August 12, 2020, https://www.standard.co.uk/culture/books/reclaim-her-name-womens-prize-for-fiction-a4522006.html.

5. Wild Woman Writing Club, "Open Letter to the Women's Prize," *Wild Woman Writing Club*, December 6, 2021, https://wildwomanwritingclub.wordpress.com/2021/04/06/open-letter-to-the-womens-prize/.

6. Horbury and Yao write, "Many stem from the online parenting website Mumsnet and the remnants of the UK Skeptics movement; Youtube has proved a popular congregating spot for the latter, which has become a notorious recruitment tool for the alt-right; as Edie Miller writes, 'Mumsnet is to British transphobia more like what 4Chan is to American fascism.'" Ezra Horbury and Christine "Xine" Yao, "Empire and Eugenics: Trans Studies in the United Kingdom," *TSQ* 7, no. 3 (August 2020): 445–54.

7. Alyosxa Tudor, "Decolonizing Trans/Gender Studies?: Teaching Gender, Race, and Sexuality in Times of the Rise of the Global Right," *TSQ* 8, no. 2 (May 2021): 243.

8. Ibid., 244.

9. Esther Wang refers to it as an "unholy alliance." See Esther Wang, "The Unholy Alliance of Trans-exclusionary Radical Feminists and the Right Wing," *Jezebel*, May 9, 2019, https://jezebel.com/the-unholy-alliance-of-trans-exclusionary-radical-femin-1834120309. Sunnivie Brydum refers to it as a "odd couple." See Sunnivie Brydum, "Right Wing Christians and Radical Feminists Form an Odd (Trans-phobic) Couple," *Religion Dispatches*, January 19, 2017, https://religiondispatches.org/right-wing-christians-and-radical-feminists-form-an-odd-transphobic-couple/.

10. Serena Bassi and Greta LaFleur, "Introduction: TERFs, Gender-Critical Movements, and Postfascist Feminisms," *TSQ* 9, no. 3 (August 2022): 311–33.

11. Maria Lugones, "The Coloniality of Gender," *Worlds & Knowledges Otherwise* 2, no. 2 (Spring 2008): 7.

12. Nuneaton Town Centre Conservation Area, "Appraisal and Management Proposals: Draft for Public Consultation," Nuneaton and Bedworth Borough Council, March 2009, https://www.nuneatonandbedworth.gov.uk/downloads/file/153/j3_-_nuneaton_town_centre_conservation_area_appraisal_and_management_proposals_2009.

13. Ted Veasey, *Nuneaton: A History* (Chichester: Phillimore, 2002), 85.

14. Nuneaton Town Centre Conservation Area, "Appraisal and Management Proposals," 13.

15. Kathleen Adams, "A Community of Interest: The Story of the George Eliot Fellowship, 1930–2000," *George Eliot Review Online*, https://georgeeliotreview.org/items/show/926, 25.

16. The Tourism Company, "Nuneaton and Bedworth Destination Assessment, 2016," 36, https://www.nuneatonandbedworth.gov.uk/download/downloads/id/2431/nbbc46_-_nuneaton_and_bedworth_destination_assessment_-_final_report_may_2016_-_nbbc.pdf.

17. John Letts, "John Letts, the Gifted Warwickshire Sculptor," *George Eliot Review* 22 (1985): 52.

18. Ibid.

19. Ibid., 53.

20. Rebecca Mead, "George Eliot's Ugly Beauty," *New Yorker*, September 19, 2013, https://www.newyorker.com/books/page-turner/george-eliots-ugly-beauty.

21. Kathryn Hughes, "George Eliot: Is This a New Portrait of the Author as a Young Woman?" *Guardian*, May 5, 2017, https://www.theguardian.com/books/2017/may/05/george-eliot-is-this-a-new-portrait-of-the-author-as-a-young-woman-.

22. Adams, "A Community of Interest," 22.

23. Kathleen Adams, "George Eliot Unveiled," *George Eliot Fellowship Review* 17 (1986): 91.

24. Margaret Bozenna Goscilo, "John Fowles's Pre-Raphaelite Woman: Interart Strategies and Gender Politics," *Mosaic* 26, no. 2 (Spring 1993): 70.

25. Julie F. Codell, "Expression over Beauty: Facial Expression, Body Language, and Circumstantiality in the Paintings of the Pre-Raphaelite Brotherhood," *Victorian Studies* 29, no. 2 (Winter 1986): 261.

26. George Eliot, "The Natural History of German Life," in *Essays of George Eliot*, ed. Thomas Pinney (New York: Columbia University Press, 1963), 268.

27. Andrew Leng, "Dorothea Brooke's 'Awakening Consciousness' and Pre-Raphaelite Aesthetic in *Middlemarch*," *Journal of the Australasian Universities Language and Literature Association* 75, no. 1 (Spring 1991): 53.

28. Letts, "John Letts, the Gifted Warwickshire Sculptor."

29. John Ruskin, *The Works of John Ruskin*, ed. E. T. Cook and Alexander Wedderburn (London, 1903–12), 12:333–35.

30. Elizabeth Prettejohn, *Beauty and Art, 1750–2000* (Oxford: Oxford University Press, 2006), 113.

31. John Ruskin, "Of Queen's Gardens," *Sesame and Lilies: Three Lectures* (Philadelphia: Henry Altemus, 1892), 135–36.

32. Kate Millet, "The Debate Over Women: Ruskin versus Mill," *Victorian Studies* 14, no. 1 (Fall 1970): 68.

33. Stuart Hall, Chas Critcher, Tony Jefferson, John Clarke, and Brian Roberts, *Policing the Crisis: Mugging, the State, and Law and Order* (London, Macmillan International Higher Education; Red Globe Press, 2019).

34. Huw Beynon and Ray Hudson, *Shadow of the Mine: Coal and the End of Industrial Britain* (New York: Verso, 2021), 64.

35. Ibid., 44.

36. Andreas Malm, *White Skin, Black Fuel: On the Danger of Fossil Fascism* (London: Verso, 2021), 277.

37. Ibid., 275.

38. Simon Jenkins, *Thatcher and Sons: A Revolution in Three Acts* (London: Allen Lane, 2006), 91.

39. Beynon and Hudson, *Shadow of the Mine*, 330.

40. Eirikur Bergmann, *Conspiracy & Populism: The Politics of Misinformation* (London: Palgrave Macmillan 2018).

41. Telford and Wilstow's claim is drawn from empirical research conducted in Teesside in Northeast England, whose economy was once bolstered by the presence of powerful coal and steelmaking industries. See Luke Telford and Jonathan Wistow, "Brexit and the Working Class on Teesside: Moving beyond Reductionism," *Capital & Class* 44, no. 4 (Fall 2019): 553–72.

42. Raymond Williams, Robin Blackburn, and Robin Gable, *Resources of Hope: Culture, Democracy, Socialism* (London: Verso, 1989), 124.

43. Beynon and Hudson, *Shadow of the Mine*, 322.

44. Moishe Postone, "Anti-Semitism and National Socialism: Notes on the German Reaction to 'Holocaust,'" *New German Critique* 19 (1980): 108.

45. Ibid., 112.

46. Michelle Hale Williams, *The Impact of Radical Right-Wing Parties in West European Democracies* (New York: Palgrave Macmillan, 2006), 60–61.

47. Beynon and Hudson, *Shadow of the Mine*, 14.

48. Florence Sutcliffe-Braithwaite and Natalie Thomlinson, "National Women against Pit Closures: Gender, Trade Unionism and Community Activism in the Miners' Strike, 1984–5," *Contemporary British History* 32, no. 1 (2018): 78–100.

49. Beynon and Hudson, *Shadow of the Mine*, 63.

50. Quoted in ibid., 5.

51. My thanks to Andrew J. Haas for this insight.

52. Klaus Theweleit, Erica Carter, and Chris Turner, *Male Fantasies: Male Bodies: Psychoanalyzing the White Terror* (Minneapolis: University of Minnesota Press, 1989), 351.

53. Jay W. Richards, "Will Left's Gender Agenda Fall Flat with Minorities and Working Americans?" *Heritage Foundation*, January 18, 2022, https://www.heritage.org/gender/commentary/will-lefts-gender-agenda-fall-flat-minorities-and-working-americans.

54. Tim Fitzsimmons, "Conservative Group Hosts Anti-Transgender Panel of Feminists 'from the Left,'" *NBCNews.com*, January 29, 2019, https://www.nbcnews.com/feature/nbc-out/conservative-group-hosts-anti-transgender-panel-feminists-left-n964246.

55. Melinda Cooper, *Family Values: Between Neoliberalism and the New Social Conservatism* (New York: Zone Books, 2013).

56. Ellen Peirson-Hagger, "How a Mary Wollstonecraft Statue Became a Feminist Battleground," *New Statesman*, July 27, 2021, https://www.newstatesman.com/politics/uk-politics/2020/11/statue-mary-wollstonecraft-feminist-battleground-maggi-hambling.

57. Julia Jacobs, "Two Transgender Activists Are Getting a Monument in New York," *New York Times*, May 30, 2019, https://www.nytimes.com/2019/05/29/arts/transgender-monument-stonewall.html.

58. Lisa Duggan, *The Twilight of Equality?: Neoliberalism, Cultural Politics, and the Attack on Democracy* (Boston: Beacon Press, 2003), 44. Italics mine.

59. Reina Gosset, Eric A. Stanley, and Johanna Burton, *Trap Door: Trans Cultural Production and the Politics of Visibility* (Cambridge, MA: MIT Press, 2017), xv.

60. Sammy Gibbons, "New York Advocates Fight for State Funds Dedicated to Transgender Health Access," *NorthJersey.com*, https://www.lohud.com/story/news/politics/2023/02/20/ny-advocates-fight-for-funds-dedicated-to-transgender-health/69908112007/.

61. Martin B. Duberman, *Stonewall: The Definitive Story of the LGBTQ Rights Uprising That Changed America* (New York: Penguin Publishing Group, 2019), 251.

62. Marquis Bey, "The Trans*-Ness of Blackness, the Blackness of Trans*-Ness," *TSQ* 4, no. 2 (May 2017): 278.

63. Ibid., 284.

64. Ibid., 283.

65. Karen L. Cox, *No Common Ground: Confederate Monuments and the Ongoing Fight for Racial Justice* (Chapel Hill: University of North Carolina Press, 2021), 29. Caroline E. Janney writes that the earliest of these statues were erected in cemeteries under the auspices of ostensibly apolitical women's memorial associations, wherein the leadership of women disguised the political intent of these statues as signs of continued allegiance to the Confederacy. See Caroline E. Janney, *Burying the Dead but Not the Past: Ladies' Memorial Associations and the Lost Cause* (Chapel Hill: University of North Carolina Press, 2008), 6–7, 40, 142.

66. Dell Upton, "Confederate Monuments and Civic Values in the Wake of Charlottesville," *Society of Architectural Historians*, https://www.sah.org/publications-and-research/sah-blog/sah-blog/2017/09/13/confederate-monuments-and-civic-values-in-the-wake-of-charlottesville. Caroline Winterer writes that

the revivification of Greek mythology in Confederate racial ideologies gave Southern women the means to justify a slave-based agricultural economy and way of life. See Caroline Winterer, *The Mirror of Antiquity: American Women and the Classical Tradition, 1750–1900* (Ithaca: Cornell University Press, 2009).

67. Rebecca Senior, "The Confederate Statues That Have Been Overlooked: Anonymous Women," *Washington Post*, July 29, 2020, https://www.washingtonpost.com/outlook/2020/07/10/confederate-women-statues-allegory/.

Kirk Savage

Toppling Pocahontas

LONG AGO POCAHONTAS had a life. But to become a heroine in the white imagination she had to lose her life, literally and figuratively.

In this respect she is similar to many other heroes in the commemorative landscape whose actual lives were distorted or erased when they were conscripted into the supposedly higher cause of representing the nation. In Pocahontas's case, however, her dispossession was more profoundly tragic, as it was emblematic of the much more sweeping dispossession of indigenous land and lifeways undertaken by the very people who turned her into a national heroine.

Pocahontas was all of ten or eleven years old when the Englishmen arrived in her land, a chiefdom of Algonquian-speaking peoples led by her father, Powhatan. At the moment she supposedly saved John Smith from execution, she was leading a child's life, largely unclothed, having fun doing cartwheels while also doing the strenuous physical labor demanded of everyone—foraging, farming, collecting firewood. She went on to marry a Native man, Kocoum, but her life with him was interrupted when she was captured by the English colonists and held hostage for a year in Jamestown. It was then that she submitted to baptism and married John Rolfe, before

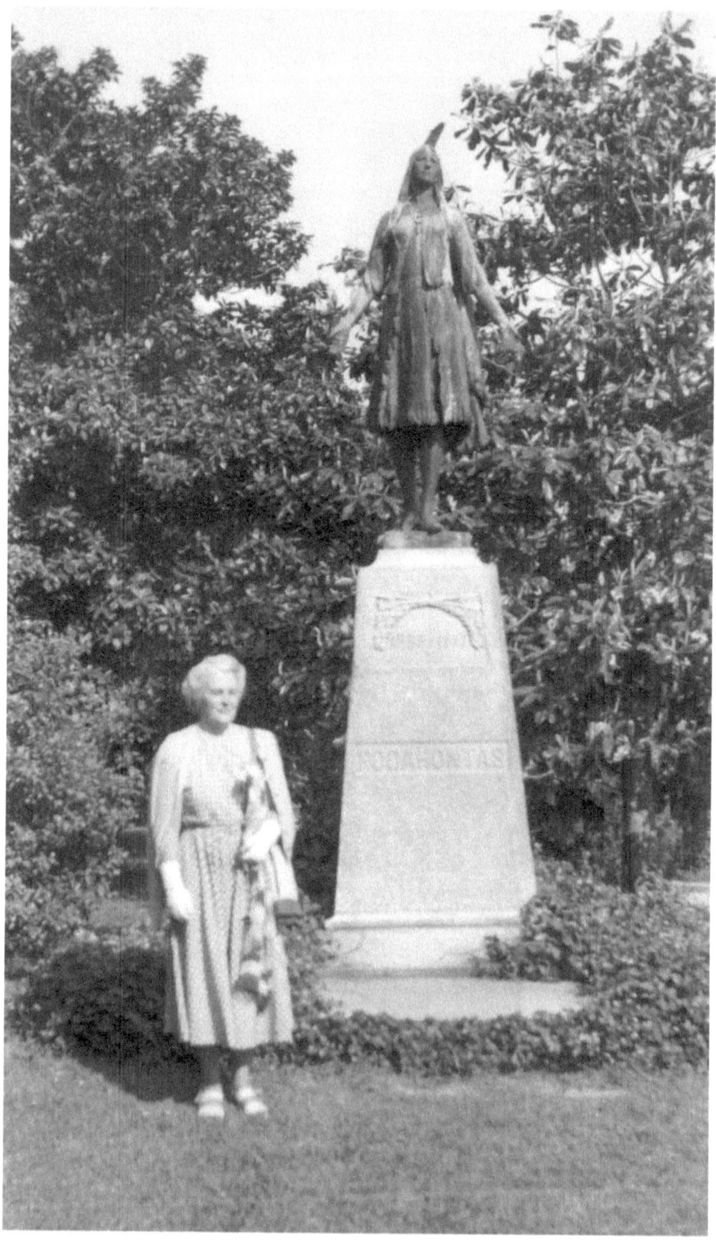

Figure 1. Margaret Julia Band with Pocahontas statue, Jamestown, Virginia, n.d., photographer unknown (http://hdl. handle.net/10464/6679). Source: Archives & Special Collections, Brock University Library, St. Catharines, Ontario.

traveling with him to England on a fundraising mission, where she met King James and later died, perhaps of dysentery.

Even these few fragments of a life we know only from the self-serving reports of white men such as John Smith. Her indigenous life remains largely unknown, although Native studies scholars have made some informed propositions and a controversial work of oral history has suggested additional details. Her purported rescue of Smith, for example, might well have been a traditional choreographed ceremony, if it happened at all; her baptism and second marriage were probably strategic moves to assist Powhatan's diplomacy.

But it is a distinctly white imagination that has shaped her image and spread it across the Anglo-American world. Pocahontas appears three times in the Rotunda of the Capitol at Washington, twice as the savior of Smith and once as a glorious convert to Christianity, resplendent in a shimmering white gown. She is a place-name for towns and counties across the United States, from Virginia to Iowa and Arkansas, named as white settlers spread westward and expelled indigenous peoples. She has chapters named after her in the leading white women's lineage organizations, the Daughters of the American Revolution and the Colonial Dames. Statues honor her in the UK in London and Gravesend, and in the United States in Jamestown, Gloucester, and Pocahontas, Arkansas. And she has an enduring place in popular culture, from the colossally frumpy 1950s "roadside princess" in Pocahontas, Iowa, to the slick and sexy New Age package of Disney's movie.

Throughout all these representations Pocahontas retains the physical signs of her otherness, whether it is her brown skin in the white baptismal gown of John Chapman's painting in the Capitol (1840) or her feathered headdress in the public statues (beginning 1922). Yet to become a heroine she had to undergo an invisible transformation. Her own inner indigeneity had to be exterminated as she became metaphysically white. Thus transformed racially, she became a true woman as well, her femininity authenticated in the story of Smith's rescue and in her attachment to Rolfe's mission. With her entry into white female respectability, her image validated white supremacy as moral truth and as empirical fact. Meanwhile, on a parallel track, the physical conquest of indigenous peoples accelerated, resulting in dispossession and expulsion.

The cult of Pocahontas began in the early nineteenth century when Indian removal took hold as federal policy. The cult reached a new stage in the early twentieth century as eugenics gained more

widespread adherence. The installation of William Partridge's graceful statue of Pocahontas in Jamestown took place two years before
Virginia's now infamous Racial Integrity Act of 1924, which legally
defined whiteness for the first time. Its so-called Pocahontas Exception enabled her elite descendants through John Rolfe to remain
legally white. This was happening as the indigenous descendants of
Pocahontas's people, who had been displaced and decimated by settler colonialists, were struggling for survival and recognition. These
descendant communities of Powhatan's chiefdom did not get federal
recognition as tribal peoples until 2018.

The heroic status Pocahontas achieved through her conscription
into whiteness went hand in hand with the delegitimizing of indigeneity perpetrated by white settler colonialism. As the nation and world
struggle to repair the damage done by this crime against humanity,
we will have to topple her fabricated heroism in order to revalue the
life taken from her—even as justice and indeed planetary survival
demand the revaluation of indigenous life everywhere.

Carolina Aguilera and Manuela Badilla Rajevic

Monument to the Chilean Women Victims of Political Repression

TWO DAYS AFTER the death of Chilean dictator Augusto Pinochet (in power from 1973 to 1990) on December 12, 2006, a memorial to the women victims of the military dictatorship was inaugurated in the center of Santiago. Impressive in size at 13 feet wide and 7 feet tall, the plaque was the result of the tireless efforts of a group of women who campaigned for over twenty years to see the memorial materialized. Made of semi-transparent acrylic, the design resembled a barcode representing a concealed identity and was dotted with empty squares echoing the black-and-white photographs kept by the relatives of those who were executed or disappeared. The memorial bore no list of names and many considered it cold, perhaps too abstract and difficult to understand. But this did not matter at the time. The work was finally in place. It was large. It was important.

The memorial was the result of the mobilization of a group of women who came together in 1992: the Comité Pro-Monumento a las Mujeres Víctimas de la Represión (Committee for a Monument to Women Victims of Repression). However, the idea only gained traction a decade later, in the context of Chile's increasing openness to memorialization processes, a cultural shift that was nonetheless rife

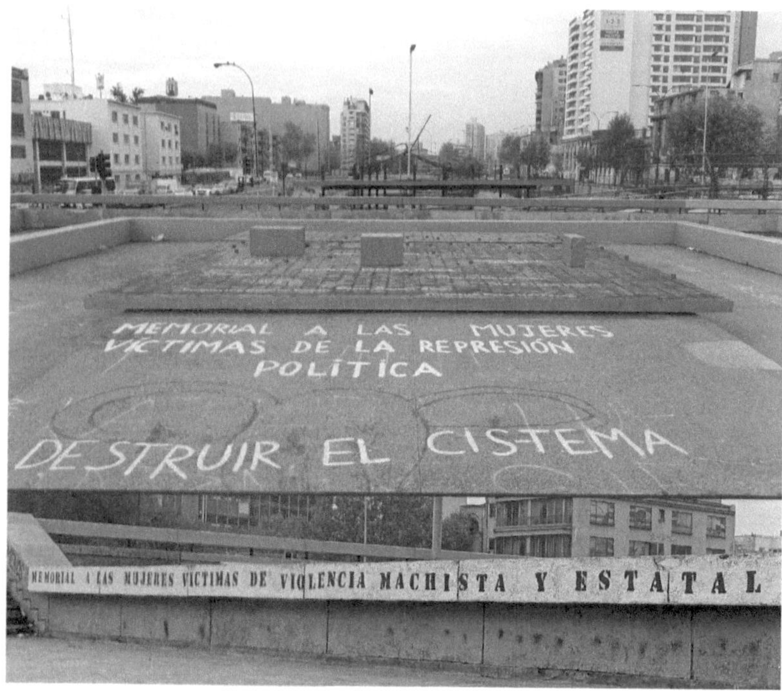

Figure 1. Monument to the Women Victims of Political Repression, Santiago de Chile. Source: Carolina Aguilera.

with conflict.[1] The state provided public funds and endorsed a location on Paseo Bulnes, a pedestrian boulevard connecting the Presidential Palace with other government buildings, providing a prime location for commemorative works of a political nature. A building permit was even granted by the then right-wing mayor of the city of Santiago, although it was later revoked.

After its inauguration in 2006, the memorial was vandalized by passersby and abandoned by the authorities. While the memorial committee has repaired and cleaned the memorial at least twice, today it languishes in a state of almost complete neglect.

How is it that a central monument, constructed with the support of the state, the city, and civil society, came to be abandoned and is now in ruins? The reasons are threefold. The first is urbanistic. With funding in place and the project underway, the memorial suddenly lost the support of the city shortly before inauguration. In response, the Ministry of Public Works had very little time to find a new location for it. In an effort to retain the central location, a site belonging to the state-owned Santiago subway system was chosen to circumvent the need for city permits. The ground-level site within the Los Heroes subway station complex was initially seen as a good option, positioned as it is at an important intersection of the pedestrian central strip of the Avenida Alameda Bernardo O'Higgins, the capital's principal thoroughfare. However, the space itself—an old, elevated walkway over the Norte-Sur urban expressway—was a dead end, disconnected from foot traffic, and used solely by the homeless and university students looking for a covert place to drink and hang out.

The second reason was that no institution took responsibility for the maintenance of the memorial. Commemorative works of this type located in public space usually fall under the purview of the city, but this was not the case here. Furthermore, although the committee that promoted the memorial made considerable efforts to keep it clean initially, it was unable to cope with the constant graffiti, vandalization, and general deterioration. Furthermore, the landowner, the public transportation agency, refused all responsibility toward maintaining the memorial.

The third and perhaps most important reason is that women have until very recently occupied a marginal position within the public memory of the dictatorship. Gender violence has not been officially recognized as a particular crime by the country's truth commissions.[2] Despite hundreds of testimonies describing sexual abuse, rape, and violence against women under the military regime, the courts have failed to bring the perpetrators to justice.[3] Moreover, the role of women, their political affiliations, and their involvement in anti-dictatorship resistance has largely been absent from the social history of the dictatorship.

The irony is that the dilapidated state of the women's memorial has changed its resonance. After years of neglect, the memorial has now once again become a meaningful space for the commemoration of the women. Recently reappropriated by the feminist movement, the monument now stands for both the female victims of the dictatorship and the ongoing victims of patriarchy and gender violence. New feminist movements arose in this context, even before the popular uprising of 2019. The now world-famous performances of the Chilean feminist collective Las Tesis are part of this surge of feminist activism. These new groups of women have reclaimed and reappropriated the memorial, or what remains of it, organizing commemorations at the site and using it as a meeting place for protests.

The ruins of the memorial represent the debt owed by society not only to the victims of the dictatorship but also to women who are sexually abused, women who protest, and women who actively fought against authoritarianism and military repression. Furthermore the ruins of the memorial represent the persistence of a patriarchal system of domination that has failed to acknowledge the role of women, their demands, and their rights in society. These ruins, as a residue of memory, have been transformed into a memorial to abused, abandoned, and neglected women, both historical and contemporary. Paradoxically, it was the ruination of the initial memorial that created a powerful representation of the ongoing struggles that women face to secure a place for themselves in both the city and society.

Notes

1. Cath Collins and Katherine Hite, "Memorials, Silences, and Reawakenings," in *The Politics of Memory in Chile: From Pinochet to Bachelet*, ed. Cath Collins, Katherine Hite, and Alfredo Joignant (Boulder: First Forum Press, 2013), 133–63.

2. Hillary Hiner, "Voces soterradas, violencias ignoradas: Discurso, violencia política y género en los Informes Rettig y Valech [Voices buried, violence ignored: Discourse, political violence, and gender in the Rettig and Valech reports]," *Latin America Research Review* 44, no. 3 (2009): 50–74.

3. Caroline Davidson, "Nunca más meets #niunamenos: Accountability for Pinochet-Era Sexual Violence in Chile," *Columbia Human Rights Review* 51, no. 1 (2019), http://hrlr.law.columbia.edu/files/2019/11/51.1.2-Davidson.pdf.

PART II
Public Women

Lauren Kroiz

3. White Marble and White Women: Adelaide Johnson's *Portrait Monument*

SCULPTOR ADELAIDE JOHNSON (1859–1955) created a white marble monument to woman's suffrage over a span of more than three decades (figure 1). Begun with portrait sittings by Susan B. Anthony in 1886, the memorial was unveiled and dedicated in the U.S. Capitol on February 15, 1921, at an event celebrating the 101st anniversary of Anthony's birth and the ratification of the Nineteenth Amendment to the U.S. Constitution enfranchising women (figure 2). The Architect of the Capitol and the Capitol's art curator tried to pin down a title for the innovative sculpture in letters to the artist. Johnson referred to it with a generalizing phrase as "Portrait Monument of and to Women," while also adding "Subjects—Lucretia Mott, Elizabeth Cady Stanton, Susan B. Anthony."[1] Indeed, the sculpture conjoins busts of two important suffragists, Lucretia Mott (1793–1880) and Elizabeth Cady Stanton (1815–1902), with a portrait of Anthony (1820–1906), as all three emerge from a huge block of Carrara marble. A couple months later Johnson called the sculpture "Portrait Monument of Women— L.M-E.C.S and S.B.A.—to Women presented by Women."[2] She also used the title "Woman Monument" and agreed to the Architect's suggestion that the work be known as *Portrait Monument to Lucretia Mott,*

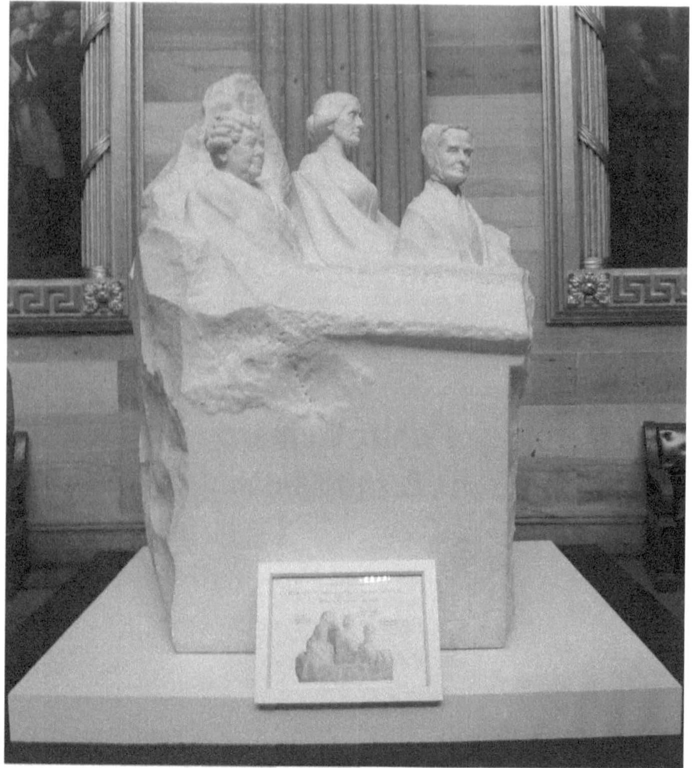

Figure 1. Adelaide Johnson, *Portrait Monument*, 1886–1920, in the Rotunda of the U.S. Capitol, 2019. Photograph by the author.

Elizabeth Cady Stanton and Susan B. Anthony, a long descriptive title that mutes the work's politics and connection to broader women's rights struggles.[3]

Throughout this chapter I will use *Portrait Monument* both for brevity and in hopes of evoking Mott, Stanton, and Anthony at the same time as Johnson's phrase centering all Women. For Johnson, an uncompromising artist and suffrage advocate, the multi-bust monument fused specific individuals and an idealized category of women. Her chosen form—three highly finished, representational busts that seem to emerge as an ensemble from an immense chunk of rough-hewn stone—also allowed a temporal collapse. Johnson physically conjoined two generations of suffrage leaders and undulating rock that represented the work remaining for future women. In so doing,

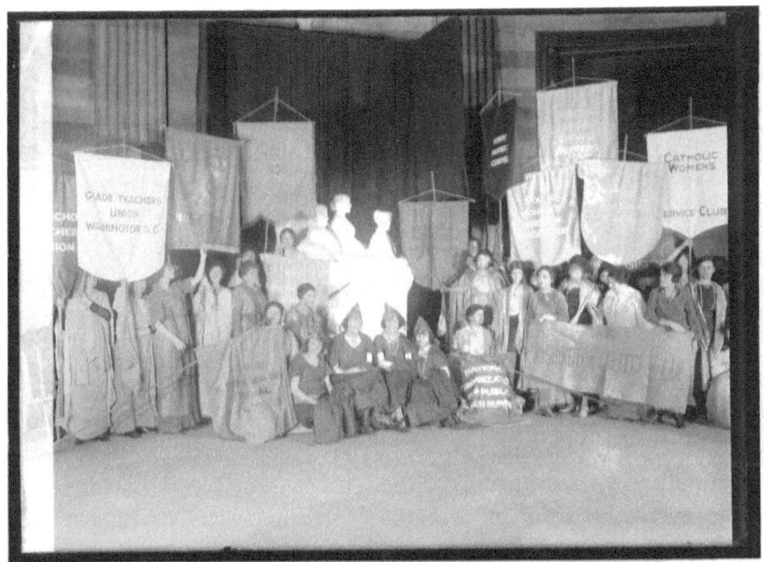

Figure 2. Unveiling suffrage memorial, 1921, unknown photographer, National Photo Company Collection, Library of Congress, Prints & Photographs Division, LC-F81-12117. Retrieved from the Library of Congress, https://www.loc.gov/item/2016822518/.

Johnson's design occluded disagreements among suffragists and distinct phases of the suffrage movement in the United States. Hers is a monument to a movement with a history that—even in 1921—was lengthy and contested, particularly, as this chapter will emphasize, with respect to the racialized strategies white women used to win the vote for themselves.

In the decades Johnson worked on elements of her portrait monument, the sculptor became close friends with Susan B. Anthony and to a lesser extent Elizabeth Stanton, who both sat for her multiple times. She worked from photographs of Mott, who had already died by the time Johnson began sculpting suffrage leaders. Anthony and Stanton suggested Mott's inclusion and recalled her fondly as "the mother of us all."[4] However, the early leader and abolitionist had split with her younger colleagues in 1867 over the campaign Anthony and Stanton launched against the Fifteenth Amendment enfranchising Black men. Johnson herself collaborated, and at times fought, with a countless number of other suffragists. By the time the sculptor had finished *Portrait Monument* in 1920 the pioneering first and second generations of female leaders she had initially worked with and sought to honor with the busts had all died. Johnson's vision was picked up by a third generation—Alice Paul (1885–1977) and the National Woman's Party—who finally raised the funds to send the sculptor to Carrara, Italy, in 1920 to create the monument she had planned for three decades. Disparate moments and visions of suffrage politics collapse in this work, as well as distinct moments of Johnson's production, which included the separate creation of three busts.

Indeed, in Carrara, when Johnson found a piece of stone that she deemed appropriate, she wrote, "Ah me! The huge block at last after thirty years is the thing to be done."[5] The block Johnson selected in Carrara measured approximately seven feet high, five feet and eight inches wide, and five feet deep. Johnson herself gave the dimensions as "about 7½ feet tall and weighs 7½ tons," a correspondence that suggested numerical significance to the sculptor who was deeply involved in alternative spiritual movements of the era.[6] The mass of marble itself formed a part of the sculptor's argument. Johnson claimed she wanted the sculpture so large that the women could not be separated, mitigating against a future threat of danger to the sculpture as part of its design.[7] Lifted by the shared block and low base, the three women also stood elevated above approaching viewers as seen in figure 2. The busts themselves are barely over life-size: Mott's portrait is twenty-four inches high, Stanton's twenty-six inches, and Anthony's thirty-five inches. Johnson imagined these figures as a kind of timeline from the beginning of the movement with Mott in the block's right front, moving backward with Stanton left front, and Anthony in the center middle toward the unfinished stone surface on the far left, which represents the work for women still to be done.

The monument's medium of large-scale sculpture, as well as its material—white marble from the famed quarries of Carrara, Italy—adhere to neoclassical conventions. However, the form created from three highly finished portrait busts emerging from a seemingly unfinished block was and remains quite exceptional. Suffrage opponents described the monument as three women buried alive, sitting up suddenly in bed, or submerged in a bathtub.[8] The problem of titling and this range of insults are symptoms of a larger tension between tradition and innovation struggling in the sculpture itself.

Johnson's *Portrait Monument* is unwieldy in many ways, but this sculpture grapples with a particular problem in building a monument to suffrage. It is worth turning back to this artwork following the centenary of the Nineteenth Amendment's ratification in 2020.

Most monuments, even recent contemporary monuments to women's suffrage, obey conventions that Johnson defies. They act as commemorations of a triumph that is finished, resolved, and thus able to be recognized through specific historical figures.[9] This choice should be striking in our contemporary moment that also offers the option of countermonuments that abandon figurative or even monumental conventions. The *Portrait Monument* derives from and belongs to its period's neoclassical language of traditional monuments, even as it stands out. For neoclassical sculptors, stone, especially marble, was understood to have a kind of aliveness. Johnson invoked a material animacy in her deliberately unfinished or non finito technique, which enlivened not only the portrait subjects but the field of whiteness from which they emerged. Differing from other neoclassical sculptors, however, Johnson left the preparatory marks of a specific technique, drawing attention to the layered process of sculptural making. The marble itself materially excluded Black women feminists and naturalized white racism in a monument to history that seems to grow from the Carrara stone itself.

"The Commemoration of an Epoch"

AS SHE FINISHED her monument Johnson herself described its broad intention, writing, "No one seems to have risen to the realization that this is something far more than the simple presentation of three busts. It is the commemoration of an epoch."[10] The remarkable form of Johnson's monument struggles to commemorate coherently an ongoing event whose past and future were, and still are, precarious. Briefly exploring aspects of that history will set the stage for the ways marble envisions and contains the breaks in this long historical span and the problems of memory.

Scholars of suffrage and the early feminist movement in the United States trace the movement's origins to the Seneca Falls Convention of 1848. Lucretia Mott and Elizabeth Cady Stanton were instrumental in the event, which was organized in Stanton's New York hometown to coincide with a visit by Philadelphia-based Mott. The event organizers were Quaker women, except for Stanton, and were all white women active in the radical wing of the movement to abolish slavery led by William Lloyd Garrison.[11] Originating in a natural rights argument for universal suffrage, Garrison's movement and the white women who convened Seneca Falls argued that voting was one of a set of rights that was universal and inalienable; such natural rights could not be revoked by a legal system. It was a radical premise that led Garrison, for example, to declare the U.S. Constitution illegal in the antebellum era because it allowed slavery.

Immediately after the Civil War, in 1866, Mott was elected the first president of the American Equal Rights Association, which united white and Black women and men to advocate for universal suffrage. In the postbellum period, the natural rights argument for the right to vote began to give way to new arguments based in expediency. Here expediency has two meanings: first, the use to which the woman's vote would be put, and second, an openness to any argument leaders deemed most effective to gaining the vote. Moving away from radicalism, this pragmatic, reformist strategy created the understanding of female suffrage that has largely prevailed, a movement of white, upper-middle-class women allied with progressive reforms, including temperance. In other words, in this second phase, women argued for the right to vote not because it was already theirs and had been unjustly taken but because they would use it dutifully and morally to reshape society.[12]

A move away from universal rights to the language of expediency marks this second phase of the movement, consolidated by 1890 and extending until the 1920 passage of the Nineteenth Amendment. This period was also marked by virulent racism against Black people within the United States and the U.S. movement for women's right to vote. The facts that follow should not obscure the many important Black women involved in advocating for suffrage, including Sojourner Truth, Ida B. Wells, and Harriet Forten Purvis, among countless others. Nor should my brief account of the conflicts around the passage of the Fifteenth Amendment occlude the fact that Black men largely lost the right to vote, especially in the southern United States, by the late nineteenth century following the end of Reconstruction.

In this shift from natural rights to expediency, some leaders, including Stanton and Anthony, turned strongly against new amendments enfranchising African American men. The Fourteenth Amendment to the U.S. Constitution was ratified in 1868 and designed to provide citizenship and equal protection to formerly enslaved people. However, the amendment specified "male citizens" in the section of the text related to voting and was the first time a constitutional amendment had explicitly excluded women. The subsequent Fifteenth Amendment was designed to address voting rights, but it also kept suffrage the domain of men. The period between the ratification of the Fourteenth Amendment in July 1868 and the ratification of the Fifteenth Amendment in February 1870 lasted less than two years, but that period pulled apart the suffrage movement that had grown from the radical abolitionist movement.

New organizations resulted. Stanton and Anthony formed the National Woman Suffrage Association (NWSA) in May 1869. They worked to oppose passage of the Fifteenth Amendment, viewing its neglect of women as intolerable. They collaborated with individuals and groups who were against Black suffrage and racial equality. Mott split with Stanton and Anthony when the two formed an alliance with one such individual, wealthy entrepreneur and politician George Francis Train, during the 1867 battle over suffrage in Kansas. Dueling campaigns around a popular vote gave Kansans the choice of whether to remove "male" or "white" from state constitutional regulations on voting; two separate ballot initiatives became a binary question of whether to enfranchise Black men or white women. While Stanton and Anthony were ideologically in favor of universal suffrage, they campaigned with Train, who was a racist and opposed enfranchising Black people because he viewed them as less intelligent. Ultimately neither resolution won the popular vote in Kansas.[13] Anthony and Stanton continued to speak and write admiringly of Train and his participation in the struggle for woman's suffrage, including in their survey of the movement, *History of Woman Suffrage*.[14] Suffrage and racial equality, once aligned, were now in contention.

To combat Anthony and Stanton in November 1869, Lucy Stone, Henry Blackwell, and Julia Ward Howe formed the American Woman Suffrage Association (AWSA), dedicated to supporting the Fifteenth Amendment. The split in the movement for the woman's vote began to subside following the 1870 passage of the Fifteenth Amendment. In 1887 the two groups began talk of reconciling. In 1890 the AWSA and the NWSA merged into a new group, the National American Woman Suffrage Association (NAWSA) with first Stanton and then Anthony as its president. The similar names and acronyms for these groups often blur their vehement period disagreements. Anthony and Stanton died in the first decade of the 1900s, but both helped compile the first four volumes of the canonical *History of Woman Suffrage* (published in six volumes between 1881 and 1922), narrating the history from their own perspective for future generations.

In the 1910s, suffrage advocates moved toward more direct public action, inspired by militant movements in England. In 1913, under the auspices of the NAWSA, Alice Paul and others helped organize a silent parade in Washington, D.C., the day before Woodrow Wilson's inauguration. A riot ensued. The resulting publicity began a new phase of the woman's suffrage movement that was less patient and more interested in direct action. Paul soon split from the NAWSA, founding the National Woman's Party (NWP) in 1916, envisioning an independent political party calling for the immediate passage of a suffrage amendment at the federal level. Returning to the United States from England in the wake of the deaths of Stanton and Anthony, Paul positioned herself as the inheritor of their mantle and attempted to energize the movement for suffrage. Whereas existing organizations focused on state suffrage, the NWP envisioned a national movement adopting a strategy of holding the party in power accountable. Committed to the kind of direct public action previously thought to be inappropriate for women, the NWP picketed the White House starting in 1917. Their continued protest, even as the United States entered World War I, finally catalyzed public pressure and led to Woodrow Wilson's 1918 presidential endorsement of the suffrage amendment.

In 1920 while Johnson completed the statue in Carrara, Italy, to celebrate the amendment's passage, this third generation of suffrage leaders, Alice Paul and the NWP, sent her letters opining about various legal challenges to individual states' ratification then working their way through the court system. Paul commissioned and deposited Johnson's eight-ton sculpture on the steps of the Capitol without certainty that the suffrage amendment would pass or that the sculpture would be accepted. Indeed, a period photograph captures the Capitol Police standing uncertainly with the partially uncrated monument (figure 3).

This gesture aligns with the NWP's direct-action strategy. The NAWSA, which had initially commissioned the monument, opposed *Portrait Monument*'s installation in the Capitol's Rotunda and boycotted the unveiling festivities, determined to retain primacy in the way suffrage history would be remembered and show their opposition to the NWP's militancy.[15] Quickly following the amendment's passage, the NAWSA dissolved into the non-partisan League of Women Voters and NWP began working for an equal rights amendment, which is still unratified. Even this brief history provides a sense of the intricate, contested, and unfinished history of the suffrage movement, a past with traces in Johnson's monument.

It would be easy and correct to critique Johnson's sculpture as a white monument commemorating white women's vision of suffrage rooted in the deployment of period ideologies of white supremacy.[16]

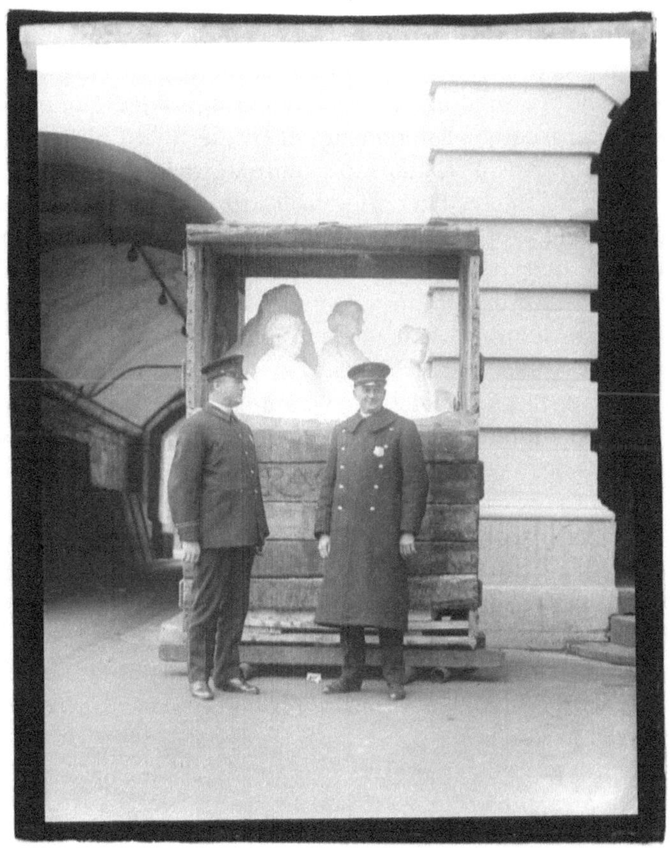

Figure 3. Suffrage memorial, 1921, unknown photographer,
National Photo Company Collection, Library of Congress, Prints
& Photographs Division, LC-F8-11906. Retrieved from the
Library of Congress, https://www.loc.gov/item/2016829725/.

In its facture the artwork also leaves clues to the ways white supremacy operates in material ways. A series of shallow holes extend across
the top and bottom of the rough horizontal edge from which the figures emerge. Bore and chisel marks also dot the non finito left side of
the sculpture's frontal plane. A line of several deeper holes near the
exact center of the block traces a curve that mimics the highly finished drapery above. Bridging the highly polished and rough marble,
it draws the viewers' eye to the contrasting surfaces. The centrality
of this portion of the monument suggests it is more than a distrac-

tion from the depicted content above. This seam of bore holes left as marks of the sculpture's facture indexes a process known as pointing, a way of reproducing sculptural form via indirect carving, allowing a model to be rendered in stone. By centering evidence of pointing, which would usually be smoothed out in the final finish, Johnson foregrounded her own relations to sculptural traditions and the ways her monument conjoined her prior busts into a new vision.

The pointing process has ancient Greek origins but reached its modern form in the early nineteenth-century practice of neoclassical Italian sculptor Antonio Canova. Using a prototype created by the artist, often, as in Johnson's case made from clay or plaster, professional stone carvers worked to mechanically transfer points from the original to the stone block. A pointing machine consists of an upright rod, often in hollow tubing with attached adjustable rods set in movable sockets. Points can be taken and transferred in all positions in three dimensions. To use the process, one marks in pencil all the projections and recessions or "points" on the model. Then the pointing rod is used to transfer the depth of the points marked on the original model to the block. Holes are drilled into the stone mass to the depth measured by the rods of the pointing machine. Finally the stone carver chisels away the stone between the holes until the depth of the holes is reached, creating a rough and potentially enlarged or reduced version of the model in stone.[17]

Johnson described the process evocatively a few weeks after she arrived in Carrara to create *Portrait Monument*:

> As the model had arrived before the marble now in the studio the ... men at once began the very mysterious—to outsiders—not to say mystical process of measuring just wherein this huge white stone. . . was to be found the "Angels" (our great women) to later be released by the long process of chiseling day by day for <u>much</u> of the great mass will be eliminated when the work is done.[18]

Johnson's language about freeing subjects from the block recalls tropes of her era, in which Renaissance artists, including Michelangelo, were understood to have actively discovered forms encased in the block through the act of carving. Michelangelo produced numerous unfinished works, in all parts of his life, that seem to demonstrate the struggle of finding figures in stone. Early understandings of non finito followed Platonic philosophy in which any work of art never completely resembled its heavenly counterpart. Later Pliny argued that viewers experience sadness when seeing an unfinished work because they assume the sculptor has died. Vasari agreed with this sense of loss, regarding the desired norm as the finished work, speculating that small errors led to abandonment. By the early twentieth century art critics took an idealist understanding of the non finito, conceiving a spiritual striving within the stone block of the figure that needed the stone carved away to free it.[19]

However, unlike Michelangelo, who generally practiced direct carving, approaching the stone with sketches and perhaps models, Johnson's description of pointing clearly demonstrates the unique ways she combined indirect carving and a mathematical precision with non finito surfaces. For Johnson, pointing techniques translated an original work that had been made in clay into stone. While creation with clay constitutes an additive process, working with stone carving requires a subtractive approach. Within the history of art this difference has sometimes led critics to question the appropriateness of copying from one material into another via indirect carving, as well as anxieties in the modern period about copying itself. The debate emerged with particular force in the work of French sculptor Auguste Rodin, who was a generation older than Johnson and whose work Johnson knew well.[20] Patrons who thought they were purchasing one-of-a-kind sculptures from Rodin were surprised to see other versions. Art historian Rosalind Krauss reframed Rodin's work as groundbreaking precisely because bronze casting became a systematic part of his artistic process. Krauss argues for Rodin's intersections with postmodernist reproduction. By contrast, Johnson foregrounded her *Portrait Monument*'s status as a reproduction of fragments in a quite different way with pointed marble. She preserved the status of the singular work of art while also materially gesturing to the three decades of suffrage history and earlier artwork that went into making this sculpture.[21]

Material History

JOHNSON WAS BORN in a small western Illinois farm town in 1859, but little is known about her life before she moved to St. Louis in 1876 to attend the Saint Louis School of Design. She joined the inaugural class at the all-female school founded by Mary Foote Henderson, a wealthy art enthusiast and president of the Missouri State Suffrage Association. Johnson's training envisioned artistic work as a path to female self-sufficiency. After finishing her studies, in 1879, Johnson moved to Chicago and soon co-opened a decorative arts firm.[22] On her way to an artistic career focused on interior design, in 1881 Johnson experienced a terrible accident, falling down an elevator shaft at Chicago Central Music Hall. The resulting injury forced her to close her design firm. Johnson sued the hall and won a $15,000 settlement, which funded her recuperation and then her study in Europe, first in Dresden in 1883 and then in Rome in 1884. In Rome, Johnson established a studio and became the pupil of neoclassical sculptor Giulio Monteverde, a professor at the Academy of Fine Arts, with whom she would work through the 1890s. During the last decades of the twentieth century, many American artists had shifted from art academies in Italy to France, and from marble to less expensive bronze, but Johnson committed to the ideal she saw represented in the history of classical and neoclassical sculpture.

Johnson returned to the United States in 1885, quickly becoming reengaged with the suffrage movement. She volunteered at the 1886 meeting of the NWSA, meeting Anthony there and proposing to create a portrait. In 1887 Johnson finished her first bust of Anthony and traveled with it to Rome where she sculpted another version. Johnson returned to the United States in 1888 for the Convention of the International Council of Women. Anthony agreed to sit for Johnson again in 1890 and 1891. In all Johnson created nine different portraits of Anthony, including seven marble busts and two medallions. In 1891 at Anthony's request Johnson also began sculpting other leaders of the suffrage movement, particularly Stanton, who sat for Johnson at least twelve times, and Mott, whose death a decade earlier forced the sculptor to work from photographs. Johnson came to see these three as a trinity, entwining art with feminism and spiritual, even religious, connotations.[23]

Johnson reached out to suffrage organizations for the funds she needed to travel to Rome to transfer the three busts into marble so that they could be exhibited at the Hall of Honor in the Woman's Building at the 1893 Chicago World's Fair. In 1891 each state chapter of the NWSA was asked to contribute $100 to support the sculpture project. The treasurer allowed: "Some have argued that the money ought to go to the [suffrage] work. . . but at this stage of our progress, this is an important part of the work."[24] Suffrage appealed to middle-class women and organizations that did not recognize the need to immortalize leaders, especially in a moment when their success was uncertain, which also created fundraising challenges.[25] Johnson's sculptures were finished and shown in the Court of Honor of the Woman's Building, alongside other portraits and allegorical figures created by women. The upper-class Board of Lady Managers responsible for the Woman's Building had disassociated themselves from suffrage issues. Johnson had a larger goal: to eventually place the busts in the explicitly political space of the Capitol Building in Washington, D.C.

Johnson created, displayed, and sold versions of the busts over the decades as she waited for them to enter the Capitol. In 1903 she moved with her artworks to New York to start a Gallery of Eminent Women, a venture that was never commercially successful. Johnson loaned versions to the Corcoran Art Gallery in Washington, D.C., and a version of Susan B. Anthony's bust entered the Metropolitan Museum of Art in 1906. In 1904, Anthony requested Johnson allow the busts to be permanently placed in the newly constructed Library of Congress. Anthony did not want them in the Capitol with "the atmosphere of tobacco, spittoons, and the class of men who roam around there."[26] Perhaps the large block Johnson selected acted as a buffer, as a type of frame, to set the busts off from their material environment, acting to extend and secure the domain of "respectable" white femininity into an environment of questionable and menacing male morality. Johnson arrived at the final idea of conjoining the busts during the International Council of Women's June 1914 meeting, where her display included cloth drapery, suggesting a new plan for the composition she photographed, sent as a postcard to friends, and published in *The New American Woman* in June 1917 (figure 4).[27]

Fundraising quickly became tangled because while the appeal for support was made at the NWSA convention, donations went to a separate Bust Fund Committee.[28] From the beginning there was conflict over the Bust Fund Committee's contract with Johnson. The sculptor was promised $3,000 but only got the first two payments and a part of the third. Anthony begged Johnson to either give back the $2,400 or take $600 and turn over the sculptures.[29] However, Johnson refused, believing the contract dictated that she could only accept full payment when the busts were delivered to the U.S. Capitol. Following the display of the three busts in Chicago in 1893 Johnson made herself their custodian. Although a version of Johnson's vision eventually came to fruition as public and political opinion shifted on suffrage, the contract dispute was never fully resolved. Anthony's biographer, Ida Harper, claimed the sculpture had been "the cause of more friction in the Association [NWSA] for nearly thirty years, than any other one subject."[30]

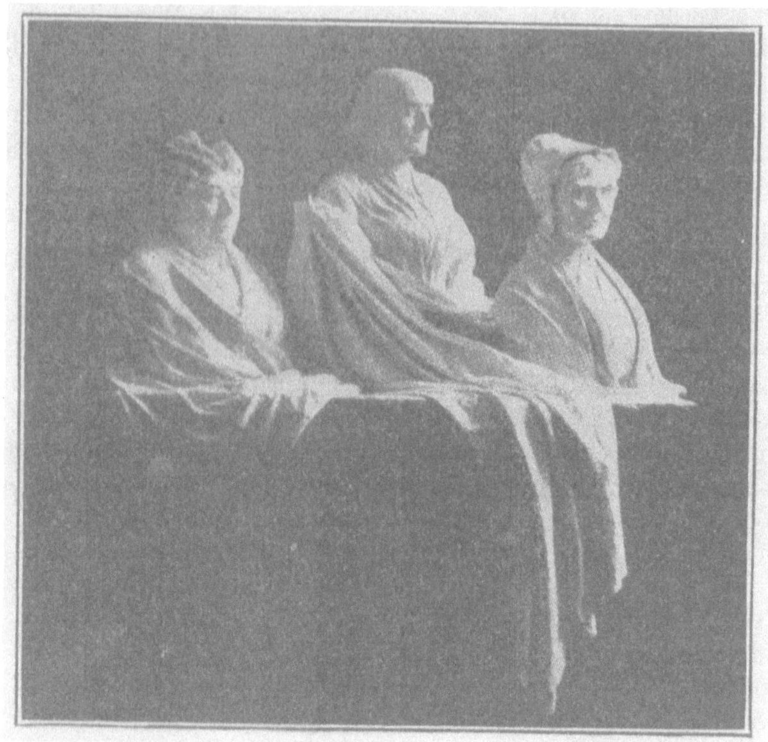

Figure 4. [Three suffragists by Adelaide Johnson], *The New American Woman* (Los Angeles, CA: C. Shortridge Foltz, June 1917). Print. Courtesy of the California History Room, California State Library, Sacramento.

In April 1920, with the suffrage amendment nearing passage, Paul and the NWP commissioned Johnson to create a new monument, in the process implicitly asserting control over memorializing the suffrage movement through the busts that had plagued the NWSA for decades. Ultimately the sculptural form Johnson arrived at in 1920 was derived from, but was radically different than, the three initial busts. In fact, when the NWP proposed a celebration of *Portrait Monument* with a display of the earlier work, Johnson deemed "dragging old long ago made works out" a "farce," arguing "the real thing [. . . was . . .] no more represented by separate busts. . . than the moon is represented by 'green cheese.'"[31] By 1920, when Johnson began sculpting the final composition in Carrara, everyone on the original 1892 Bust Fund Committee and the subjects of the busts had died. Nonetheless, frictions continued.

Reception and Critique

OVER THE YEARS Johnson's busts were subject to criticism, both for their representation of individuals and later for the unorthodox composition of *Portrait Monument*. These condemnations evidence shifting, often misogynistic period language around female bodily appearance and image. Interestingly, no one seems to have had any memory of, attachment to, or objections regarding Johnson's depiction of Mott. Perhaps her visibly antiquated form derived from a well-known photograph saved her bust from attack. Mott's natural rights argument may have appeared as antiquated as her bonnet by 1920. Aesthetic judgments often paralleled political and personal disagreements within the movement and between individuals, as changing relationships became projected onto Johnson's busts.

Sharp criticism began while Anthony and Stanton were still living. First in 1895, after publication of Stanton's controversial *The Woman's Bible*, Anthony turned against her friend. Stanton's book was viewed by many, including Anthony, as a heretical challenge to traditional religious ideals about women that would harm the suffrage movement. The NWSA disavowed the book and Stanton was never invited to take its convention stage again. Anthony disapproved of both Stanton's book and the NWSA's resolution against it. In a difficult personal and political moment, Anthony complained to Johnson about the bust, writing, "the fact is that she is not a good figure for a bust and you ought never to have attempted to make one," adding "the curls looked just like bananas."[32] Of course, Johnson was shocked because Anthony had insisted that she sculpt Stanton. This anecdote demonstrates how changing feelings about individuals shaped critiques of their depictions.

In 1920, as plans for the final sculpture unfolded, Stanton's figure continued to be the source of much critique. Alice Paul relayed criticisms from Stanton's daughter and others:

> her hair should be less formal and rigid, and should lie in loose waves instead of the tight curls which were used in the earlier busts. Mrs. Blatch says that her mother never wore her hair in the way in which it is shown in the earlier busts, and even if she did, it would seem more attractive to make the bust show her hair without the tight curls. Can you not also make Mrs. Stanton less fat? She must have been more slender at some period of her life and it seems to me that we should preserve her in a more idealized form than shown in the earlier busts.[33]

Johnson never sculpted standing figures. Her continued avoidance, even as *Portrait Monument* reached full-figure scale, may have served her negotiation of the changing ideas of appropriate bodily appearance and morals for women. The sculptor repeatedly heard from Paul sentiments along the lines of "it would be easier to raise the money if Stanton is more Idealized." In her defense, Johnson pointed out that with the exception of Stanton's daughter no one sending critiques "had ever seen Mrs. Stanton and none had ever seen the bust."[34]

Similar criticisms were levied against the bust of Anthony. Paul asked:

> Cannot Miss Anthony be made without such an excessively pronounced bosom as shown in the earlier busts? Her bosom in the bust at Mrs. Belmont's home, makes her seem very stout while in reality I understand she was not very stout. It seems to me that if she could be made with a straight front as you have given Mrs. Stanton and Mrs. Mott in the earlier busts, it would improve her.

Johnson scribbled in the margins of the letter "Ye Gods!!!" and "Ignorant Fools."[35]

Harper, who had known Anthony well, agreed with Johnson's assessment, writing that Paul's advice and questions "would make the Gods laugh." Addressing Paul, Harper wrote,

> I do not know the source of your understanding but she weighed 175 lbs. and had almost an abnormally large bust. Mrs. Johnson's marble is made from the exact measurements to a quarter of an inch. Miss Anthony was very proud of her figure and the suggestion that she should be made "with a straight front" could be exceeded only by one that a figure should be made of her with the narrow short skirt of the present day.[36]

Harper's invocation of measurements recalls the pointing process framing the bust as a precise reproduction of Anthony's body. Johnson complained more pointedly of those who suggest Anthony be depicted as if she did not wear a corset. Reminding Paul that Anthony herself said the bust "is the best thing ever done of me," Johnson flatly refused to give Anthony "the sloppy slutty look predominating today."[37] While Paul and NWP sought to update Anthony to fit their own image of a female leader, Johnson pushed back in the language of personal connection, realism, and respectability.

On the eve of debates about the amendment's passage, debates over the sculpture became a proxy for how the suffrage movement would be remembered. Worried about individual portraits, but also about *Portrait Monument*'s unorthodox form, Paul continuously requested photographs to show to dubious artist experts who might help secure funding and the sculpture's installation in the Capitol. Johnson objected that "<u>any committee must see the work itself</u>" rather than a photograph of it.[38] After the monument's unveiling Johnson explained,

> If I had brought you something like the Three Graces with arms twined around each other, you might have had an easy time of it. But a thousand years from now you would have seen no groups standing by the monument asking questions. If I had brought you something mediocre instead of something of distinction, it would have attracted no comment. The work will stand.[39]

Johnson designed her monument to provoke questions, particularly questions about the relationship of the real and the ideal. Some did praise Johnson. As sculptor Lorado Taft wrote to Johnson: "Your bust of Miss Anthony is better than mine: I tried to make her real, but you have made her not only real, but ideal."[40] Taft pointed to a tension embedded in neoclassical portraiture, especially portraits of women. Art historian Joy Kasson traces the rise of what she terms "ideal" sculpture in the United States between 1830 and 1880. Noting the preponderance of female subjects, Kasson recovers the way fictional subjects and allegories—like the Three Graces—encoded an ambivalent anxiety about women and their social roles in chaste, dramatic subjects that predominated in neoclassical marble in the United States.[41]

Inheriting this ideal, but turning it toward representation of historical women leaders, Johnson's sculpture signals a tension between the real and the ideal extant within the suffrage movement's broader commemorative landscape. Second-generation suffrage leaders, Anthony and Stanton had created an idealized story that centered themselves and downplayed or edited out disagreements in the movement, as discussed above. In the third generation, Paul urged Harper to idealize the past as well, asking about an article she had written on the monument:

> Would it not be better to change the second paragraph in which you write "Miss Anthony, as was characteristic of her, insisted

that the busts of her co-workers, Lucretia Mott and Elizabeth Cady Stanton, should be made at the same time."

It occurs to me that the families of Mrs. Stanton and Lucretia Mott may not be satisfied with this statement. Would it not be possible to simply state that the making of the three busts was undertaken, and not to discriminate among the individuals.[42]

For a congressional publication about *Portrait Monument*, Paul urged, "It seemed to me that it would be better to omit all references to controversy with the National American Woman Suffrage Association and all explanation and interpretation of the woman's movement."[43] Should history be idealized to accord with family memory or an understanding of suffrage and female solidarity devoid of disagreement? As the fight for a federal woman's suffrage amendment succeeded, who and what were being commemorated?

Johnson dismissed Paul's ideas, negotiating her own path through realism and idealism in ways that return us to the central detail of pointing marks. The pointing process looked back to the bust's origins, but leaving these marks is one part of Johnson's non finito technique. Johnson bridged the real and ideal by envisioning a history that was incomplete and unstable, progress that might move forward or be rewound. The unfinished, innovative qualities of Johnson's sculpture coincided with uncertainty that the amendment would carry enough states to be ratified and uncertainty about what would happen to the woman's rights movement if ratification did occur.[44] Minutes from the 1920s of the NWP's Executive Committee reveal the group to be unsure where to go next. Several suffrage leaders, including Paul, shifted to champion an equal rights amendment, returning to the language of natural rights with which the agitation for suffrage began. The unfinished sense of Johnson's work commemorates that ongoing struggle.

Following its unveiling in the Capitol Rotunda in 1921, officials moved Johnson's sculpture to the first-floor Crypt, a storage area so named because it was designed to hold George Washington's remains. The monument remained in the basement until it was shifted back to the Rotunda to honor the seventy-fifth anniversary of the Nineteenth Amendment. When the possibility of relocation was featured in the *Washington Post* in 1995, the article reported Newt Gingrich's aide had declared the Speaker of the House to be in favor of suffrage, as if opposition to female franchise was still possible.[45] The non finito of *Portrait*

Monument and its implications for the dual motion of history continue to be unsettling.

Monuments ask us to understand history as moving forward in a series of triumphs or losses to be built upon. Johnson's narration is less clear. Debates about this monument help us consider what can and cannot be included in Johnson's commemoration. In 2003, congressional leaders proposed carving a portrait of Sojourner Truth on the rear unfinished portion. In 2009, Truth was honored by a separate sculpture in the Capitol Visitor Center created by Artis Lane, a Black female Canadian sculptor. The suggestion that Truth's bust could be simply added to *Portrait Monument* seems to demonstrate how naive Congress is about art but also the ways in which monuments constrict memory and visions of justice. We cannot simply add Black women without grappling with the ways many white suffragists turned against Black people at critical junctures in our history, giving up universal equal rights for expediency. Acknowledging the ways period visions of whiteness constrain Johnson's sculpture, can we imagine the appearance of a different U.S. monument to radical universal suffrage or to the natural rights that exceed legal codes?

Notes

1. Elliot Woods (Architect of the Capitol) to Adelaide Johnson, March 17, 1921, Adelaide Johnson Papers, Manuscript Division, Library of Congress, Washington, DC (hereafter AJ Papers); Adelaide Johnson to Charles Fairman (Art Curator, United States Capitol), April 28, 1921, Suffrage Group Files and Adelaide Johnson Files, Architect of Capitol, Washington, DC (hereafter AOC Papers). The AOC also retains reproductions of relevant correspondence from the Library of Congress's more extensive archive of Johnson's papers. While critical accounts of Johnson's sculpture are few, my own is indebted to Ann Lyman Henderson, "Adelaide Johnson: Issues of Professionalism for a Woman Artist" (PhD diss., George Washington University, 1981); Edith Mayo, "Adelaide Johnson's Suffrage Statue and the Political Uses of History," *Capitol Dome* (Spring 2006): 11–18; Richard F. Novak and Catherine Novak Davidson, *Adelaide Johnson's Portrait Monument* (Rockford, IL: SW Publishing, 2013); Sandra Weber, *The Woman Suffrage Statue: A History of Adelaide Johnson's Portrait Monument at the United States Capitol* (Jefferson, NC: McFarland, 2016); Rikki Sierra Rooney, "Monumental Women: Gender, Place, and Heroism in American Public Statues, 1980–2018" (PhD diss., Stony Brook University, 2019); and Teresa Bergman, *The Commemoration of Women in the United States: Remembering Women in Public Space* (New York: Routledge, 2019).

2. Johnson to Charles Fleisher, July 3, 1921, AOC Papers. Johnson wrote to compliment Fleisher's editorial "Are Women Free?" in the *New York American* the previous day.

3. Fairman to Johnson, May 19, 1926, and Johnson to Fairman, May 20, 1926, AOC Papers.

4. Adelaide Johnson, "Lucretia Mott," AJ Papers.

5. Diary, Adelaide Johnson, July 16, 1920, AJ Papers.

6. Fay Stevenson, "Woman Suffrage Memorial Monument, Chiseled by a Noted Woman Sculptor," *St. Louis Post-Dispatch*, January 28, 1921, 31.

7. Johnson, "The Great Three"; Johnson to Alice Paul, June 23, 1920; and Johnson to Ida Harper, June 23, 1920, all in AJ Papers.

8. Note, Adelaide Johnson, AJ Papers; "Suffrage Statues Get Place in the Capitol," (Washington) *Evening Star*, February 10, 1921, Suffrage Group: Presentation File, AOC Papers. There were existing works by female sculptors in the Capitol when Johnson's arrived, including Sarah Fisher Ames, *Abraham Lincoln*, 1868 and Vinnie Ream Hoxie, *Abraham Lincoln*, 1866–71. Criticism of Johnson's monument focused on its unique composition rather than explicitly critiquing Johnson's gender or the gender of her sitters.

9. For example, sculptor Alan LeQuire's Tennessee Woman Suffrage Memorial in Knoxville (2006) and his Tennessee Woman Suffrage Monument in Nashville (2016), as well as artist Gillian Wearing's London memorial to British suffrage leader Millicent Fawcett (2018), and sculptor Meredith Bergmann's *Women's Rights Pioneers* (2020) featuring Stanton, Anthony, and Sojourner Truth in New York's Central Park.

10. Johnson to Harper, October 17, 1920, AOC Papers.

11. Mott and Stanton had met at the World Anti-Slavery Convention in London in 1840, where women were only permitted as observers. For a biography of Garrison, see Henry Mayer, *All on Fire: William Lloyd Garrison and the Abolition of Slavery* (New York: St. Martin's Press, 1998).

12. These interpretations are based on the pathbreaking work of Aileen Kraditor, *The Ideas of the Woman Suffrage Movement, 1890–1920* (New York: Columbia University Press, 1965). Tracing this transition, Faye E. Dudden points out that "Garrisonian abolitionists were peculiarly ill-suited to assess political strategy" because their American Anti-Slavery Society had long prized "moral suasion" over direct politics. Faye E. Dudden, *Fighting Chance: The Struggle over Woman Suffrage and Black Suffrage in Reconstruction America* (Oxford: Oxford University Press, 2011), 75.

13. The state did ratify the Fifteenth Amendment in 1870 and in 1912 became the eighth state to allow women the right to vote. Dudden, *Fighting Chance*, 108–32.

14. Elizabeth Cady Stanton, Susan B. Anthony, and Matilda Joslyn Gage, eds., "The Kansas Campaign—1867," *History of Woman Suffrage* (Rochester: Susan B. Anthony and Charles Mann Printing, 1887), 2:243–62.

15. Minutes of the Meeting of the Executive Committee of the Woman's Party, May 14, 1920, "Correspondence 1899–1921," AOC Papers.

16. Art historian Charmaine Nelson considers the racial implications of neoclassical white marble in her excellent *The Color of Stone: Sculpting the Black Female Subject in the 19th Century* (Minneapolis: University of Minnesota Press, 2007). Recent accounts by historians of ancient art have noted ways the monochrome

material distances the viewer from the bodily, muting sex or race. Jennifer Stager, "The Unbearable Whiteness of Whiteness," *Art Practical*, January 16, 2018.

17. Jack C. Rich, *The Materials and Methods of Sculpture* (New York: Oxford University Press, 1947), 271. This is the understanding of pointing and Canova that would have circulated in Johnson's period; for a more recent interpretation of Canova's materials, see Sarah Betzer, "Canova, 1816: Marble, Plaster, Surface," *Sculpture Journal* 28, no. 3 (2019): 315–30.

18. Diary, Adelaide Johnson, July 18/19, 1920; Johnson to Paul, July 22, 1920, both in AJ Papers.

19. Creighton E. Gilbert, "What Is Expressed in Michelangelo's 'Non-Finito,'" *Artibus et Historiae* 24, no. 48 (2003): 54–64.

20. While Johnson admired Michelangelo, when period critics found the influence of Auguste Rodin in her work she vehemently disagreed. She recorded a visit from Professor Ettore Ferrari, president of the Royal Institute di Belle Arti of Italy, who saw Rodin's influence in *Portrait Monument*, as well as her own reaction: "Heaven forbid, I do not have one feeling in common with his life or his work." Henderson, "Adelaide Johnson," 99.

21. Rosalind Krauss, "The Originality of the Avant-Garde: A Postmodernist Repetition," *October* 18 (Autumn 1981): 47–66.

22. Henderson, "Adelaide Johnson," 17–23.

23. Ibid., 30–33. During her lifetime Johnson participated in many alternative spirituality movements, including having her 1896 marriage officiated by the medium Rev. Cora Richmond, founder of Chicago's Church of Soul. This religious experimentation likely informed her conception of the feminist trinity. The inscription Johnson stenciled on the verso of *Portrait Monument* began with praise for "the three great destiny characters of the world whose spiritual import and historical significance transcend that of all others of any country or age," infuriating viewers who felt Johnson was placing Anthony, Stanton, and Mott above the Holy Trinity. The inscription was removed by September 1921. Weber, *The Woman Suffrage Statue*, 41, 112.

24. Jane Spofford to Mrs. Warren, July 4, 1891, AJ Papers, quoted in Weber, *The Woman Suffrage Statue*, 44.

25. Henderson, "Adelaide Johnson," 189.

26. Harper to Johnson, March 10 and March 17, 1904, AJ Papers, quoted in Weber, *The Woman Suffrage Statue*, 49.

27. Weber, *The Woman Suffrage Statue*, 122; Jean B. Cook Smith, "Life in Marble—Speech in Silence: Adelaide Johnson and Her Work," *The New American Woman* (Los Angeles: C. Shortridge Foltz, June 1917): 5–6.

28. Weber provides an account of this controversy: *The Woman Suffrage Statue*, 43–50.

29. Anthony to Johnson, March 4, 1895, AJ Papers.

30. Harper to Paul, June 27, 1920, AJ Papers.

31. Johnson to Paul, October 17, 1920, and Johnson to Harper, October 7, 1920, AJ Papers.

32. Anthony to Johnson, March 20, 1904, AJ Papers.

33. Paul to Johnson, September 25, 1920, AJ Papers.

34. Johnson to Harper, October 17, 1920, AOC Papers. Johnson summarized the letters she had been receiving from Paul.

35. Paul to Johnson, September 25, 1920, AOC Papers.

36. Harper to Paul, November 8, 1920, AOC Papers.

37. Johnson to Harper, October 17, 1920, AOC Papers.

38. Ibid.

39. Johnson quoted in Weber, *The Woman Suffrage Statue*, 119.

40. Johnson, "Unsolicited Remarks from Correspondents," AJ Papers, quoted in Weber, *The Woman Suffrage Statue*, 35.

41. Joy Kasson, *Marble Queens and Captives: Women in Nineteenth-Century American Sculpture* (New Haven: Yale University Press, 1990), 1–4.

42. Paul to Harper, October 9, 1920, AOC Papers.

43. Paul to Johnson, May 21, 1921, AOC Papers.

44. Johnson to Harper, October 17, 1920, AOC Papers.

45. Cindy Loose, "They Got the Vote, but Not the Rotunda," *Washington Post*, August 19, 1995.

Sierra Rooney

4. "We Shall Beg No More": Helen Keller, Politics, and Commemorations in the National Statuary Hall

AS THE UNITED States grapples with the proliferation of problematic and troubling monuments and artworks in public spaces, arguably one of the most nationally significant of these spaces is the U.S. Capitol. Inside the vaunted halls of the Capitol building in the nation's capital city of Washington, D.C., stands an assortment of imposing statues of Confederate leaders.[1] They are part of the National Statuary Hall, a collection of figurative portrait statues that honor prominent and influential Americans throughout history (figure 1). Over the past five years, the National Statuary Hall has increasingly been the focus of public outcry.[2] Critics claim it enshrines white supremacy and gender, ethnic, and racial disparities in its collection of honorees.

The commission and dedication of the Helen Keller statue (figure 2) in the National Statuary Hall by the state of Alabama in 2009 is a case study for the contentious cultural territories of gender and the politics of public memory. The statue raises difficult questions about the limits of commemorative artworks to redress inequities within the civic sphere. Its accession to the Statuary Hall typifies the fraught, still-incomplete effort to address issues of equity through artistic interventions in this collection.

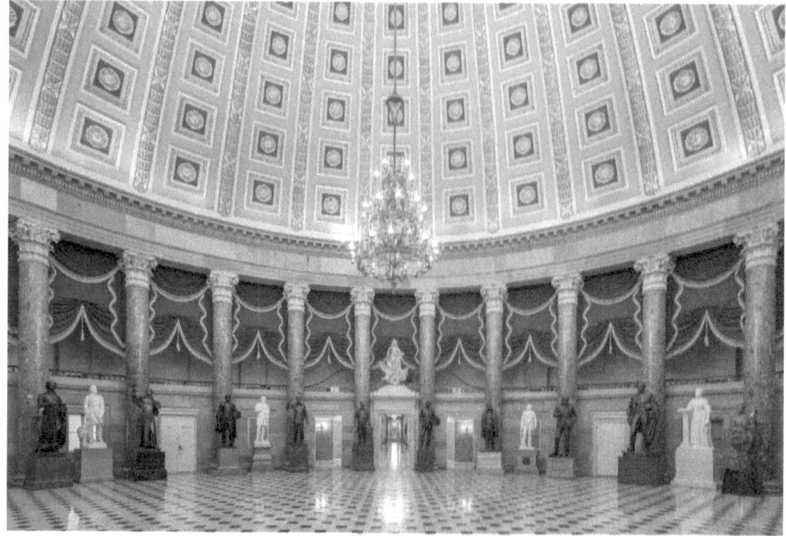

Figure 1. National Statuary Hall. U.S. Capitol, Washington D.C. Courtesy of Architect of the Capitol.

Keller's statue foreshadowed many themes that would soon emerge in the raucous exchange over American public monuments and the feminist activism of the #MeToo movement. The confluence of feminism and public commemoration now informs the cultural conversation, as women demand equal representation in our public landscapes. Such activists today might find comfort in Keller's speech to delegates of the New Woman's Party in 1916:

> We have prayed, we have coaxed, we have begged, for the vote, with the hope that men, out of chivalry, would bestow equal rights upon women and take them into partnership in the affairs of the state. We hoped that their common sense would triumph over prejudices and stupidity. We thought their boasted sense of justice would overcome the errors that so often fetter the human spirit; but we have always gone away empty handed. *We shall beg no more* [emphasis added].[3]

Keller's crashing of the boy's club of Statuary Hall is a step toward breaking the bronze ceiling and bringing gender parity to the national collection of monuments. However, her admission to the hoary halls of the Capitol invites a more considered analysis of when, why, and

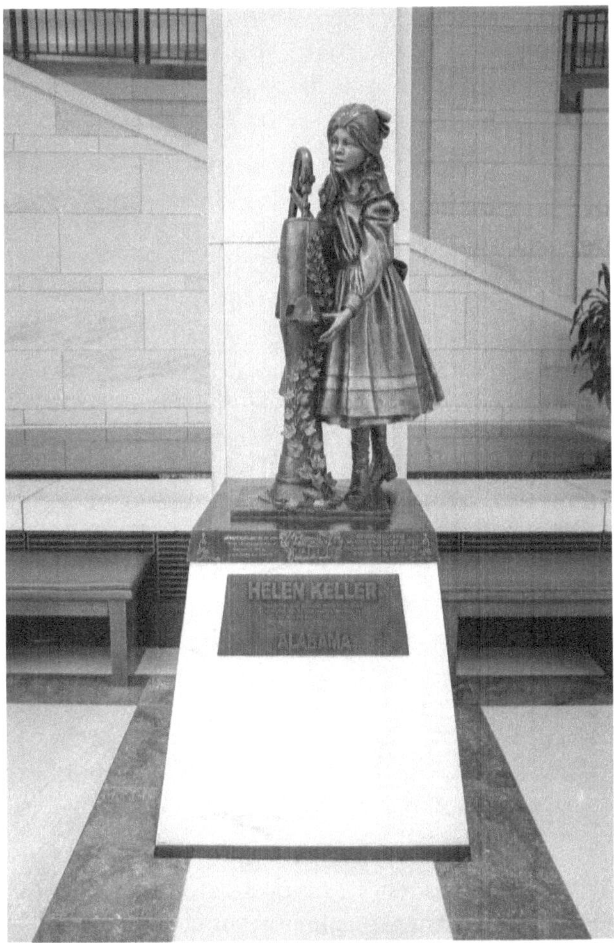

Figure 2. Edward Hlavka, *Helen Keller*. National Statuary Hall, given by Alabama in 2009. Courtesy of Architect of the Capitol.

how governments choose to integrate female figures into public history. Including Keller within the Statuary Hall is a powerful, official endorsement of a new narrative, one that acknowledges the historical contributions of women and people with disabilities. But it also demonstrates the degree of obfuscation that monument stakeholders are willing to go to on a life story that happens not to align with prevailing political orthodoxy. At the Capitol and in the state of Alabama,

Keller's lifelong and influential career in social and political activism was neglected in favor of a narrative that freezes her life at a young age. This chapter examines the stated political goals as well as the ableist and infantilizing rhetoric of the stakeholders who produced these commemorations.

The History of the National Statuary Hall

To understand the implications of the Helen Keller statue, it is important to establish a brief history of the National Statuary Hall in the U.S. Capitol as a collection, a site of display, and a political framework for public monuments. The Capitol, as both a public museum and the seat of the federal government, is a crucial space for the intersection of commemorations and politics, which was apparent at its inception. Statuary Hall began as both a practical necessity and a symbolic gesture of national unity during a time of warring regional divisions. The concept for the hall originated in 1857 when the House of Representatives moved from the Old Hall, a semicircular room designed by Henry Latrobe, to their present chambers in the House wing.[4] The Old Hall became a neglected thoroughfare between the central Rotunda and the House wing that was "draped in cobwebs and carpeted with dust [and] tobacco."[5] In 1864, amid the factional conflict of the Civil War, Vermont representative Justin Morrill introduced a bill to turn the neglected space into a grand unified display for statuary. The resolution called for the president to:

> invite each and all States to provide and furnish statues, in marble or bronze, not exceeding two in number for each state, of deceased persons who have been citizens thereof, and illustrious in their historic renown or for distinguished civic or military services, such as each State shall determine are worthy of national commemoration.[6]

An initial draft of the bill specified "distinguished men" but was amended in committee to "persons," suggesting the lawmakers had anticipated the nomination of both men and women honorees.[7]

The shortage of public money during the Civil War required creative solutions for any new aesthetic improvements in the Capitol. Morrill framed the bill as a "simple and inexpensive" way to acquire new artworks by having the then thirty-six states assume commissioning costs of the new collection.[8] It was a pragmatic choice, but

Morrill held lofty goals for his bill and hoped that by honoring its distinguished citizens, "the Union will clasp and hold forever all its jewels—the glories of the past. . . in one hallowed spot."[9] Such a hall of jewels would heal the "patriotic heart of the nation" in the aftermath of the divisive Civil War.[10]

Statuary Hall would add to the building's robust arts collection, which included Constantino Brumidi's frescoes and John Trumbull's Rotunda paintings. The Capitol arts program, as Vivien Green Fryd has documented, was developed and supervised by federal authorities throughout the early to mid-nineteenth century.[11] However, unlike previous artistic projects, the Statuary Hall would afford the states, rather than the federal government, the opportunity to contribute to a national collection of art. The text of the bill conferred total control to the states. Proceedings for a statue's donation usually began in the state legislature with a representative enacting a resolution naming a citizen to be commemorated. Such a resolution would often specify a separate, nongovernmental committee to oversee the commissioning process, including obtaining the necessary funds.

Once completed, the statue would then be donated to the collection and formally accepted by the Joint Committee on the Library (JCL), a congressional body with the authority to commission, accept, and place works of art in the building.[12] Once the statue was unveiled, it became the property of the federal government and could not be removed or replaced without the permission of the JCL.[13] In 1876, Congress created the office of the Architect of the Capitol (AOC), which it tasked with the superintendence of the Capitol building, including artworks housed therein, and to act as an advisory body to the JCL.[14] The role persists to this day, with the AOC assisting the states by providing guidelines that standardize statuary design, including material, pedestal, inscriptions, size, weight, and patina.

Representative Morrill, hoping to create a hall that resonated with the aspirational virtues of the country at large, called upon the deeply heterogeneous states to send him a new pantheon of American heroes to embody the nation's democratic ideals. What he got—and what we see in the collection even now—is a fractious assortment of state-specific local stories and values. The first gift to the hall came in 1870, when Rhode Island donated its statue of Nathanael Greene, but it wasn't until 2005, with New Mexico's Po'pay, that every state filled their two-statue quota. The heroic figures span nearly five hundred years of American history, with subjects donning everything from early colonial attire to spacesuits. Most figures honor political and military leaders, such as George Clinton and James Garfield; but the hall also includes religious figures and inventors, such as Father Damien and Thomas Edison; and artists and performers, such as Charles Marion Russell and Will Rogers.

Within this national space, the collection of statues has mirrored commemorative trends at play throughout the country: for all its history, the hall has been dominated by elite white men. States were slow to nominate people of color and women, just as they were slow to honor them within the public spaces of their cities and towns. Historian Teresa B. Lachin notes both the regional and temporal patterns in the dedication of Statuary Hall works. Northern states commemorated colonial leaders and patriots of the American Revolution, donating most statues from 1870 to 1919. Midwestern states primarily honored politicians, and mostly between 1886 and 1920, while southern states selected heroes of the Confederacy between 1910 and 1939, the same period when Confederate monuments were being erected throughout the South. Western states were among the last to fill their quota, dedicating the majority of their statues to pioneers after World War II.[15] By tracing commemorative patterns, Lachin effectively illuminates shifting conceptions of heroism as expressed through distinct regional identities. Before Alabama nominated Keller, all eight statues to women had been donated by midwestern and western states, which aligned with broader patterns of commemoration. These states were among the first in the Union to grant female suffrage, thereby recognizing women as public figures.

Throughout the 1990s, there were increasing calls for Statuary Hall to better reflect the demographics and values of contemporary Americans. Yet, with most states having already filled their allotted two figures in the hall, there was little they could do without an amendment to the original 1864 legislation. Responding to mounting public pressure, Congress passed a bill in 2000 that allowed states to replace their previously donated statues in the hall.[16] Now permitted to swap out outdated figures, states could refashion their public image by contributing statues that reflected a more diverse view of the country's history. Though the legislation intended to modernize Statuary Hall, it did not immediately open the floodgates for equal representation. Helen Keller was the first and, to date, the only woman to enter the collection as a replacement statue; she is also the last woman to be inducted into the hall, bringing the ratio of women to nine out of one hundred, or less than one-tenth of all the figures it contains.[17]

The fragmented display of the statues in the Capitol similarly belies an equitable national narrative. The Statuary Hall collection outgrew its designated space as early as 1933, requiring the scattering of sculptures to different areas of the Capitol; consequently, only forty-one statues remain in Statuary Hall itself, with others relegated to the Rotunda, the Crypt, and the House corridors. The collection grew even more dispersed with the opening of the new Capitol Visitor Center (CVC) in 2008, which dramatically expanded the Capitol's exhibition space.

Located below the East Front of the Capitol Plaza, the CVC is a massive, three-story subterranean complex used as the main public entrance to the Capitol and a gathering point for tours. The central chamber of the CVC, which serves as its grand focal point, is lined with statues from the Statuary Hall collection, including, eventually, Helen Keller (figure 3). Originally named the "Great Hall," Congress passed legislation in 2007 designating the space "Emancipation Hall" to recognize the contributions of enslaved laborers who helped build the Capitol.[18] Emancipation Hall added much-needed usable space that afforded the opportunity to display rarely seen art from the JCL collection, including statues from the Statuary Hall collection that had previously been on display outside the hall in low-trafficked areas.

With its sleek modern design, the CVC encompassed a very different viewing experience than the neoclassical Statuary Hall. Displayed under a half-dome coffered ceiling and flanked by Corinthian columns, steps away from the House Chamber, the statues in Statuary Hall accrued a sense of historical and political import from their surroundings. The implicit hierarchy in the exhibition spaces conferred more prestige to the statues in the actual hall (predominantly white men) than those in the CVC (whose statues reflected a greater diversity, like Keller).

Commissioning the Helen Keller Statue

THE HELEN KELLER statue's journey to the Capitol began in 2001, when the JCL approved Alabama's request to replace one of their two statues in the hall. To make room for Keller, Alabama retired Jabez Lamar Monroe Curry, a Confederate officer and American diplomat. Originally donated in 1908, the marble statue of Curry, by artist Dante Sodini, was part of the widespread proliferation of Confederate commemoration, both in the hall and throughout the South, that occurred

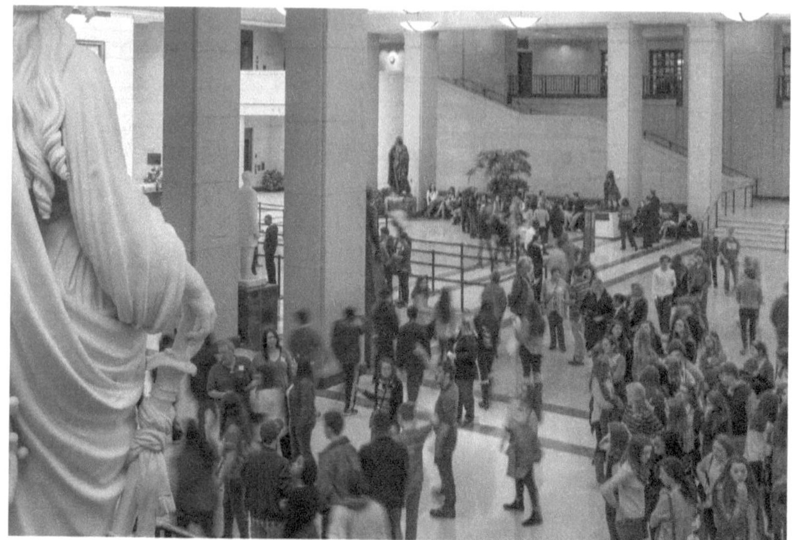

Figure 3. View of statue of Helen Keller in Emancipation Hall, Capitol Visitor Center. Courtesy of Architect of the Capitol.

in the first decades of the twentieth century.[19] Alabama's choice to supplant Curry, however, predated the public outcry over Confederate monuments that emerged in the wake of the deadly shootings in Charleston, South Carolina, in 2015, and the Charlottesville protests, in 2017.[20] When the state of Alabama voted to remove Curry's statue from the hall, they did not suggest that he was no longer worthy of such an honor; their justification rested entirely on Curry's relative obscurity in the twenty-first century. As then Alabama governor Bob Riley explained, "This is not to diminish Mr. Curry at all, but I think Helen Keller is as recognizable nationally and internationally as anyone who has been born and raised in Alabama."[21]

Honoring Keller, who was born and raised in Tuscumbia, Alabama, also provided the state with an opportunity to donate the first statue of an American with an acknowledged disability to the hall.[22] The idea to send Keller to the Capitol originated with Governor Riley and his wife, Patsy Riley, who helped pass the necessary resolution in the state legislature to replace Curry. Once the legislation passed, the Helen Keller Campaign and Artist Selection Committee was assembled to oversee the selection of the artist and design for the statue and to help raise private funds to pay for the commission. The governor's press releases explicitly stated that no state funds were being used for

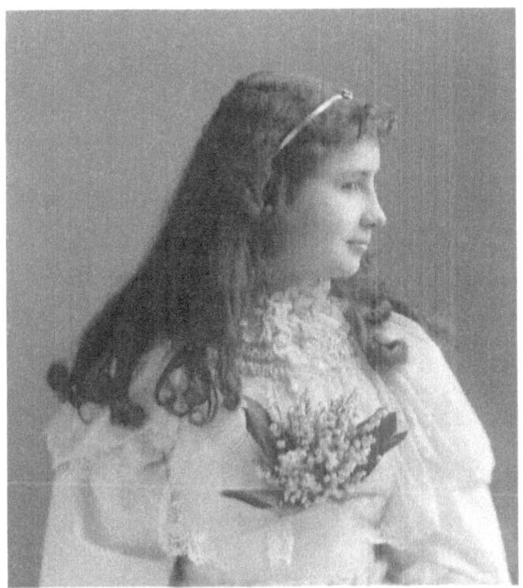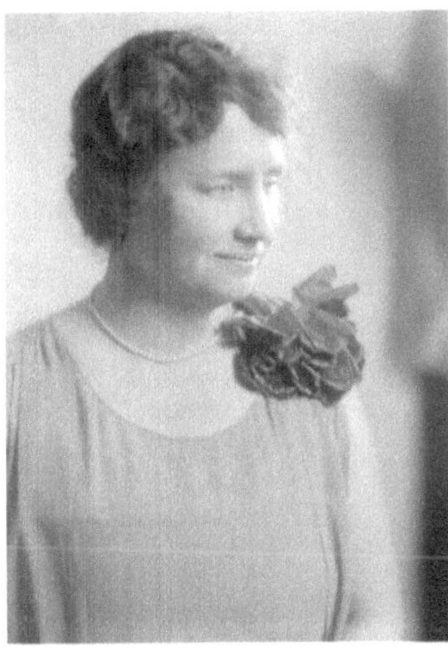

Figure 4. (*left*) Helen Keller, 1891. Library of Congress Prints and Photographs Division, photograph by C. M. Bell [reproduction number, LC-DIG-bellcm-04511]. (*right*) Helen Keller, between 1905 and 1945. Library of Congress, Prints and Photographs Division, photograph by Harris & Ewing [reproduction number, LC-DIG-hec-21484].

the statue.[23] The First Lady served as the honorary chairperson of the committee, with Dr. Joe Busta, vice president for Development and Alumni Affairs at the University of South Alabama, and Elmer Harris, retired CEO of Alabama Power Company, acted as its cochairmen.

As Alabama's governor and First Lady, the Rileys exerted considerable influence on the commission and design and expressed a strong belief that the statue should represent Keller as a young girl and not as an adult (figure 4). This preference was indicated in the Request for Proposals, which states that the committee's preference was for a statue depicting the well-known story of Keller at a water pump, when her awakening to objects and words first took place.[24] After an open competition overseen by the Sculpture Committee and in cooperation with the Alabama State Council on the Arts, Utah-based sculptor Edward Hlavka was chosen for the project. While many Alabamians expressed surprise that neither a southern nor a woman artist was selected, Hlavka was apparently the only artist out of the forty-five submissions to portray Keller as a child, the Rileys' and the committee's stated preference.[25]

The scene at the well is a foundational moment in Keller's mythology, which was first recounted in her 1903 autobiography and popu-

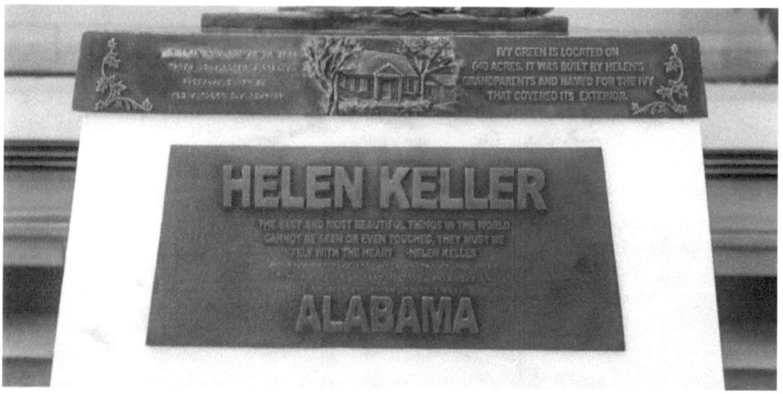

Figure 5. Edward Hlavka, *Helen Keller* (detail of base). National Statuary Hall, given by Alabama in 2009. Photograph by Dan Muse.

larized in the 1962 film *The Miracle Worker*: the moment when Keller, deaf and blind, first learned to communicate with the outside world. In the statue, Keller is portrayed as a young girl. With a large bow in her ringlet curls and nineteenth-century-style dress, she stands at an ivy-covered pump with her left hand beneath the spout, as if to feel the flow of water. Her face registers a look of astonishment, and her mouth is agape as she connects the sign for "water" with the physical phenomenon. The pedestal of the statue, made of Alabama white marble, included a small bronze bas-relief of the house featured prominently on the front and quotes by Keller written in Latin and braille letters wrapping around the square base (figure 5).

Upon seeing the initial design of the statue, the AOC initially expressed ambivalence.[26] While all the other statues in the hall depict their subjects as adults at the height of their influence and careers, Keller would be the only child in the hall. The majority of the male figures in the hall conform to the gendered paradigm of heroic statuary: standing erect either in contrapposto or in a pose that conveys they are active agents. Keller, by contrast, is shown in a moment of passive awakening. Her diminutive size is dwarfed by the standing men in the Statuary Hall collection.

Responding to the apprehension of the AOC, the state of Alabama maintained that the sculpture needed to depict Keller at a young age because "in every important book, article, or movie about her, the focus is always on this one moment as the most important in her life."[27] This is evidenced in Keller's public statues: of the five other portrait monuments dedicated to Keller in the United States, all but one depict her as a young girl. And, given that the statue captures a moment that occurred in Alabama, it is understandable that the state would want to highlight this specific time in Keller's life, especially since she moved elsewhere as an adult. "At this moment when Helen Keller was a child," explained Alabama's First Lady, "she showed us the power of a determined human spirit and reminded us all that courage and strength can exist in the most unlikely places. That child from Alabama is worthy of being celebrated and Alabama takes great pride in being Helen Keller's home state."[28]

Freezing Keller as a young girl allowed Alabama to conveniently sidestep any mention of Keller's political engagement as an adult. An avowed women's rights activist, pacifist, and Socialist, Keller's liberal ideology drastically departs from the political conservatism dominant in Alabama today.[29] Requesting that Keller be represented as a child, the governor and First Lady, both of whom are Republican, cannily defanged Keller as an influential woman with her own held political beliefs—beliefs that conflict with the prevailing leanings of Alabama's legislators. The troublesome woman Keller became is effectively hidden behind the innocent mien of a child.

The Capitol statue is part of a larger depoliticization of Keller within her home state. In her birthplace of Tuscumbia, Keller is treated as a hometown hero and heavily featured throughout city tourist promotions. Residents celebrate Keller with an annual festival and a yearly theatrical performance of *The Miracle Worker*. Her childhood home of Ivy Green has been transformed into the Helen Keller Birthplace Museum, displaying images and artifacts from Keller's life. Visitors also have the opportunity to touch the storied well-pump. What visitors will not find in the museum are her membership card in the Socialist Party, her letters praising the work of Planned Parenthood founder Margaret Sanger, her antiwar essays, or any mention of her work as one of the founders of the American Civil Liberties Union.[30] The museum director justified these omissions by maintaining that if Keller held extreme liberal beliefs as an adult, it was only because she was unduly influenced by the radicals around her: "We've got to remember, Helen, being deaf and blind, someone always had to be the one talking with her, telling her views, telling her feelings."[31] Unable to reconcile Keller's politics as an adult, the museum director cast the adult Keller as a helpless victim of leftist associates in order to square her commemoration with the contemporary political landscape of the state.

Alabama turned to Keller with the hope of eliciting civic pride, yet the state's interests did not exist in an economic vacuum. In the wake of deindustrialization, cities and towns across the country increasingly turned to heritage tourism and monument-building as a vital revenue source, capitalizing on their local history to boost investment and consumer spending.[32] Alabama had clear financial stakes in capitalizing on Keller's renown through public commemorations. An article published in *The Lion* at the University of South Alabama—where sculpture committee cochairman Joe Busta served as vice president for Development and Alumni Affairs—warned that Keller's status as an American icon was in danger, lamenting that teachers no longer assigned Keller's book *The Story of My Life* as part of their curriculum. However, the article comforted its readers that "Keller's legacy is certainly assured among Lions," citing that the Lions helped establish and maintain the Helen Keller Memorial Park at Ivy Green and are among its most frequent visitors. The Helen Keller Birthplace Museum directly stated that attendance at Ivy Green increased as the unveiling neared, acknowledging, "This brings a lot of positive attention to the birthplace, to the Shoals, to Alabama, and the nation."[33] It is notable that few if any local articles of the time mentioned that Helen Keller's final resting place was not at Ivy Green or even in Alabama but at the Washington National Cathedral, just a few miles away from the Capitol building. She was interred in 1968 alongside her teacher Anne Sullivan in the Cathedral crypt, with a small bronze plaque, written in braille, denoting her grave. The Cathedral's website honors Keller as an author, feminist, and advocate for the handicapped.[34]

Centering attention on Ivy Green—and not on Keller's life after she left the state—gave conservatives permission to support the statue, despite Keller's left-leaning beliefs. Rather than focusing on Keller as a feminist or a political activist, local press framed Keller's achievements within conservative values of personal responsibility rather than social services. Such framing is explicitly articulated in *The Lion* article: "Keller's rising above her disability resonates with Lions who help others help themselves and try to give people at a disadvantage the opportunity to prosper. Given a chance by Sullivan, Keller proved to be the ultimate champion of self-improvement."[35] The ableist narrativization of Keller's life as one of "self-improvement" and "rising above her disability" was maintained by Joe Busta, the sculpture committee's cochairman and a Lion himself. In his initial letter to the JCL, requesting review and approval of the sculpture of Keller, Busta submitted a "Chronology of Life and Selected Quotes of Helen Keller" that was compiled by Robert Morris and Carol Dollar of the Helen Keller Eye Research Foundation in September 1993. In the document there is no mention of Keller's progressive politics, including her association with the Socialist Party, the ACLU, or Planned Parenthood.

However, not every conservative was mollified by the selective narrativization of Keller's legacy, particularly in the context of contemporary debates over the passage of the Affordable Care Act—colloquially known as Obamacare—which ignited fears of a "socialist" takeover of the United States. The federal statute, which was signed into law by President Barack Obama in 2010, expanded national health care and was pilloried by conservative Republicans as socialized medicine. In an editorial titled "Red Helen in Capitol, but No Bear"—in reference to University of Alabama football coach Paul "Bear" Bryant"—the author called out Keller for being a "big backer of the Bolshevik revolution and even displayed a red hammer-and-sickle flag in her office," and went on to claim that "it's a safe bet that she'd also be an avid supporter of President Obama's health-care reform."[36] The battle over Keller's legacy was a proxy for the battle over the political future of the United States.

The statue of Keller was dedicated on October 7, 2009, and was permanently sited in the CVC, alongside the more recently accepted statues in the Statuary Hall collection. Hlavka gave a second casting as a gift to the governor and First Lady that will be displayed in the Alabama Capitol building in Montgomery. In addition to congressional leadership and the Rileys, Tuscumbia mayor Bill Shoemaker, the Colbert County Tourism Director, members of the Helen Keller Museum Foundation Board, and students from the Alabama Institute for Deaf and Blind were in attendance. A *New York Times* article called out the spirit of political harmony during the dedication ceremony: "The Republican and Democratic leaders agreed on at least one thing today: a statue of Helen Keller better suits the halls of Congress than one of a Confederate officer."[37]

Following the ceremony, AOC Barbara Wolanin wrote to Busta requesting a small-scale version of the statue for visitors to touch to comprehend the whole. Busta replied that the maquette had been promised to Ivy Green and recommended that the real sculpture be made more accessible by a small step platform.[38] It does not appear this suggestion was ever taken. Yet, if blind visitors did touch the statue, they would find a typo in braille. In the quote "The best and most beautiful things in the world cannot be seen or

even touched, they must be felt with the heart," "world" is spelled
"wolrd."

ARGUABLY, KELLER IS an ill-fitting representative for Alabama and the
dominant conservative ideology held by the state legislature at the
present moment, yet for better or worse her nomination to Statuary
Hall encapsulated all of the messy contradictions of government-
sponsored commemorations of women. As the first person, male or
female, with an acknowledged disability to be included in the hall,
Keller's statue is representative of the millions of Americans with disabilities. To honor her, however, necessitated a skillful reshaping of
Keller's legacy that arrested her life at the water pump in Tuscumbia.

The legislation in 2000 opened the door of the National Statuary
Hall for the great women of history to take their place within the
American pantheon. With a total of twelve statues dedicated to Confederate leaders in the hall at the time of the bill's passage—*notably,
greater than the number of women overall*—the legislation presented an
opportunity for a systematic rethinking of American history that
rewrites stories of oppression and inequality.[39] That evolution was
almost entirely notional for the better part of two decades. No state
mounted a serious effort to replace a Confederate statue until 2017,
after Charlottesville, when several state legislatures began that process, including Florida, Arkansas, Utah, and Nebraska. At the time of
this writing, a further five years on, Keller remains the only female
figure to enter the hall as a replacement. Paradoxically, the states taking this progressive step are some of the most politically conservative
in the country. Though the changes are slow, the present makeup of
the Statuary Hall collection signals a significant advancement in representation toward inclusion of women and other underrepresented
minorities into the country's collective past.

However, the particular contradictions of Alabama's circumspect
commemoration of its daughter Helen Keller are not limited to this
one statue. As the country continues to reckon with its public history
through monuments and memorials, it is clear this commemorative
reconsideration is not a purely ameliorative process. Correctives will
be needed, elisions will be rectified, but there will also be new obfus-
cations. The question of who is honored, in the end, can be less telling
than how and why.

Notes

1. The Capitol as a contentious space for politics and commemorations was thrust into the forefront of national consciousness after the attack on the building and its legislators on January 6, 2021. The art and architecture of the Capitol, including the works of Statuary Hall, served as the background for some of the horrifying images from that day. In the specter of a mob espousing racist, anti-Semitic, and anti-democratic views, these artworks raise difficult questions, among them: How do we reckon with the imagery embedded in the Capitol and its relationship to the enduring legacy of white supremacy on full view during the riot?

2. Jennifer Steinhauer, "Search for Confederate Symbols Finds Them Aplenty in Washington," *New York Times*, June 25, 2015, https://www.nytimes.com/2015/06/26/us/politics/search-for-confederate-symbols-finds-them-aplenty-in-washington.html; Thomas Kaplan, "Call to Remove Confederate Statues from Capitol Divides Democrats," *New York Times*, August 17, 2017, https://www.nytimes.com/2017/08/17/us/politics/pelosi-confederate-statues-capitol.html; Nicholas Fandos, "House Votes to Purge Confederate Statues from the Capitol," *New York Times*, June 29, 2021, https://www.nytimes.com/2021/06/29/us/politics/house-confederate-statues-vote.html.

3. Helen Keller, "Speech to the Delegates of the New Woman's Party, June 11, 1916, Chicago," quoted in *Love This Life: Quotations by Helen Keller* (New York: American Foundation for the Blind Press, 2000), 55.

4. Jacob R. Straus and R. Eric Peterson, "National Statuary Hall Collection: Background and Legislation in Congress," Congressional Research Service, November 6, 2012, 1.

5. Justin Morrill quoted in Rep. John Rice et al., "The Old House Hall," House debate, *Congressional Globe*, 38th Cong., 1st Sess., vol. 24, part 2 (April 19, 1864), 1736.

6. 13 Stat. 347, July 2, 1864.

7. Rice et al., "The Old House Hall," 1736.

8. Morrill quoted in ibid.

9. Ibid.

10. Ibid.

11. For a history of the development of the Capitol art collection, see Vivien Green Fryd, *Art and Empire: The Politics of Ethnicity in the United States Capitol, 1815–1860* (New Haven: Yale University Press, 1992). See also William C. Allen, *History of the United States Capitol: A Chronicle of Design, Construction, and Politics* (Honolulu: University Press of the Pacific, 2001).

12. The Joint Committee on the Library also oversees the Library of Congress as well as the U.S. Botanic Gardens. Its membership consists of both House and Senate members and includes: the chairman and three other members of the Committee on House Administration, the chairman of the House Appropriations Legislative Branch Subcommittee, and the chairman and four other members of the Senate Committee on Rules and Administration. The chairmanship of the committee alternates between the House and Senate with each Congress. "Joint

Committee of Congress on the Library," https://cha.house.gov/jointcommittees/joint-committee-library.

13. Architect of the Capitol, "The Origin of the National Statuary Hall Collection," May 2014, 2, Records of the Architect of the Capitol [hereafter AOC Records], National Statuary Hall.

14. Architect of the Capitol, "Defining the Architect of the Capitol," https://www.aoc.gov/defining-aoc.

15. Teresa B. Lachin, "Worthy of National Commemoration: National Statuary Hall and the Heroic Ideal, 1864–1997," in *The United States Capitol: Designing and Decorating a National Icon*, ed. Donald Kennon (Athens: Ohio University Press, 2000), 280.

16. P.L. 106-554, 114 Stat. 2763A-119, December 21, 2000.

17. As of this chapter's writing, the statues of women included in the Statuary Hall collection are: Frances E. Willard, donated by Illinois, 1905; Maria L. Sanford, donated by Minnesota, 1958; Dr. Florence Rena Sabin, donated by Colorado, 1959; Esther Hobart Morris, donated by Wyoming, 1960; Mother Joseph, donated by Washington, 1980; Jeanette Rankin, donated by Montana, 1985; Sakakawea, donated by North Dakota, 2003; Sarah Winnemucca, donated by Nevada, 2005; and Helen Keller, donated by Alabama, 2009.

18. H.R. 3315, 110th Cong., December 18, 2007, was cosponsored by Jesse L. Jackson and became P.L. 110-139, 110th Cong., December 18, 2007. Enslaved laborers are also recognized within Emancipation Hall with the "Slave Labor Commemorative Marker," which is comprised of a block of sandstone that was once a part of the East Front portico.

19. Karen Cox, *No Common Ground: Confederate Monuments and the Ongoing Fight for Racial Justice* (Chapel Hill: University of North Carolina Press, 2021).

20. "Confederate Monuments Are Coming Down across the United States," *New York Times*, updated August 28, 2017, https://www.nytimes.com/interactive/2017/08/16/us/confederate-monuments-removed.html.

21. Andrew Seaman, "Helen Keller Honored in Capitol," *USA Today*, October 7, 2009, AOC Records, Statuary Hall, Alabama, Helen Keller.

22. Disabilities are not always visible; Keller is the first subject honored in the hall whose disability was publicly acknowledged, but in retrospect it is crucial to allow for the possibly unrecognized disabilities of other honorees.

23. "First Lady Patsy Riley Announces Artist Selection for Helen Keller Statue," State of Alabama, Office of the Governor, Press Office, September 26, 2005, AOC Records, Statuary Hall, Alabama, Helen Keller.

24. "Helen Keller Monumental Sculpture: Call for Artists," AOC Records, Statuary Hall, Alabama, Helen Keller.

25. "First Lady Patsy Riley Announces Artist Selection for Helen Keller Statue"; John Hollenhorst, "Utah Artist's Statue Gaining National Attention," *KSL.com*, November 2, 2009, AOC Records, Statuary Hall, Alabama, Helen Keller.

26. Joseph Busta to Rep. Robert Ney et al., Chairman Joint Committee of the Library, April 8, 2005, AOC Records, Statuary Hall, Alabama, Helen Keller; Mary Orndorff, "325,000 Donated for Helen Keller Statue," *Birmingham News*, December 20, 2008, AOC Records, Statuary Hall, Alabama, Helen Keller.

27. Busta to Ney et al., April 8, 2005.

28. "First Lady Patsy Riley Announces Artist Selection for Helen Keller Statue."

29. Kim E. Nielsen, *The Radical Lives of Helen Keller* (New York: New York University Press, 2009).

30. Carla Crowder, "Historians Take a Look at the Left Side of Helen Keller," *Washington Times*, May 16, 2005, AOC Records, Statuary Hall, Alabama, Helen Keller.

31. Carla Crowder, "Helen Keller's Liberal Leanings Often Forgotten," *Tuscaloosa News*, May 16, 2005, http://www.tuscaloosanews.com/news/20050516/helen-kellers-liberal-leanings-often-forgotten.

32. Sierra Rooney, "Monumental Women: Gender, Place, and Heroism in American Public Statues, 1980–2018" (PhD diss., Stony Brook University, 2018), 30–32.

33. Bernic Delinksi, "Keller Statue to Be Unveiled," *TimesDaily.com*, October 4, 2009, AOC Records, Statuary Hall, Alabama, Helen Keller.

34. "Helen Keller," Washington National Cathedral, https://cathedral.org/what-to-see/interior/helen-keller-2/.

35. Jay Copp, "'Helen Keller Who?' She Died 40 Years Ago This Month and Young People Don't Know Who She Was," *The Lion*, June 2008, 19–21.

36. Mitch Chase, "Red Helen in Capitol, but No Bear," *Decatur Daily*, August 7, 2009, AOC Records, Statuary Hall, Alabama, Helen Keller.

37. Janie Lorber, "Keller Statue Replaces Confederate Soldier," *New York Times*, October 7, 2009, AOC Records, Statuary Hall, Alabama, Helen Keller. The statue of the Confederate officer Curry was first moved to Samford University in Birmingham, and subsequently donated to the Alabama Department of Archives and History, where it is held at an off-site facility.

38. Barbara Wolanin email to Joe Busta, November 6, 2009, AOC Records, Statuary Hall, Alabama, Helen Keller.

39. As of writing, there are now nine Confederate statues in the Capitol. In June 2021, the House voted to remove these statues and others honoring white supremacist leaders from display in the Capitol and allow states to send replacements. The House had passed the legislation for the first time the year prior in July 2020 in response to the global protests against police brutality and anti-Black racism in the wake of the murder of George Floyd. However, the then Republican-controlled Senate refused to take it up. Nicholas Fandos, "House Votes to Purge Confederate Statues from the Capitol," *New York Times*, June 29, 2021, https://www.nytimes.com/2021/06/29/us/politics/house-confederate-statues-vote.html.

Katherine Hite

Monument to Sojourner Truth

ON AUGUST 26, 2020, on the west side of the popular Walkway over the Hudson, then-lieutenant governor of New York Kathy Hochul presided over the unveiling of the Monument to Sojourner Truth. The Walkway stretches across the Hudson River, connecting Dutchess County to Ulster County, Sojourner Truth's birthplace. Refusing to join other northern states in abolishing slavery from the outset of the republic, New York remained a slave-owning state until 1827, and the Hudson Valley counties possessed the largest number of enslaved people after New York City.[1] This fact seems little known to New Yorkers. Sculptor Vinnie Bagwell's seven-foot-tall monument of Truth captures the tremendous power of her countenance and stature, and in more subtle visual ways, it depicts Truth's enslavement as well as her transcendence (figure 1).

The Ulster County unveiling was the first of Hochul's two Sojourner Truth commemorations that day; the second took place in New York City for the *Women's Rights Pioneers Monument*. There Truth joins Elizabeth Cady Stanton and Susan B. Anthony as Central Park's first statue of real women. Hochul's most recent Sojourner Truth commemorative event happened on February 28, 2022, the last day of Black History Month, when now governor Hochul returned to the banks of the Hud-

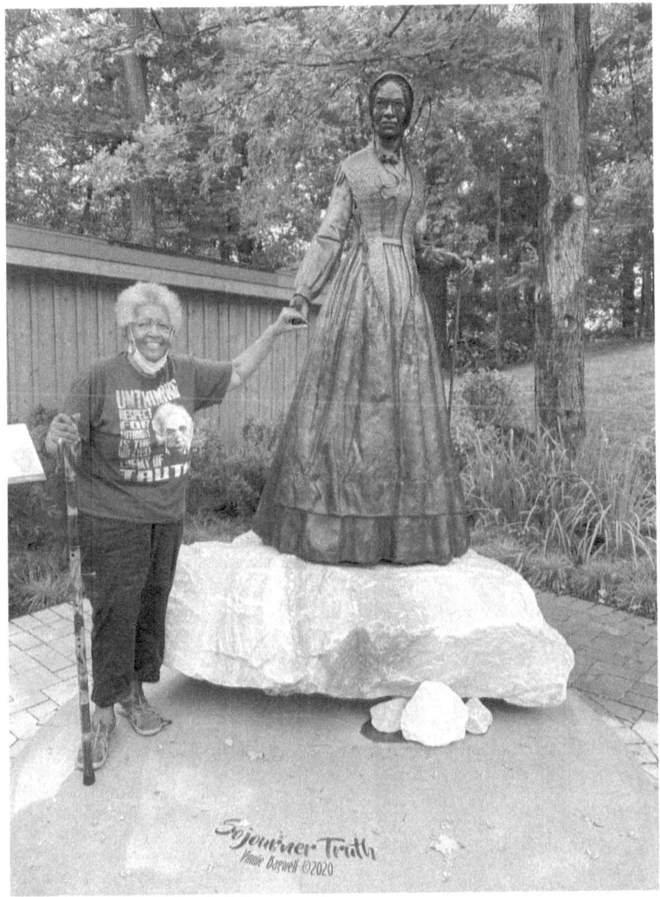

Figure 1. Monument to Sojourner Truth with the Poughkeepsie-based community organization Celebrating the African Spirit cochair, Carmen McGill. Photograph by the author.

son River in Ulster County to announce the opening of the Sojourner Truth State Park. Like the last-minute addition of Sojourner Truth to the Central Park suffragists' monument,[2] it has proved a rather late proliferation of official New York commemorative representations of Sojourner Truth, a rather late political embrace.

Born Isabella Baumfree in approximately 1797, Sojourner Truth experienced horrific early brutality. She was sold and separated at nine from her parents, beaten and whipped repeatedly over the period of her enslavement, sold twice more, denied the right to marry her first love, and raped by her last slave owner, John Dumont, who fathered one of her five children and illegally sold another before Truth could secure her freedom. In 1828, Truth successfully challenged Dumont's sale of her son Peter in court, becoming one of the first Black women in the United States to win a legal case. Truth rose to national acclaim as an abolitionist, women's activist, orator, and land rights organizer. In 1850, Truth published *Narrative of Sojourner Truth, A Northern Slave,*[3] and from the proceeds of her book and a photographic portrait whose copies she also sold, Truth purchased a home and supported the purchase of land for other formerly enslaved men and women. At the bottom of her photograph for sale, Truth placed the motto, "I sell the shadow to support the substance."[4] In many ways, this loaded phrase haunts today's New York commemorative celebrations, which now emphasize Truth's achievements while downplaying the state's history of slavery and its racist legacies.

Yet the force of Vinnie Bagwell's portrayal of Truth lies in the fullness of the rendition: the realism of Truth's face and distant gaze, her height and stance, and the pattern and folds of her dress, the bas-reliefs that metaphorically capture critical moments of her life. These include Ghanaian Adinkra symbology, a "Negroes for sale sign," an enslaved mother and child, a pointing hand to represent Truth's successful legal case, translations of her "I sell the shadow to support the substance" quote into Dutch and braille, and in English, her words, "Truth is powerful and it will prevail." Bagwell is clear that her sculptures of Black people are purposely representational, that it is imperative that Black people see the beauty and strength of themselves, the realness of who they are in her work, and that non-Black people get better at seeing Black people this way.[5] In her remarks at the Truth unveiling, Bagwell said, "Artistry is a powerful and useful tool for social transformation."[6] Indeed, as activists around the country and the world mobilize to remove white supremacist monuments, Bagwell's Sojourner Truth represents a hopeful turning point, a proper monumentalizing for the here and now.

Notes

1. New York Public Library, "The Material Realities of Slavery in Early New York," https://www.nypl.org/blog/2016/04/12/slavery-early-nyc.

2. Alisha Haridasani Gupta, "For Three Suffragists, a Monument Well Past Due," *New York Times*, August 6, 2020, https://www.nytimes.com/2020/08/06/

arts/design/suffragist-19th-amendment-central-park.html#:~:text=In%20
New%20York's%20Central%20Park,for%20women's%20right%20to%20vote.

3. *The Narrative of Sojourner Truth, A Northern Slave*, dictated by Sojourner Truth (ca. 1797–1883), ed. Olive Gilbert (Boston: The Author, 1850).

4. There is a robust literature on the remarkable life of Sojourner Truth. Several important works include Nell Irvin Painter, *Sojourner Truth: A Life, A Symbol* (New York: W. W. Norton, 1996); Margaret Washington, *Sojourner Truth's America* (Urbana: University of Illinois Press, 2009); Carleton Mabee, *Sojourner Truth: Slave, Prophet, Legend* (New York: New York University Press, 1993). For a very useful discussion of Truth's use of her photographs, as well as many photographs, see Darcy Grimaldo Grigsby, *Enduring Truths: Sojourner's Shadows and Substance* (Chicago: University of Chicago Press, 2015).

5. Panelist, "Monuments, Memorials, Markers: In the Museum and in the Community," Frances Lehman Loeb Center for the Arts, Vassar College, November 16, 2020.

6. Jennifer Warren, "New Sojourner Truth Monument Unveiled," *Hudson Valley Press*, September 2, 2020.

Marita Sturken

Fearless Girl, New York City

A YOUNG WHITE girl stands with arms defiantly on her hips, looking up and forward, with confidence, at a very large bronze bull charging toward her. She is about eight or nine, her dress and hair appearing to blow in the wind, her high-top sneakers planted firmly on the ground, her face implacable, calm, self-assured. She is the *Fearless Girl*, a statue that was placed in lower Manhattan in 2017 in front of the well-known *Charging Bull*.

On the face of it, the statue appears straightforward. Her gendered semiotics seem specific and contained—in front of the bull, who represents the ferocious power of Wall Street and the stock market, she courageously demands to be seen; in the face of the winds of finance, she confidently confronts Wall Street. She is empowered.

The story of *Fearless Girl* and, indeed, even the story of the *Charging Bull* that she confronts are, however, not so simple. Neither artwork is what it seems, and their stories involve legal conflicts, public petitions, relocation, vandalism, and contestations about artist rights. Neither was created or is owned by New York City or was sanctioned by Wall Street or the New York Stock Exchange (NYSE). Both were intended to be temporary and were surreptitiously put into place and have only been allowed to remain because they were

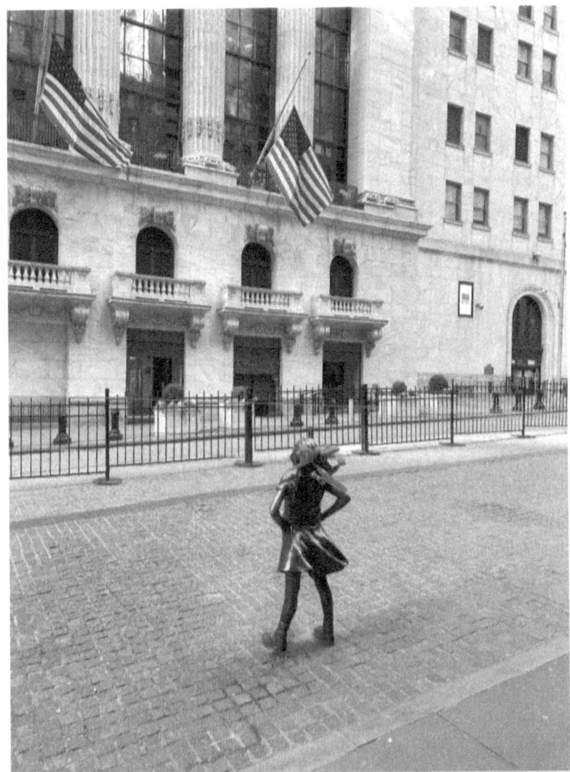

Figure 1. *Fearless Girl*, facing the New York Stock
Exchange, January 2022. Photograph by the author.

hugely popular. Both are the product of guerrilla acts of public art,
though not by radical artists.

Charging Bull, which weighs in at 7,000 pounds, was made by Soho-
based Italian artist Arturo Di Modica and placed near the NYSE in the
dark of night on December 14, 1989. It was quickly impounded by the
city and then, following a swell of public opinion to retain it, was placed
at Bowling Green, a few blocks away. Di Modica, who died in February
2021 at the age of eighty, saw it as a symbol of the American "can do"
spirit and the "virility and courage" that was needed as an antidote to
the stock market crash of 1987.[1] It is broadly understood as a symbol of
a bull market. Not surprisingly, it is a key tourist attraction in New York
and has been the source of several replicas, one by Di Modica in Shang-
hai and others replicating it without permission, as well as numerous
other temporary additions and occasional vandalism.

Fearless Girl was commissioned by a financial firm, State Street Global Advisors, and designed by artist Kristen Visbal, as a kind of guerrilla marketing ploy intended to convey the company's advocacy for increasing the representation of women in the boardrooms of financial firms. The statue was surreptitiously "dropped" into place, also at night, on March 7, 2017, and, as intended, became an immediate social media sensation.[2] It too was moved, after a year, away from the bull to Broad Street behind the NYSE and debates continue about whether and where it should be permanently placed. While the statue has been critiqued for its kitsch aesthetic, like that of the bull, it's hard not to be moved by the images of young girls interacting with it and posing for pictures with it.

Empowered girls have been the source of enormous public commentary and interest over the last two decades in both advertising and education. However, *Fearless Girl* is mired in controversy that has little to do with what it depicts and a lot to do with how it came into being. Artist Visbal was contacted by the ad agency McCann about creating a statue on short notice in honor of International Women's Day, and only found out later that it was being commissioned by State Street Global. Issues of rights, intellectual property, and trademark have been contested between the parties ever since, with extended legal battles. State Street Global has been accused of using the statue as a shallow corporate marketing ploy, while Visbal has been actively selling replicas and posters. The city, meanwhile, does not own the piece and has multiple city agencies that are all assigned to weigh in on whether and how long it can stay where it is. Should they approve the corporation's legal standing as the entity that trademarked the name or affirm the artist's copyright to extract the work from its marketing intent and bring it back into the realm of public art?[3] The city's Public Design Commission is weighing its final location.

As a work of public art, what does *Fearless Girl* advocate for? Its removal away from the bull has certainly made its meaning less specific. Standing alone on the street, she confronts the building of the NYSE, but the visual impact is gone. A small plaque states that the statue is intended to celebrate gender diversity in corporations, though Visbal proposes a much broader meaning of women's equality.[4] For the tourists who continue to photograph the statue and give it a presence on social media, *Fearless Girl* may not need the NYSE or the bull to have meaning; she is just a strong little girl, standing in the world without fear.

Notes

1. http://www.chargingbull.com/history/.

2. Bethany McLean, "The Backstory behind That 'Fearless Girl' Statue on Wall Street," *Atlantic*, March 13, 2017, https://www.theatlantic.com/business/archive/2017/03/fearless-girl-wall-street/519393/.

3. This is what Visbal and others, including public art advocate Todd Fine, are recommending. Sheelah Kolhatkar, "The Ongoing Saga of the 'Fearless Girl' Statue," *New Yorker*, January 7, 2022, https://www.newyorker.com/business/currency/the-ongoing-saga-of-the-fearless-girl-statue. See also Todd Fine, "New York City's Treatment of the 'Fearless Girl' Harms Artist Rights," *Hyperallergic*, January 5, 2022, https://hyperallergic.com/704481/new-york-citys-treatment-of-the-fearless-girl-harms-artist-rights/.

4. Jen Carlson, "The Fight Is On to Make Fearless Girl Independent," *Gothamist*, December 15, 2021, https://gothamist.com/arts-entertainment/fight-make-fearless-girl-independent.

Mechtild Widrich

Monument to the Empress
Maria-Theresia, Vienna, Austria

"*IDENTITARIANS* ATTACH BURKA to Maria-Theresia monument!" read the headline in Viennese news outlets on November 29, 2016, the 236th anniversary of the empress's death.[1] Undisturbed by police, the right-wing group had used a crane to place their protest against the "Islamification" of Europe atop the sixty-two-foot-high statue located between the Kunsthistorisches and Naturhistorisches Museum in Vienna's former imperial residence quarter.[2] We should certainly be suspicious when extremists pitch historical figures as bulwarks against the influx of people from Islamic countries. But, even when the monument opened with a big ceremony on the ruler's 171st birthday on May 13, 1888, it was immersed in political strategy. More than a hundred years after the death of the empress, the enormous statue offered a nostalgic look back to the golden times of the monarchy before economic difficulties, the emergence of various political parties, nationalist and often separatist movements in the Slavic parts of the empire, and the partial sovereignty Hungary had negotiated in 1867. The calculated fame of the *Landesmutter* or "Mother of the People" (read: *all* peoples), who ruled the Habsburg dominions from 1740 to 1780, was a much-needed narrative at the beginning of the end of the empire. At

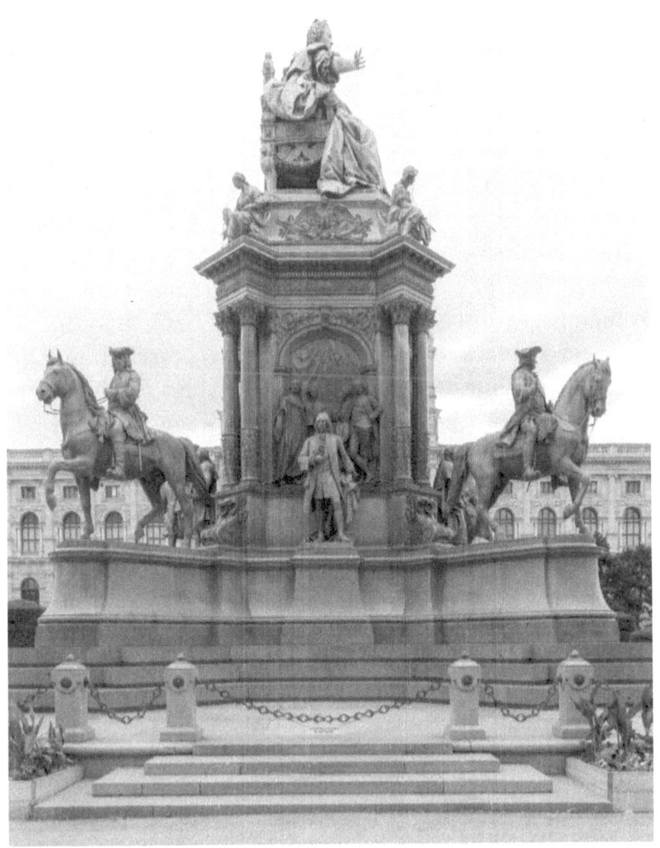

Figure 1. Monument to the Empress Maria-Theresia,
Vienna, Austria. Source: Creative Wikimedia Commons.

that time, Maria Theresia monuments strategically sprang up all over
the fading monarchy. Many of them were swiftly removed after World
War I, when the monarchy ended.

The Vienna monument was planned by the artist Caspar Zumbusch
and architect Carl von Hasenauser, together with various administrative bodies, including the State Archive under Alfred von Arneth,
who put together parts of the iconographic program. Maria Theresia holds the scepter and the "Pragmatic Sanction" her father inaugurated, the legal document that allowed women to become rulers
in the absence of male offspring. The change in the legal system was
signed in 1713, before her birth, and its main purpose was to assert

direct family lineage rather than gender equality. The art historical literature focuses on the complicated iconographic program of this ensemble monument, which includes female figures standing for the cardinal virtues, four generals on horseback, and four reliefs acknowledging advisors, officials, the military, and the arts and sciences together (Mozart and Haydn take second billing after court doctor and reformer Gerard van Swieten). Above all of them Maria Theresia presides on her throne. The bombast of the 1888 inauguration ceremony inspired then-empress Elisabeth ("Sissi") to write a sarcastic poem in her diary wondering where the monarchy and its narrow-minded members were headed.[3] Unintendedly, the monument staged a dramatic confrontation of Habsburg past and present under the aegis of a charismatic monarch with populist leanings (such as her public use of Viennese dialect), ruling an empire of bureaucrats.[4]

In the decades before the burka appeared, the monarchy and its history had comfortably come to rest in nostalgic films and tourist attractions. There had been little challenge to its history of absolutism, class and ethnic exploitation, and anti-Semitism. Seen simply as a monument to an exceptional female leader, Zumbusch's ensemble was thus able to serve as a rare exception to the rule that female figures in public commemoration mainly represent virtues or abstractions. But as the example of the equestrian statue of Maria Theresia in Pressburg a decade later attests (or for that matter the Queen Victoria Monument placed before Buckingham Palace), these female monarch monuments fit into the prevalent conventions of public commemoration. Amid today's debates on omissions in public commemoration and the call for broader representation of marginalized persons and histories, this sculpture does not provide an easy example of what to do or avoid. Certainly, the genre of the conventional monument, as we see it here in a particular bombastic version, already hints at what we must suspect. Maria Theresia's reign did not expand women's rights. She ruled the Habsburg empire solely based on birthright, a pragmatic basis to stabilize an embattled empire. Far from being a trailblazing revolutionary figure, as a passionate Catholic she passed restrictive legislation against Jews and attempted to police sexual morality. The cultural ferment that led to achievements like Mozart's emerged from her advisors' surreptitious reforms.[5]

Notes

1. See *Heute*, https://www.heute.at/s/identitare-verhullten-maria-theresien-denkmal-mit-burka-19889913; *Vienna.at*, https://www.vienna.at/identitaere-haengen-maria-theresien-denkmal-burka-um/5035774; and José Pedro Zuquéte, *The Identitarians: The Movement against Globalism and Islam in Europe* (Notre Dame, IN: University of Notre Dame Press, 2018), who argues the action was imitated by identitarians in other countries.

2. The Maria-Theresien-Platz is outside the palace complex gate (*Burgtor*), but it lay at the time between the palace and Imperial Stables (now the Museum Quarter). Still, its location on the Ring made it, and the museums, a most public part of Imperial Vienna.

3. "Die Enthüllung des Maria Theresia-Denkmals," *Neue Freie Presse*, no. 8520 (May 14, 1888): 1–3, here p. 2. The article noted that a "not insignificant aspect" of the ceremony was to bring together harmoniously the Austrian and Hungarian halves of the government. For Sissi's rude poem, see *Kaiserin Elisabeth: Das poetische Tagebuch*, ed. Brigitte Hamman (Vienna: Verlag der Österreichischen Akademie der Wissenschaften, 1984), 339–40.

4. On her notorious announcement of the birth of an imperial grandson to the Burgtheater audience in Viennese dialect, see Max Mayr, *Das Wienerische* (Vienna: Wiener Drucke, 1924), 10.

5. Which is not to deny any connection with neoconservatism: Nicholas Parsons, in *Vienna: A Cultural History* (Oxford: Oxford University Press, 2009), 5, is probably right to note that "like Mrs. Thatcher, she was incapable of irony, a figure of speech on which the Viennese thrived."

PART III
Women Warriors

Nathaniel Robert Walker

5. The Myth of the Passive Woman in Confederate Monuments

IN 1932, THE *Confederate Defenders of Charleston* was unveiled in White Point Garden, a popular public park occupying the dramatic southern tip of the urban peninsula of Charleston. The tall statue faced the vast harbor and island fortresses where the American Civil War had begun and waged for four long years (figure 1). It was the fruit of a careful process that started with the bequest of one hundred thousand dollars for a Confederate waterfront memorial by local businessman and philanthropist Andrew Buist Murray, and then proceeded through the work of a committee of local men. These men had promptly engaged the expertise of the National Sculpture Society in the hope that the final artwork would be world-class—more in league, as historian Thomas J. Brown argued, with recent World War I memorials than with typical, and often provincial, Civil War sculptures.[1] Prominent New York–based sculptor Herman A. MacNeil was given a free hand to design it, and he chose to employ the ancient and symbolic rather than the prosaic and literal.

The monument features a tall bronze group of two classical figures, cast in Paris. They stand upon a massive pedestal of Bavarian granite designed in collaboration with the architecture firm Delano

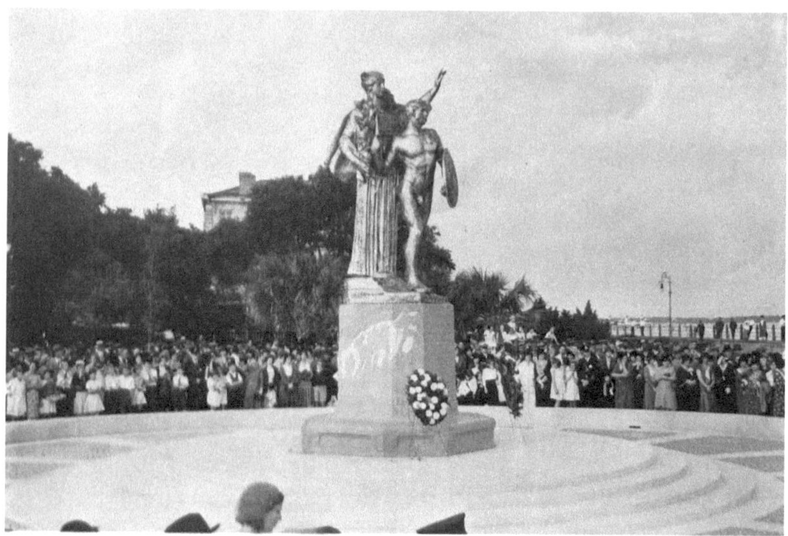

Figure 1. The unveiling of the *Confederate Defenders of Charleston* monument, by Herman A. MacNeil with Delano and Aldrich, White Point Garden, Charleston, 1932. Courtesy of Special Collections, College of Charleston Libraries.

and Aldrich, also of New York. The pedestal is sculpted in low relief with the only literal wartime image: a scene of muscular Confederate soldiers piling sandbags on the crumbling walls of Fort Sumter. The bronze figures towering above were meant to capture the larger essence of Charleston's Civil War history; the first is a heroically nude male warrior, with shield raised and sword drawn, poised to protect the tall, motherly, placid, gracefully robed female figure standing behind him. He is the island stronghold of Fort Sumter, and she is, the newspapers announced, "the spirit of Charleston," embodying a city that, like many others, has a long tradition of being represented allegorically as a woman.[2] In the past, Charleston was a proud and powerful woman—an armed "Warrior Queen of Ocean" who watched over her citizens. The woman in this statue, however, has been disarmed, and her hand now feebly clutches nothing more than a laurel for her male champion. As if to reinforce her meek nature, the newspaper jokingly reported that, during installation, a workman had been observed "standing on the head of the huge allegorical lady."[3]

Despite her stature as the tallest figure in the monument, the Warrior Queen had been reduced to a passive role, and this fact was not lost on the three thousand citizens who gathered for the monument's unveiling. One of the last living Confederate veterans in Charleston stood up and announced that the women of the South had a valor different from that of soldiers. Quoting the 1673 sonnet *When I Consider How My Light Is Spent* by John Milton, in which the English poet struggled against feelings of uselessness after losing his eyesight, the southern veteran declared: "They also serve who only stand and wait."[4] The main speaker at the unveiling was Gerald W. Johnson, a prominent Baltimore journalist and writer who a few years before had published *The Undefeated*, a book about sculptor Gutzon Borglum's tortured efforts to create the enormous Confederate monument at Stone Mountain in Georgia. In his lengthy and rousing speech, Johnson was sufficiently independent in his thinking to question the political judgment of antebellum slaveholders—a bold move for a guest to the birthplace of secession—but when it came to the monument before him, only the military gallantry of the active, heroic male figure received any attention. He declared that the monument was a testament to the sole form of "indestructible wealth" that a nation can possess: "the deeds of her illustrious sons," which raised "our estimate of the honor of being a man." He then pivoted to the present, summoning the dire threats to American liberty that had been gathering since the start of the Great Depression, whether from communists and fascists abroad or from despair and defeatism at home, to argue that the monument was at least as much about today and tomorrow as it was about yesterday: "This great bronze. . . stands not to honor men whose heroism has lifted them far above our power to honor, but to remind us from what race we are sprung. It is not. . . merely a new decoration added to an old and beautiful city. . . . it is a stern question, as well. It perpetually demands, 'What manner of men inhabit the city of Charleston today?'"[5]

With this statement, the irony of the sculpture's gendered composition was made complete. In the past, it was the Confederate defenders of Charleston who posed the greatest threat to the city; Southern militants not only started the Civil War but also, at the end of the conflict, tried to incinerate their "Warrior Queen" and its remaining population of mostly women and children rather than surrender her to the Northern enemy. Furthermore, at the time the monument was erected, Charleston was the site of a mighty struggle led by women in defense of the city against her own men, many of whom were laboring to abandon or violently alter Charleston in the name of economic modernity. For this monument to speak the truth about either the past or the present, the Warrior Queen would need to be armed and standing in resistance to a towering male bent upon ruin and spoliation. The image of the passive Southern woman waiting upon and exalting valiant men had, however, become a theme in Civil War monuments in recent decades, even as women across the region and beyond were forcefully challenging the restrictions of their traditional spheres and roles. Considering the history of these monuments in their historical context shines light on the ways that public art and architecture were drafted into efforts to consolidate and uphold an old social order during several decades of profound instability and change, in a manner perhaps similar to the desperate Confederate sandbagging of Fort Sumter. It also throws into relief the work of women who refused to play the passive part modeled for them in these prominent sculptures. In the city of Charleston, in fact, women had long claimed the right to shape and celebrate public memory and had recently intertwined that endeavor with the politics of suffrage. The Warrior Queen had grown tired of waiting; she had a city to defend.

The Guardian Loses Her Spear

THE TRADITIONAL FIGURATION of Charleston as a woman has long had an impact on the way its citizens think and speak about the city and its architecture, as the politics of gender weigh upon debates over the moral character of the relationship between the citizens and their city. The history of the icon of the Warrior Queen of Ocean is, as David C. R. Heisser traced, tied to the official seal of Charleston (figure 2).[6] The first seal proposed in the colonial period would have featured a "woman of cheerfull [sic] countenance, an Olive branch in one hand" and a friendly parrotfish "in the other."[7] The British, however, refused to grant a seal, so when Charleston finally incorporated after the Revolutionary War, it is perhaps not a surprise that the woman representing the city had exchanged the parrotfish and olive branch for a spear, usually with a liberty cap on its point. With a view of the Charleston skyline composing the background, the Warrior Queen is perched, like a fortress, on one of the harbor islands, and she accordingly claims the duty of protecting, as her Latin motto indicates, the city's "buildings, customs, and rights."

The urban vista in the seal would have cued citizens to imagine the whole fabric of Charleston, as this was the primary approach to the city from the sea and had been the perspective of choice in paintings

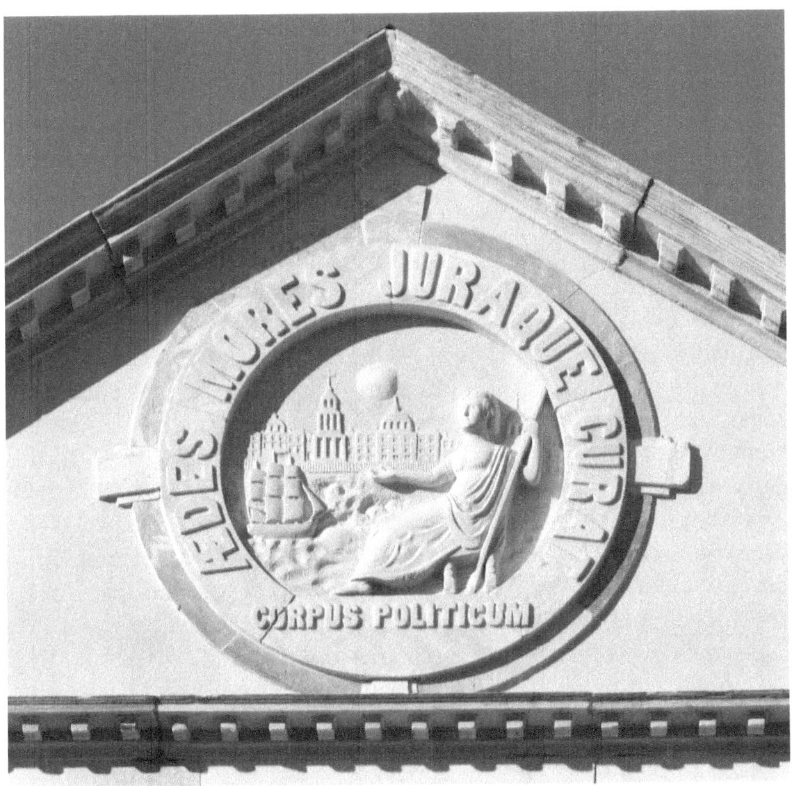

Figure 2. The Warrior Queen of Ocean in the seal of the City of Charleston, as installed in the pediment of Charleston City Hall, ca. 1839 (building originally from 1804). Photograph by the author.

and engravings of Charleston from the colonial period onward. In the early nineteenth century, this seal was used by the city government as well as local newspapers, and over the subsequent two centuries it was deployed in many other locations, including, for example, Charleston's manhole covers, the interior decoration of the massive 1809–11 Second Presbyterian Church, and commemorative monuments such as the 1877 sculpture in White Point Garden honoring the Revolutionary War era defenders of Fort Moultrie. In these images, the Warrior Queen is reliably seated and usually has one arm outstretched to welcome visitors to the city—but that arm is also extended in a gesture of protection, for she always cradles a weapon in the other. While the liberty cap on her spearpoint may have softened its visual impact, a cap covering the sharpened tip of a weapon is still strongly associated with successful armed liberation, linked as it was with the drawn daggers of Brutus following the assassination of Julius Caesar. By the middle of the nineteenth century, images of the Warrior Queen tended to push her liberty cap out of frame, most likely because that symbol was then being regularly deployed by the abolition movement and thus became anathema to Southern slaveholders.[8] The martial power of the liberty cap was not openly brandished in the streets of Charleston again until the Fifty-fifth Massachusetts Colored Regiment marched victoriously through the liberated city in 1865, with their Union army caps jubilantly raised on fixed bayonets.[9]

During the Civil War, even as the name "Warrior Queen of Ocean" was made famous, Charleston's sons insisted she throw down her spear and consign her fate to their hands, as the notion of an armed woman no longer suited the needs of a paternal order at war. In the early years of the conflict, many women were evacuated against their will from the besieged and bombarded city, with one "venerable lady of sixty" declaring "she would prefer that [the Confederate] General. . . should send her a musket instead of an order to leave."[10] In the final days of the devastating Union siege there were, however, still thousands of women living in Charleston, alongside many children and thousands of people of color of all genders and ages. As it became clear that the Southern cause was lost, and as federal forces enveloped the city, including many African American troops, Charleston native and Confederate soldier Paul Hamilton Hayne (1830–1886) penned a poem that would go on to have broad appeal throughout the South: "Calmly beside her tropic strand, / An empress, brave and loyal, / I see the watchful city stand, / With aspect sternly royal; / She knows her mortal foe draws near, / Armored by subtlest science, / Yet deep, majestical, and clear, / Rings out her grand defiance. / Oh, glorious is thy noble face, / Lit up by proud emotion, / And unsurpassed thy stately grace, / Our Warrior Queen of Ocean!"[11] Emphatically gendering the beleaguered city as a woman, Hayne described her architectural fabric as a "beauteous form" and a "loving breast," inspiring her residents with her "life-pulse" and "virgin banner." He then took the metaphor in an ominous direction by insisting that, as the Union army closed in, the virgin queen must "bend, despairing, pale / Where thy last hero slumbers, / Lift the red torch, and light the fire / Amid those corpses gory, / And on thy self-made funeral pyre, / Pass from the world to glory." Another Charleston defender, writing at the same desperate time and to the same despairing purposes, called Charleston his "mother" and declared "her" urban body "hallowed hearth," before insisting: "From all her fanes let solemn bells be tolled; / Heap with kind hands her costly funeral pyre, / And thus, with paean sung and anthem rolled, / Give her unspotted to the God of Fire."[12]

These soldier-poets were not just being histrionic with their pens. As they withdrew from the city, the Confederate defenders of Charleston took up torches and began planting explosives, preparing for the Warrior Queen to commit urban suicide rather than be delivered into the hands of the Union. Remaining citizens were not, however, content to wait in their homes until the flames carried them into "unspotted" martyrdom, so even as the Southern army lit their fuses, the women of the city took their fate into their own hands and filled the streets seeking food for their families. The consequences were devastating. Local commentators struggled to imagine that their own fellow Southerners would try to raze Charleston in a mixture of scorched-earth military tactics and sheer spite, as the destruction that ensued seemed like an inscrutable combination of manic policy and ghastly accident:

> About one hundred and fifty persons, including men, women and children, were either instantly killed or perished in the flames and about two hundred wounded. . . . The explosion was tremendous, and shook the whole city. . . . The spectacle which followed was horrible. In an instant the whole building was enveloped in smoke and flames. The cries of the wounded, the inability of the spectators to render assistance to those rolling and perishing in the fire, all rendered it a scene of indescribable terror.[13]

Fire after fire was set across Charleston over that brief but awful period, resulting in a large amount of death and destruction, falling primarily on women and children. As one female eyewitness explained: "our provisions were exhausted and we were informed that the commissary stores were being given [to citizens]. . . . Crowds of frightened women and children, white and black, came running towards us. . . saying 'Don't go there,' 'you'll be blown to pieces.'"[14] In the words of a white officer in the Twenty-first United States Colored Infantry Regiment, which was the first Union force to enter the city, "Public buildings, stores, warehouses, private dwellings, shipping, etc., were burning and being fired by armed rebels. . . . it is estimated that not less than 200 human beings, most of whom were women and children, were blown to atoms."[15] The city government would later publicly decry how "before the evacuation by Confederate troops numerous fires were kindled in different sections. . . by persons who, animated by a reckless patriotism, desired to destroy the City."[16] Charleston was only saved because the mayor entreated Union troops, "in the name of humanity," to "save the city from utter destruction," and so they quickly landed their boats and worked with the populace, including many Black citizens, to put out fires and guard Charleston's warehouses and public buildings from further attack.[17] This turn of events puts the so-called Confederate defenders of Charleston in an entirely new light; furious at their defeat, they distorted the metaphor of the city as a woman, exchanging the resilient stature of the armed Warrior Queen for the bent and despairing form of a widow preparing to self-immolate, and then set about incinerating the town and its civilians, many of them women. The Queen of Ocean's promise to protect her "buildings, customs, and rights" was kept only, in the end, due to the aid of the enemy, who, in the words of the city's remaining leaders, defended Charlestonians "even against themselves."[18]

The painful events of these final days were never completely forgotten, but they were persistently distorted or left out of official commemorations of the war. The consecration of Confederate graves and monuments in Charleston in the late 1800s and early 1900s repeatedly rang with the phrase "Virgin to the Last!" to describe a city valiantly defended by her gallant sons, weaving that myth into the militant white supremacist culture and politics of the so-called Lost Cause, which asserted that the cultural nobility of the prewar slaveholding South was true and vital and would evolve and endure thanks to white Southerners' sacrificial struggle.[19] The women of the city—or at least, those who had survived—were instructed to express a particular gratitude: "Let the citizens, and specially the ladies of Charleston, express their sympathy for the 'Lost Cause' by their goodly presence. Let the mound and monument be decked with evergreens and flowers. . . . With it will come the proud recollection that through the constancy and courage of Charleston's defenders this city was kept 'Virgin to the last'—was never taken!"[20] Such proclamations were often tied to contemporary events, such as one prominent white, male Charlestonian's assertion in 1915 that no valor shown in World War I could ever compare to that of the Confederacy: "Charleston, the supremely glorious, unconquered and unconquerable. Virgin to the last. . . . new instruments of death and destruction, all doomed to utter defeat before the marvelous intrepidity and unswerving faith of her own sons. . . . Charleston! Whatever one may win of the world's applause. . . truly, indeed, would it add to the glory of his honor if it may be said of him,

'He was born in her.'"[21] This was publicly reprinted in 1932 to mark the dedication of the *Confederate Defenders of Charleston* monument.[22]

When one recollects the events that actually took place at the close of the doomed Southern rebellion, the composition of the bronze figures seems calculated in its comprehensive inversion of the facts. The Warrior Queen of Ocean, her traditional power and weaponry conspicuously removed, is depicted as the beneficiary of "protection" from an armed youth who represents a band of rebels who had, in fact, actively worked to turn her into ash. With the truth in mind, the Queen's outstretched hand might be reinterpreted by viewers today as the city's summons to Union troops to restore her rightful power after the violent usurpation of her reckless, embittered sons. In 1932, however, the myth of the passive Confederate woman held sway. It had been persistently lauded in public histories and cast in stone and bronze by other monuments in nearby communities, even as real women were gaining more influence in the region thanks, in large part, to the politics of memory.

A Community of Monuments in Fort Mill

IN ADDITION TO the tradition of assigning the female gender to the city of Charleston, there was also a well-established American tradition of associating the task of memorialization with women, as suggested by the exhortation to Charleston's ladies, quoted above, to bedeck Confederate monuments with "evergreens." The perpetuation of memory was a crucial component of women's domestic duties, speaking to filial and marital devotion, the education of children, and the keeping of family order. This trope was given public, visual manifestation in Charleston before the Civil War, as attested by tombstone engravings such as that of Oliver L. Dobson, who died in 1850 and was buried in the prominent urban graveyard of St. Phillip's Church. His marker features a weeping woman looking up at a funerary urn (figure 3). Whether this figure was meant to evoke his wife, daughter, sister, or simply a generic lady in mourning, it was not specified, and presumably did not matter. The salient fact was that she was standing and waiting in sorrowful devotion and would thus guarantee that Dobson's memory and honor were perpetuated. The public nature of this image also indicates a civic dimension to the female domain of memory-keeping—in the words of Susan M. Stabile, American women would collectively build, through the successful keeping and honor-

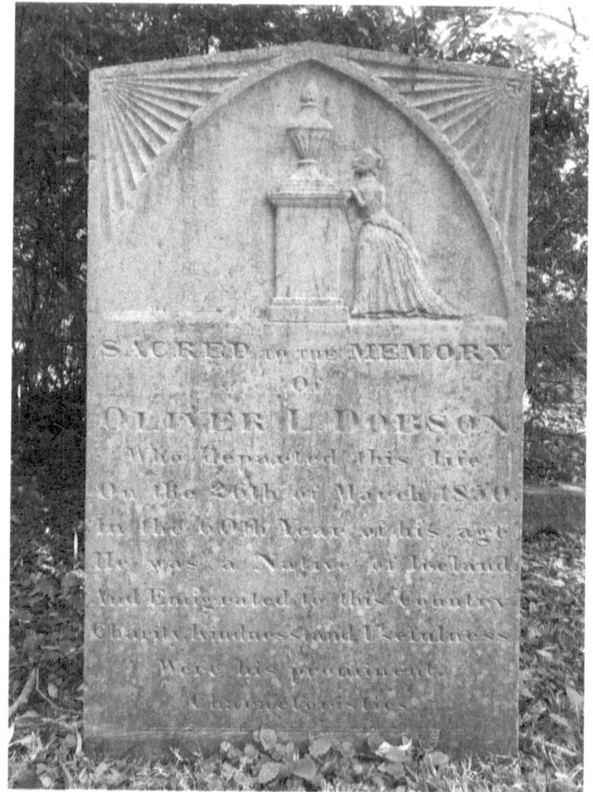

Figure 3. Lady in mourning on the tombstone of
Oliver L. Dobson, St. Phillip's Episcopal Church
graveyard, 1850. Photograph by the author.

ing of family memory, "the foundation of national memory."[23] This
dimension would grow in the years following the Civil War, because
the loss and destruction from that conflict were so vast, until collective female memory-keeping had unexpected political consequences.

Even as the politics of gender began to shift, a number of other
urban Civil War monuments unveiled in southern communities in the
late 1800s and early 1900s celebrated women for intrepidly playing
the supporting roles of waiting and remembering. The first rose in the
early industrial village of Fort Mill in York County, South Carolina, a
well-known stronghold of the Ku Klux Klan. That statue is part of a
remarkable group of monuments, all commissioned by Samuel Elliott
White (1837–1911), a proud Confederate veteran, wealthy industri-

alist, and president of the Jefferson Davis Memorial Association. He installed these sculptures within a few years of each other, and all in a single, prominent public space. These monuments quickly became famous across the nation, praised in the South and often lambasted in the North. A growing number of scholars and journalists have discussed them, but the careful and meaningful way in which they were arranged as an urban ensemble, and thus the way in which they create the image of a community, has not received sufficient attention.[24] Seen together, these statues present a nostalgic vision of the prewar social order and, as an artful public representation in stone, hold that order aloft as exemplary and prescribe its perpetuation.

White purchased a gently sloping piece of land on Main Street, bound by trees and shrubs at its rear and flanked by a building on one side and railroad tracks on the other, christened it Confederate Park, and donated it to Fort Mill. In 1891, the park received its first monument, a fairly standard statue of a Southern infantryman by local sculptor L. D. Childs. Placed near Main Street where the park is highest, it still enjoys a public and prominent site. A pavilion bandstand erected later puts visitors under the soldier's watchful gaze. At the widely reported unveiling of the infantryman, White declared his intentions to add more monuments to the grassy space, asking the town to "consider during the next year a project to erect a monument to the noble Confederate women of Fort Mill Township."[25] A few years later, he completed his plans for the second phase of Confederate Park, and newspapers across the nation published stories about the imminent installation of "two noble monuments, one to the women of the Confederacy, and the other—a most unique and happy idea—to the loyal slave."[26]

Both monuments feature female figures. As Caroline E. Janney argued, the "loyal slave" sculpture may have been inspired by the literary eulogies, then being published with growing frequency, to docile, obsequious enslaved African Americans of prewar years.[27] White Southerners were perfectly aware of the fact that this increasingly popular trope was a modern weapon against the political rights of living Black people, as declared in the South Carolina newspaper *The State* in 1903:

> The old South. . . gave birth to a new type of romantic character—the faithful slave. . . . No foolish notions of equality, social or political, have come to corrupt him. He is a slave, yet paradox of paradoxes, he is merry. His heart is loyal, and whether he is

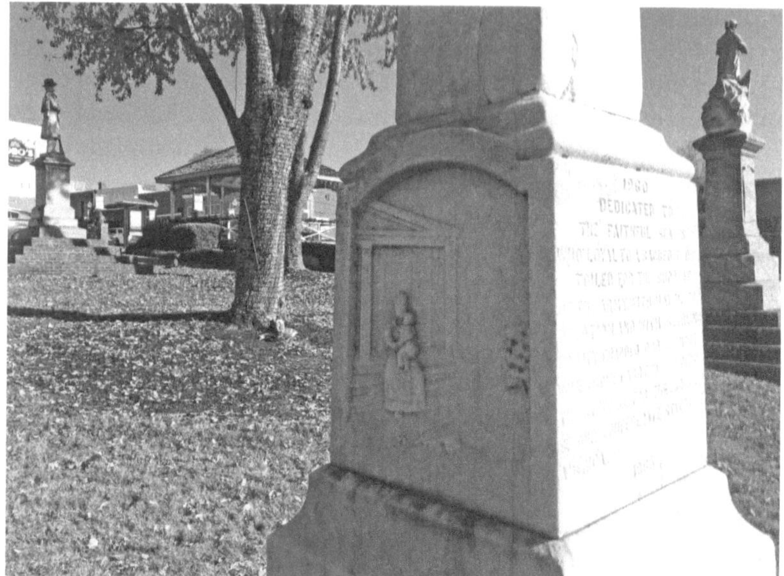

Figure 4. The enslaved, female domestic worker on the "Faithful Slaves" monument, Confederate Park, Fort Mill, South Carolina, 1895. Photograph by the author.

> blacking his master's boots or saving that master's life at the risk of his own, he is still only a negro. . . . a child's mind with a hero's heart, [and] his appeal is irresistible.[28]

The Fort Mill monument to "Faithful Slaves" features a modest obelisk rising from a pedestal with two relief carvings, probably locally engraved, of an enslaved but relaxed and contented male field laborer on one side, and on the other, a female house worker—a stereotypical "Mammy"—sitting on a porch and cradling a white child in her arms (figure 4). The enslaved man faces Main Street and is therefore the more public of the two, while the enslaved woman is on the rear of the monument and is thus positioned as more private or secluded in nature. The monument itself is conspicuously lower than any of the others and is pushed some distance away from Main Street, resting downhill by a set of railroad tracks and behind the Confederate soldier and Confederate woman. It is a visual representation of the political disenfranchisement and lower social rank of Black people, with the African American woman very last in place. Even the final monument placed in Confederate Park, erected in 1900 to honor the local Catawba Native Americans who fought for the Confederacy, is higher than that of the loyal slaves; it is much further from the sidewalk—pushed, as it is, into the trees in the back of the property, as if to suggest the Indian was receding into the primal forest—but it faces Main Street, while the image of the Black woman faces only grass and the train tracks.

The statue of the Confederate white woman was brought directly to the edge of Main Street and is, in fact, even nearer to the public thoroughfare than the Confederate soldier, although she is also conspicuously lower in height. While he stands, she is on her knees with hands uplifted in a position of submissive supplication (figure 5). She has thrown herself atop the furled banner of the Confederacy while praying "for the war to cease."[29] Newspapers across the region reported on this monument, praising it as "a magnificent piece of art." In contrast with the other statues, Samuel White had commissioned an Italian workshop to craft his ideal Southern belle for the hefty sum of two thousand dollars. Her diminutive, subservient status in the overall composition of the park ensures that this outlay presents her as a precious, luxurious ornament on the paternal order. She waits, but she does not even stand.

Perhaps White's monument to Confederate women had been inspired by "Our Women in the War," a weekly series of personal memories of the conflict solicited from women across the South and published in Charleston's *Weekly News and Courier* in the 1880s. When the series was finished, it was gathered together and reprinted in book form. Because it contained the actual memories of real women, there is considerable diversity among its narratives—including the account, cited above, of a woman running from explosions during the Confederate wrecking of Charleston—but the male editors set the stage for the dominant reception of the book by announcing it offered "the simple tales of heroism, suffering and patriotism" of Confederate women, and asking readers to love and honor those "who remained and suffered at home during the four years of strife."[30] Popular publications such as this ensured that many people were interested in White's efforts to celebrate the passive valor of Southern women, and a large audience attended the unveiling of his monument. In a manner similar to the *Confederate Defenders of Charleston* unveiling, the dedication speech by a close friend of White insisted that the message of the statue was about the present as well as the past: this "monument in marble" was "an open book, teaching its deathless lesson to the rising generation."[31] This sentiment was reciprocated by the local branch

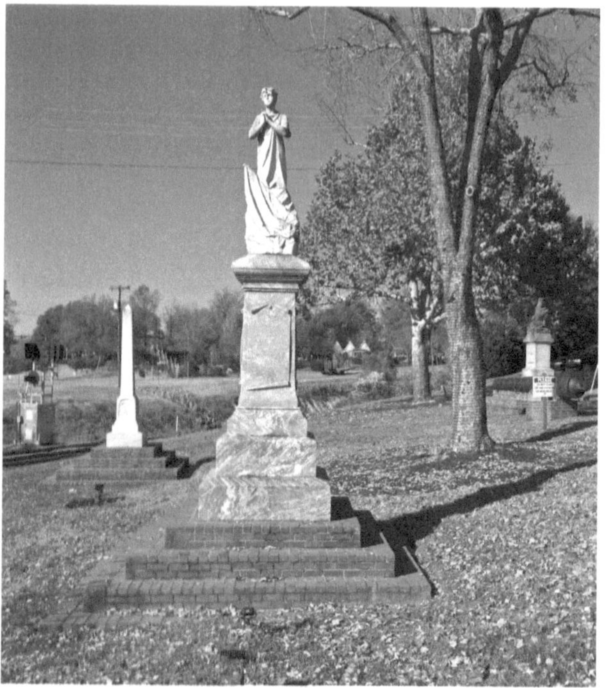

Figure 5. Monument to Confederate women,
Confederate Park, Fort Mill, South Carolina, 1895;
on the left is the "Faithful Slaves" monument, to the
right is the monument to Catawba Native Americans.
Photograph by the author.

of the Ladies' Memorial Association, which showed up in force to the statue's debut and passed a resolution of gratitude for it, declaring that they "desire to reiterate our devotion to the principles for which these noble women suffered."[32]

A proposal emerging a few years later for a fifth monument in Confederate Park honoring the Ku Klux Klan reinforces the idea that many people in Fort Mill saw their community of statues and its hierarchies of race and gender as an image of an ideal society of the present. This scheme emerged in the wake of the phenomenal success of the racist 1915 film *The Birth of a Nation*. Based upon the novel *The Klansman*, written by Thomas Dixon Jr., a man who grew up in the region of Fort Mill, the violent movie rekindled the zeal of surviving Confederate veterans and inflamed the passions of white supremacists with its grotesquely caricatured scenes of African American depravity and viciousness. Gender was a major issue in the plot, as the Ku Klux Klan was put forward as the only defender of the sexual purity of white women against the dangerous lust of African American men, with one scene depicting a white, female character preserving "her virtue by jumping to her death" rather than submit to violation by a former slave. In another scene, the KKK saves a white woman who had chastely fainted at the prospect of a Black husband and then been bound, gagged, and imprisoned by her suitor; in a close-up of her meekly terrified face, black hands menace her restrained form.[33] Fort Mill was so proud of their local connection to Dixon and enthusiastic about *The Birth of a Nation* that one year after the movie was released, the local Chamber of Commerce proposed erecting the monument to the Ku Klux Klan in Confederate Park.[34] Despite vocal support from Confederate veterans and the Daughters of the Confederacy, it was never built, but if it had been, it would have weighed forcefully upon the other monuments, embodying a triumphant afterlife for the failed Confederate veteran, keeping a savage eye upon the diminutive loyal slaves and presumably turning its back to the marginalized Catawba while watching over the figure of the stooping female supplicant, whose brittle, placid body could only be kept "virgin to the last" by the weapons of white men or, failing those, suicide.

By the turn of the century, however, the vision of the helpless, paralyzed Confederate lady was becoming harder for southern women to countenance. As Anne Firor Scott, Marjorie Spruill Wheeler, Catherine W. Bishir, and others have argued, the decades following the Civil War brought profound change into the lives of southern women, broadening their horizons and opening opportunities.[35] In *Burying the Dead but Not the Past*, Caroline E. Janney showed how the Ladies' Memorial Associations that formed across the South to bury and honor the vast numbers of Confederate dead—they reinterred 72,000 corpses in Virginia alone—steadily became political and cultural forces of profound power and influence.[36] The effects were varied. On the one hand, they were instrumental in perpetuating the racist ideology of the Lost Cause, and women-led memorialization efforts took reliably racist turns, as in the infamous case of the 1920s campaign for a "Mammy" memorial statue in Washington, D.C., that was defeated only by vociferous resistance largely led by Black Americans.[37] On the other hand, the increasingly public nature of women's demonstrations of devotion, whatever their political intent, meant that their collective impact on the civil and political fabric of their communities was growing far beyond the traditional domestic realm. The 1850 image of an individual, anonymous lady mourning by an urn on a Charleston tombstone had, by 1890, given way to the vision of veritable armies of women, with formal leadership hierarchies and structured operations, working together to craft and broadcast the memories of entire communities, and thus helping to shape their future destinies. This shift is attested by the fact that while the white ladies of Fort Mill expressed approval of a kneeling, submissive statue, they did so by voting through a resolution as an organized group that attended the unveiling in unison. Even the proximity of the monument to the Main Street of the city—a deliberate choice in a carefully composed park—is subtly suggestive of women's increasing command of public space and life.

Sitting, Waiting, and Preparing to Fight

AFTER YEARS OF public calls for a regional expansion of Samuel White's monumental recognition of Confederate women, the press announced in 1906, with considerable fanfare, that Irvine Walker of Charleston had launched an initiative with the United Confederate Veterans to install bronze *Women of the Southern Confederacy* monuments in every southern capital.[38] Walker proposed pooling the resources of every state together so that a truly beautiful design could be commissioned, replicated, and erected "from the Potomac to the Rio Grande." As Cynthia Mills has shown, many women of the South protested against the idea of a monumental statue—one lady publicly disparaged the vision as a "heap of stones"—calling instead for scholarships or for schools for women, but the Confederate veterans insisted upon their scheme, perhaps in a bid to burnish their chivalry, still tarnished by the failure of the war, and perhaps in an effort to compete with growing female authority over public memory.[39]

Walker's proposed design was, however, too bold for the men he had rallied to the project. Developed by Washington-based sculptor Louis Amateis, it featured a nine-foot-tall standing woman with a face that was "highly, purely, strongly womanly, gentle yet determined." She held a sword in one hand and a flag in the other and urged her menfolk to take them both up and carry them to victory (figure 6).[40] Below, one bronze relief panel would have depicted a Southern woman waiting anxiously at home for news of the war, while another would have shown her as a nurse on the battlefield tending to a casualty.

The government of South Carolina promptly and decisively rejected the design, as the steadily growing female suffrage movement had inspired a backlash across the state and within the ranks of the United

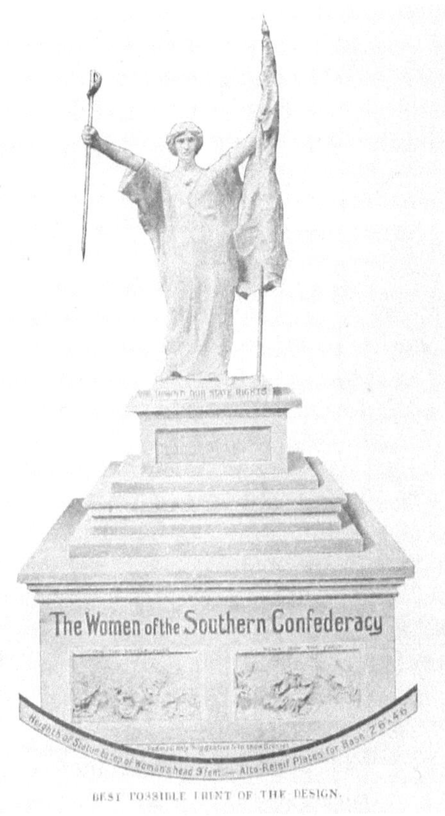

Figure 6. Proposed design for *The Women of the Southern Confederacy* monument to be replicated and installed across the South. Louis Amateis, 1906; from *Confederate Veteran* 17, no. 4 (April 1909): 150. Courtesy of the University of Florida George A. Smathers Libraries.

Confederate Veterans.[41] An attack on the proposed monument published in the *Confederate Veteran* journal in 1909 reveals the political tension then attending women's increasingly forceful claims to political power:

[This sculpture] violates every canon of art or good taste or historic condition. In brief, it presents the typical woman of the Confederacy standing in defiant pose upon a pedestal something after the manner of that other "I Will" Chicago travesty that confronted Exposition visitors except that this brawny Southern Amazon. . . is brandishing an antique sword. . . . Not a line of womanly grace or tenderness, not a hint of the dear home keeper and home builder of the Southland, not a reminder of the sweet and gentle minister of mercy and comfort. . . . Think of the sweet little home body of the Southland, brandishing a big sword. . . and declaiming like a candidate for the Legislature an oration upon State rights!. . . I am tolerably sure that the Confederate woman does not care to be reincarnated in bronze as a composite of the classic Amazon, the Wagnerian Brunehilda, and Carrie Nation!. . . this besworded symbol [is] a kind of Southern woman that never existed and I pray never may exist.[42]

The "'I Will' Chicago travesty" to which this scandalized southerner referred was the female allegory of that city created for the 1893 Columbian Exposition and prominently displayed above the fair's entrance gates. Bold, strong, and armored like a warrior, this woman was too much like the increasing ranks of suffragettes, demanding their right to vote and hold office. One can imagine the horror when, in 1913, a real-life Brunhilda in the form of German actress Hedwig Reicher donned armor and took up the standards of a warrior to help lead a female suffrage march in Washington, D.C. There, thousands of American women from across the nation deployed their organizational skills and the iconography of armed struggle to put on a military parade, claiming the roles of "organizers, sponsors, promoters, symbols, and foot soldiers."[43]

Confederate veterans found this kind of woman intolerable, and many other attacks against Walker's proposed sculpture were forthcoming. Some argued that a lady would only hurt herself holding a sword. The plans for a unified memorial program eventually fell apart. Seven different southern states slowly erected their own unique monuments featuring female forms in much more docile positions; two of them, Tennessee and Mississippi, relied upon the work of the southern female sculptor Belle Kinney, but most chose to use male artists.[44] In 1912, when the men of South Carolina finally approved their design, it featured a sitting, immobile woman who was so passive as to be almost divested of life. Flanked by cherubic children and limply holding a book with a blank stare on her face, even her motherly labors were deprived of energy. Her role is that of a memory-keeper rather than an active maker and transmitter of public remembrance— she is dedicated almost solely to the meek ardors of waiting. At the official unveiling in Columbia, all of the women present were chastened to "not forget that you are not, and cannot, be men, and that love and admiration are as well worth winning as. . . cold respect."[45] As architectural historian Lydia Mattice Brandt pointed out, even the Daughters of the Confederacy opposed this vein of memorialization, believing it diminished their actual wartime work and undermined their increasing desire for the vote.[46] That desire was at this very moment gaining organized force in Charleston, where a long tradition of female activism in the preservation of public memory was feeding into the growing movement for political rights.

The early efforts of Charleston women to steer the city's monumental landscape had, in previous decades, produced a series of substantive urban interventions that were often compromised by embarrassing sculptures. Accounts of the rise of the American historic preservation movement usually begin in Charleston with the formation in 1853 of the Mount Vernon Ladies' Association dedicated to the preservation of George Washington's home. Even at this early point, organized efforts such as these meant that "Charleston's elite white women were present in the public sphere."[47] Accordingly, female appeals for preservation echoed contemporary publications by authors such as George Burnap and Louise Tuthill that insisted women's concern for history and art, including architecture and public spaces, was crucial to lifting American culture above the banal, materialistic male concerns of business and industry.[48] The saving of old homes in particular was also akin to traditional female duties in service of domestic memory such as the flowering of graves and therefore, in the words of Patricia West, proved "appealing to conservative as well as activist women."[49]

Hardly one month after the launching of the Mount Vernon effort, another group of Charleston women bound together to create a monument to the recently deceased white supremacist politician John C. Calhoun. Thomas J. Brown recounted how those women outlasted the Civil War and overwhelmed a rival male society to finally unveil a Calhoun monument in Charleston's Marion Square in 1887.[50] The sculpture was originally meant to feature a proud Calhoun uplifted by three allegorical female virtues, but when scheduling and budget limitations reduced those three ladies to one, the already awkward scheme degraded into a gendered hierarchical binary that was ridiculed by the public, especially African Americans, who renamed the sculpture "Calhoun and his wife."[51] The Ladies' Calhoun Memorial Association melted it down as quickly as possible and then erected a second monument. Lifted high into the air on a great column and entirely devoid of female figures, this bronze likeness of Calhoun glared down upon the city until the local government, responding to a series of Black Lives Matter protests, removed it to a warehouse in 2020.

After the female-led construction of the Calhoun monument, other women in the city organized to save two colonial-era landmarks: the small gunpowder magazine of 1713 and the massive Exchange Building of 1767–71. The latter was saved by the Daughters of the American Revolution in 1913, not long after the passive Confederate women monument was unveiled in Columbia. The notoriously violent and racist Senator Ben Tillman made a small contribution to their herculean effort by convincing the federal government to surrender the decaying building to their care. He later congratulated the women's success in restoring it by presenting them with a bronze bust of himself.[52]

The following years were crucial to Charleston. As bronze women were cast in a humiliating fashion and melted down, and as bronze men proliferated, two distinct visions of the city's future emerged. While many women were striving to preserve the old urban fabric of the city, many men were working to abandon or destroy it, even as outlets such as the *New York Times* increasingly recognized Charleston for its "architectural wealth" of "hundreds of admirable and characteristic" buildings.[53] Destruction took many forms, including an increasingly rapid pace of demolition of old structures for automobile infrastructure. This was attended by efforts to pull white families out of the ancient, mixed-race downtown and install them in new, racially "hygienic" suburbs. Advertisements for the popular streetcar suburb of Hampton Park Terrace, for example, boasted about its exclusive whiteness and "virgin soil," attacking the old city's density, frequent flooding, and "negro hovels."[54] The huge automobile suburb of North Charleston also advertised its rejection of density and Black people; its developers, a group of leading professionals and businessmen including a former mayor, hoped North Charleston would initiate a bold new future for the whole region as white families depopulated the old city and dispersed across the hinterlands.[55] Even in downtown, a wide new waterfront street was designed, built, and zoned so that only large, detached, expensive, suburban-style, single-family houses could be built upon it, and only whites would own them. This was named Murray Boulevard after the local philanthropist who donated money to see the project to completion—the very same philanthropist who donated money for the *Confederate Defenders of Charleston* monument, which was placed exactly where the new boulevard met the old harbor line. As Gerald W. Johnson insisted upon its unveiling, the statue asks: "What manner of men inhabit the city of Charleston

today?" In the increasingly suburban city of 1932, the old Confederate warrior was echoed by the fiercely independent white, male motor-
ist and homeowner, who, like the Ku Klux Klansmen in *The Birth of a
Nation*, carried forth the Confederate "Lost Cause" by standing between
his womenfolk and the corrupting dangers of ravenous Black men or
parading suffrage zealots in the tangled, uncontrollable old streets of
Charleston.

The resistance to this architectural violence was led by Susan Pringle Frost (1873–1960), director of the local Female Suffrage League.
A resident of one of downtown's historic homes, she was enraged by
the careless demolitions taking place around her, as well as by the
despoliation of old buildings as unscrupulous—and usually male—
owners stripped them of their valuable ironwork and woodwork and
then left them to rot.[56] She became the city's first female real estate
agent and set to work restoring downtown and filling its homes with
families. In 1920, the same year that women achieved the right to
vote nationwide, Frost leveraged her political experience, community connections, and personal charisma to launch the Society for
the Preservation of Old Dwellings. The gutting of Charleston hit a
wall of resistance as Frost and her allies militantly laid claim to the
dense, complicated old streets, saving huge swathes of urban fabric
and finally convincing City Hall to adopt the world's first historic district zoning ordinance in 1931, effectively saving the city one year
before the unveiling of the huge passive lady in White Point Garden.
Henceforth, the society steadily gained force, attracting female and
male members partly by leveraging the old allegorical conception of
Charleston as a living woman.

In the 1940s, Frost pleaded with citizens not to be "cruel" to the
city's architecture.[57] A cartoon published by the society in 1961
depicts a weeping house brought back to blushing cheer by restoration, with stereotypically feminine eyelashes teased out of its window
jack arches and rosy brick cheeks (figure 7). Frost's cousin announced:
"Charleston is like a woman of many moods! Like such a woman she
is swayed by the views of every passing critic. If she is not to fly apart,
she must soon decide where it is she wants to go? What it is she wants
to be? She cannot be all things to all men, and remain a whole city."[58]
In 1933, when Frost ally Herbert Ravenel Sass wrote the introduction
to a book of Charleston woodcuts by Charles W. Smith, he explained
that a Charlestonian who knows and loves his city refers to it as "she
(he does not think of Charleston as 'it')."[59] The Preservation Society
summoned the Warrior Queen of Ocean herself in 1953 by placing

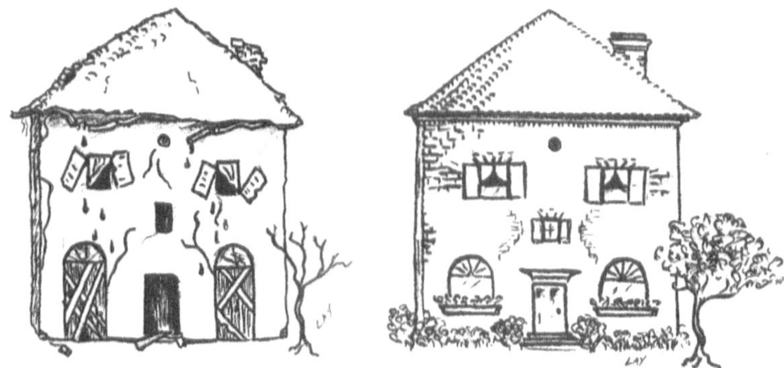

Figure 7. Illustrations representing the return of an anthropomorphic house to health and good cheer by restoration, from *Preservation Progress* 6, no. 2 (March 1961): 6. Courtesy of the Preservation Society of Charleston Archives.

her on the bronze plaques they continue to present to winners of their Carolopolis Award. Affixed to well-restored historic buildings all over the city, they mark the victories that the Warrior Queen has won defending her buildings against the enemies of Charleston.

The achievements of Susan Pringle Frost and the Preservation Society were not perfect. Even as businessmen continued to try to pull white families into white suburbs, some of the restoration work taking place downtown resulted in the eviction of Black families, who had few places to turn for a new home. The one-hundred-year anniversary of the Preservation Society celebrated in 2020 also marks a century of unjust gentrification on the Charleston peninsula. Nonetheless, the city would have been cleared beyond recognition if not for its valiant women, who survived the attempted destruction of their "virgin" metropolis by hysterical men at the end of the Civil War and then overcame its male-driven defacement and neglect by deploying the political power they had gained as guardians of collective memory and suffragist reformers. The Warrior Queen of Ocean was saved not by her sons but by her daughters, who picked up the spear that had been dashed from her hands and charged forward to protect her "buildings, customs, and rights." The monuments that rose in Charleston and across the South in order to cast in bronze the myth of the timid woman clutching a laurel and demurely waiting for either salvation or death were never honest recollections of the past—they were, and they remain, fantasies of a society that never was and never could be.

Notes

1. Thomas J. Brown, *Civil War Canon: Sites of Confederate Memory in South Carolina* (Chapel Hill: University of North Carolina Press, 2015), 174–77.

2. "Borings Finished for Monument," *News and Courier*, Thursday, September 10, 1931, 14.

3. "Did You Happen to See-?" *News and Courier*, Friday, October 7, 1932, 16.

4. "Memorial Bronze Presented to City," *News and Courier*, Friday, October 21, 1932, 7.

5. "Fort Sumter Great Monument to the Ideals of Defenders, Johnson Says," *News and Courier*, Friday, October 21, 1932, 7.

6. David C. R. Heisser, "'Warrior Queen of Ocean': The Story of Charleston and Its Seal," *South Carolina Historical Magazine* 93, no. 3/4 (July–October 1992): 167–95.

7. Bruce T. McCully, "The Charleston Government Act of 1722: A Neglected Document," *South Carolina Historical Magazine* 83 (October 1982): 308–9.

8. Yvonne Korshak, "The Liberty Cap as Revolutionary Symbol in America and France," *Smithsonian Studies in American Art* 1, no. 2 (Autumn 1987): 52–69.

9. "'Marching On!' The Fifty-fifth Massachusetts Colored Regiment Singing John Brown's March in the Streets of Charleston," *Harper's Weekly* 9, no. 429 (March 18, 1865): 165.

10. "Our Noble Women," *Charleston Courier*, December 2, 1862, 4.

11. Paul Hamilton Hayne, "Charleston," in *Poems of American History*, ed. Burton Egbert Stevenson (Boston: Houghton Mifflin, 1922), 515–16; for an example of the poem's appeal in the postwar years, see "Paul Hamilton Hayne: The Elegant Reception by the Macon Athenæum Last Night," *Macon Daily Telegraph*, Friday, May 21, 1886, 5.

12. John Dickson Bruns, "The Foe at the Gates," in *Poems of American History*, ed. Burton Egbert Stevenson (Boston: Houghton Mifflin, 1922), 515–16.

13. "Evacuation of Charleston," *Daily Courier*, Monday, February 20, 1865, 1.

14. Pauline Dufort, "Charleston during the Siege," in *Our Women in the War: The Lives They Lived; The Deaths They Died* (Charleston: News and Courier Book Presses, 1885), 52.

15. A. G. Bennett, Report No. 273, in Daniel S. Lamont, George B. Davis, Leslie J. Perry, and Joseph W. Kirkley, eds., *War of the Rebellion: A Compilation of the Official Records of the Union and Confederate Armies*, ser. 1, vol. xlvii, part 1: reports (Washington, DC: Government Printing Office, 1895), 1019.

16. "Mortuary: Charles MacBeth," in *Year Book, 1881* (City of Charleston and the News and Courier Book Press, 1881), 254.

17. Bennett, Report No. 273, 1020.

18. "Mortuary: Charles MacBeth," 254.

19. "The Sword of Beauregard," *News and Courier*, Friday, March 17, 1893, 1; "The Flag of the First Regulars," *News and Courier*, Wednesday, January 17, 1894, 2.

20. "The Memory of Ripley," *News and Courier*, Monday, April 3, 1893, 8.

21. William G. Mazyck, "There Were Giants in Those Days," *News and Courier*, Monday, March 29, 1915, 4.

22. "Fort Sumter," *News and Courier*, Thursday, October 20, 1932, 4.

23. Susan M. Stabile, *Memory's Daughters: The Material Culture of Remembrance in Eighteenth-Century America* (Ithaca: Cornell University Press, 2004), 4; see also Brown, *Civil War Canon*, 52–53.

24. Kirk Savage, *Standing Soldiers, Kneeling Slaves* (Princeton: Princeton University Press, 1997), 155–60; Caroline E. Janney, *Remembering the Civil War: Reunion and the Limits of Reconciliation* (Chapel Hill: University of North Carolina Press, 2013), 210–11; Brown, *Civil War Canon*, 114–15; Ethan J. Kytle and Blain Roberts, *Denmark Vesey's Garden: Slavery and Memory in the Cradle of the Confederacy* (New York: The New Press, 2018), 147–50; for a thoughtful and comprehensive survey of recent local and national debates over these monuments, see the online petition and article "It's Time to Stand against White Supremacy, Fort Mill," *End White Supremacy Fort Mill*, June 14, 2020, https://medium.com/@endwhitesupremacyfortmill/its-time-to-stand-against-white-supremacy-fort-mill-ac9d93a84e0e; my research on Fort Mill benefited from a research paper that I cowrote and copresented with Patricia Ploehn, then a College of Charleston undergraduate student: "On the Loyalty of Slaves: Black History, White Supremacy, and Public Monuments in South Carolina," Ninth Biennial Urban History Association Conference, October 2018.

25. "All Honor to Fort Mill," *News and Courier*, Saturday, December 26, 1891, 6.

26. "Facts from Fort Mill," *The State*, Saturday, Saturday, July 27, 1895, 6.

27. Janney, *Remembering the Civil War*, 209–10.

28. "The Home of Romance: The South's Primacy in Literature," *The State*, Sunday, August 30, 1903, 5.

29. "Capt. S. E. White: Patriot," *Charlotte Observer*, Friday, May 22, 1896, 1.

30. *Our Women in the War*, iii.

31. "Monument to the Slaves," *Greenwood Daily Journal*, Thursday, May 28, 1896, 1.

32. "Capt. S. E. White: Patriot," 1.

33. Eric Olund, "Geography Written in Lightning: Race, Sexuality, and Regulatory Aesthetics in 'The Birth of a Nation,'" *Annals of the Association of American Geographers* 103, no. 4 (July 2013): 935.

34. "Fort Mill after Monument to the Ku Klux Klan," *Evening Herald*, Wednesday, December 6, 1916, 3; see also the online petition "It's Time to Stand against White Supremacy, Fort Mill."

35. Anne Firor Scott, *Natural Allies: Women's Associations in American History* (Urbana: University of Illinois Press, 1991); Marjorie Spruill Wheeler, *New Women of the New South: The Leaders of the Woman Suffrage Movement in the Southern States* (New York: Oxford University Press, 1993); Catherine W. Bishir, "'A Strong Force of Ladies': Women, Politics, and Confederate Memorial Associations in Nineteenth-Century Raleigh," in *Monuments to the Lost Cause: Women, Art, and the Landscapes of Southern Memory*, ed. Cynthia Mills and Pamela H. Simpson (Knoxville: University of Tennessee Press, 2003), 3–26.

36. Caroline E. Janney, *Burying the Dead but Not the Past: Ladies' Memorial Associations and the Lost Cause* (Chapel Hill: University of North Carolina Press, 2012).

37. For a discussion of this effort with a focus on gender, see Micki McElya, "Commemorating the Color Line: The National Mammy Monument Controversy of the 1920s," in *Monuments to the Lost Cause: Women, Art, and the Landscapes of Southern Memory*, ed. Cynthia Mills and Pamela H. Simpson (Knoxville: University of Tennessee Press, 2003), 203–18.

38. "Suggestions of Gen. Walker," *The State*, Wednesday, March 7, 1906, 1.

39. Cynthia Mills, "Gratitude and Gender Wars: Monuments to the Women of the Sixties," in *Monuments to the Lost Cause: Women, Art, and the Landscapes of Southern Memory*, ed. Cynthia Mills and Pamela H. Simpson (Knoxville: University of Tennessee Press, 2003), 186–87.

40. "State Monuments to Women of South," *Charleston Evening Post*, March 13, 1909, 7.

41. Brown, *Civil War Canon*, 113.

42. H. M. Hamill, "Confederate Woman's Monument," *Confederate Veteran* 17, no. 4 (April 1909): 150.

43. Annelise K. Madsen, "Columbia and Her Foot Soldiers: Civic Art and the Demand for Change at the 1913 Suffrage Pageant-Procession," *Winterthur Portfolio* 18, no. 4 (Winter 2014): 283–310.

44. Mills, "Gratitude and Gender Wars," 189.

45. Brown, *Civil War Canon*, 124.

46. Lydia Mattice Brandt, "South Carolina Monument to the Women of the Confederacy," in "Monuments on the South Carolina State House Grounds," online tour by Historic Columbia: https://www.historiccolumbia.org/tour-locations/south-carolina-monument-women-confederacy.

47. Stephanie E. Yuhl, *A Golden Haze of Memory: The Making of Historic Charleston* (Chapel Hill: University of North Carolina Press, 2005), 28–29.

48. Nathaniel Robert Walker, "Life and Breath to the City: Women, Urbanism, and the Birth of the Historic Preservation Movement," in *Suffragette City: Women, Politics, and the Built Environment*, ed. Elizabeth Darling and Nathaniel Robert Walker (Abingdon: Routledge, 2019), 58–64, 71.

49. Patricia West, *Domesticating History: The Political Origins of America's House Museums* (Washington, DC: Smithsonian Institution Press, 1999), 2.

50. Brown, *Civil War Canon*, 36–90.

51. Ibid., 84.

52. "Celebrated by D.A.R.," *Evening Post*, Monday, June 30, 1913, 10.

53. "City's Architectural Wealth Hailed by Magazine Writer," *News and Courier*, Monday, November 2, 1931, 10.

54. "Hampton Park Terrace" advertisement in the *Charleston Evening Post*, Saturday, December 30, 1991, 13.

55. Nathaniel Robert Walker, *Victorian Visions of Suburban Utopia* (Oxford: Oxford University Press, 2020), 479–82.

56. Sydney Bland, *Preserving Charleston's Past, Shaping Its Future: The Life and Times of Susan Pringle Frost* (Columbia: University of South Carolina Press, 1999); Walker, "Life and Breath to the City," 72–79.

57. "History of Society to Preserve Old Dwellings Recited," *News and Courier*, Sunday, January 14, 1941, 10.

58. Eleanor Pringle Hart, "Editorial: Charleston," *Preservation Progress* 7, no. 1 (January 1962): n.p.

59. Herbert Ravenel Sass, "Charleston," in Charles W. Smith, *Old Charleston: Twenty-Four Woodcuts* (Richmond, VA: Dale Press, 1934), iv.

Tania Gutiérrez-Monroy

6. Firearms, Flowers, and Barricades: Women's Reinscriptions in the Mexican Landscape of Monuments

THIS CHAPTER TRACES women's presence in the Mexican landscape of monuments from postrevolutionary to present times, considering the transformation of the narratives originally inscribed in these monuments into spatial dialogues. The first section analyzes the memorials built to honor the working-class women who participated in the Mexican Revolution. It examines the symbolic relationship between the figure of the revolutionary woman, war, and urban geographies, observing an everyday that remains unacknowledged in the original design of these monuments.[1] The second section explores more recent forms of engagement with these memorials by feminist collectives, as well as subversive forms of commemoration emerging throughout the country. I argue that both of these challenging practices transform urban and memorial geographies as they open up a space of visibility for an everyday that calls for historical recognition and contemporary political action. The apparently immobile narratives inscribed in the landscape of memory become dialogues that invite movement and open up new discursive and political spaces.

Writing Women

THE MEXICAN REVOLUTION was the first of the twentieth century. Started in 1910, it was a period of socioeconomic, political, and cultural transformation in the country. In the words of historian Susie Porter, it was "a violent adjustment in the way different sectors of society negotiated conflict and access to resources" that developed in the midst of "larger historical processes of industrialization, migration, and urbanization."[2] Accounts of the revolution often trace its timeline as defined and directed by renowned battles in places all over Mexico. Since all generals were men and only a few women attained the rank of *coronelas*, or colonels, both scholarly and popular narratives understand the revolution as a masculine event (or series of events). As female insurgents and civic leaders are increasingly seeing their histories unearthed, the built commemorations of the working-class and peasant women who participated in the struggle, the *soldaderas*, help expand the history. Soldaderas traveled with armies and tended to the food, shelter, and health-care needs of soldiers. They have since been celebrated as the builders of the temporary homes that sustained both federal and rebel military columns.[3]

Making use of the household objects they carried, soldaderas transposed domestic space onto the battlefield. They reconfigured sites, most visibly as unwalled homes in trains, camps, pathways, and even battlegrounds. They carried hotplates, grinding stoness, blankets, and packages in baskets or wrapped in their shawls. These women used them to assemble and construct the temporary dwellings of the war. Frequently, they would buy, find, and steal additional materials. Soldaderas gave form to the mobile domesticities of military camps through cyclic spatial practices of settling, building, dwelling, dismantling, leaving, and building anew.[4] Their work persistently reshaped the boundaries between the geographies of home and war.

The two best-known monuments honoring these camp followers stand in the northern cities of Chihuahua and Torreón. They are among the few exceptions in the masculinist landscape of monuments to the revolution across Mexico. Both bronze figures bear the name Adelita, often used to refer to revolutionary camp followers.

The *Torreón soldadera* (Vladimir Alvarado, 1980) (figure 1) is located on the periphery of the city, at the intersection of Avenues Ávila Camacho and Ramón Méndez. Facing the end of Ramón Méndez, the sculpted figure turns her back on the adjacent city airport. Diagonally

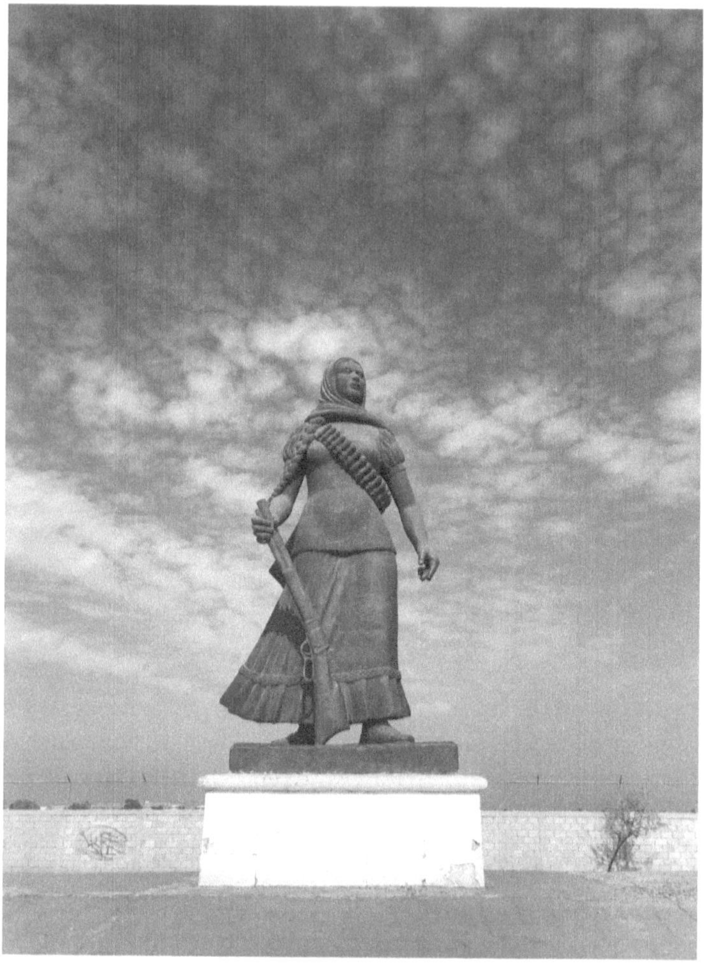

Figure 1. *Torreón soldadera*, 2019. Photograph courtesy of Cristina Casas.

on her right used to stand the Corona Stadium (demolished in 2009). Before the closure of this public venue, celebrations of victories of the Torreón soccer team were the few occasions that brought city dwellers in contact with the monument—other than the quick encounter with the roundabout while driving or riding public transit.

The soldadera's location feels marginal in relation both to the city center and to other sites that accommodate sculptures of Mexican heroic figures, such as the major thoroughfare, Boulevard Revolu-

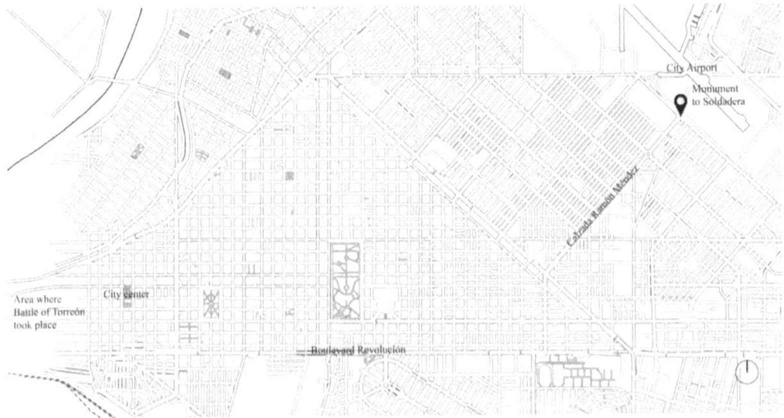

Figure 2. Map of Torreón. Drawing by the author.

ción (figure 2). More importantly, she stands on the side of the city opposite to the area where the renowned Battle of Torreón took place and where prominent male revolutionaries are commemorated.[5] This remoteness is worth noting because the Torreón and the Chihuahua soldaderas were created in or near areas where important confrontations of the revolution took place: the Battle of Torreón and the Battle of Ciudad Juárez (Chihuahua, the capital of the state where significant revolutionary activity took place, is around 220 miles away from Ciudad Juárez).[6] Whereas the crucial role of soldaderas in the civil war must have inspired their immortalization in these key cities, the emplacement of their memorials, far away from the very sites of the historical episodes, is striking.

The *Chihuahua soldadera* (Ricardo Ponzanelli, 1998) (figure 3) was placed at the intersection of the avenues Tecnológico and División del Norte (figure 4). The latter street is the name of a major revolutionary army and accommodates further west a monument to the famous general who led that army, Francisco Villa. At the point where this statue rises, División del Norte crosses Avenida Universidad. Besides sitting on a generous plinth and base, the Villa landmark is axially connected to the city's main square, where Avenida Universidad stretches southeast under the name Venustiano Carranza, another male revolutionary. The main square contains an additional memorial to Francisco Villa. Merely two blocks south, a third piece honors Villa in front of the building called Heroes of the Revolution—still on Avenida Venustiano Carranza. As strategic points in the city, the three monuments

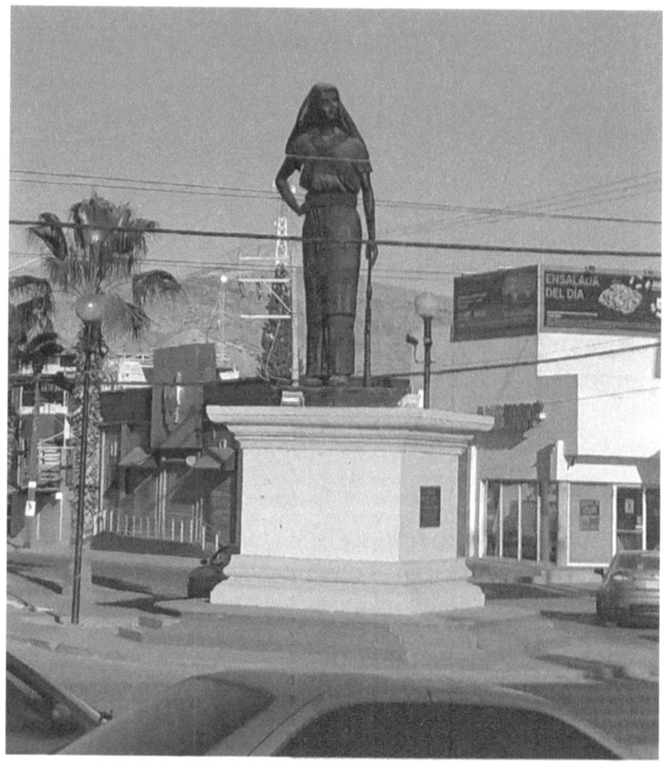

Figure 3. *Chihuahua soldadera*, 2019. Photograph courtesy of Martín Ramírez.

give form to a "spine" of built commemorations dedicated to the same historical figure along a key axis of Chihuahua, not counting the space within the Government Palace where another statue of Villa is part of a group of figures evoking the Mexican Revolution. In this light, the *Chihuahua soldadera* feels located in a marginal space as well.

The design decisions connecting the soldadera monument to its immediate surroundings are equally revealing. The location of each of the Francisco Villa memorials traces an axis, not only ensuring visibility but also creating a meaningful relationship between the built object and the city dwellers. One of these Villa sculptures is the central element of a park named Francisco Villa's Horseride. The horizontal panels of another memorial to Villa embrace Chihuahua's Plaza Mayor. The first Villa monument mentioned, which mirrors the position of the soldadera in relation to the university campus, stands on

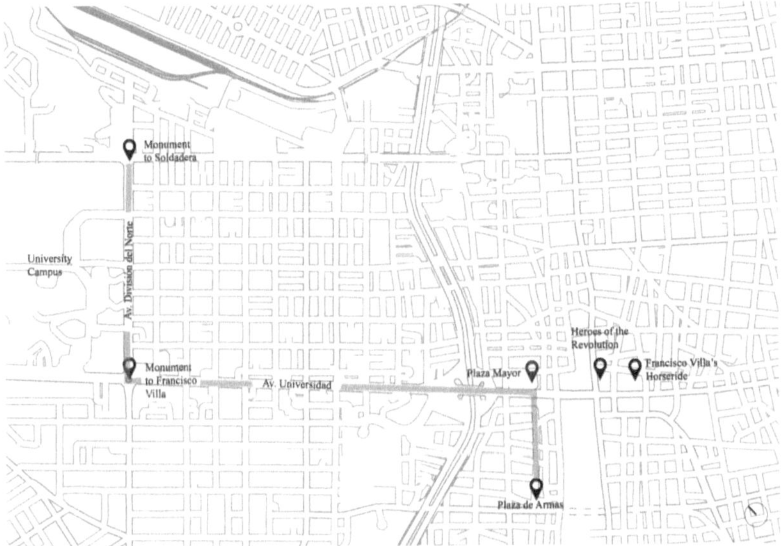

Figure 4. Map of Chihuahua showing new axis created by protesters. Drawing by the author.

a spacious, more celebratory roundabout and bears an axial relation with the city center and the other monuments to him.

The urban and visual symbolism of the soldadera monuments reveals the masculinist values that the people who crafted and commissioned them embraced.[7] Both women stand proudly and use one hand to hold a rifle that rests on the ground. The Chihuahua soldadera places the opposite hand on her waist and bears bandoliers across her chest, as well as around her waist. One bandolier crosses the upper body of the Torreón soldadera, who directs her gaze slightly above the horizon. Neither figure is represented with an item that recalls her home-building task: we see no hotplates, no baskets, no bedrolls.

The double roles of female soldier and camp follower often blurred boundaries in the war labor of soldaderas.[8] In their bronze memorials, however, the soldaderas stand on their plinths bearing only firearms. The household items that they carried and that shaped much of their war labor are left out of the built commemoration. The celebration of the figure of the female warrior creates a blind spot for the role of the homemaker, overlooking how the actions of these revolutionaries actually merged home and war spaces. The chosen symbolism of the sculptures arguably results from a patriarchal negotiation of subject, space, and gendered agencies. This negotiation reflects the masculinist view of urban space as more easily associated with war than with domesticity, an urban space believed by the monuments' male creators and commissioners to "resist" representing the homemaking actions of soldaderas.[9]

This conventional association between urban space and war is legible in abstract and in concrete examples. The soldaderas, in creating an intersection between war and domestic spaces, upset pervasive narratives of war and its commemorative representation. Yet the imagined boundaries between home and war still drive the narrative of the revolution as a masculine event, shaped by the actions of male generals and warriors, and far from the supposedly feminized family dwelling.[10] Here, the contrived home front–war binary parallels the private-public binary, where one sphere is understood as feminine and the other as masculine. The consideration of public sites as welcoming to military symbolism is legible not only in the portrayal of soldaderas and revolutionary men with their weapons but also in the placement of artifacts such as cannons on streets, in the decision to name avenues after famed generals, and even in the military parades that are common in cities around the world.[11]

Design revisions to the Torreón monument reveal the stakeholders' adherence to a conventional understanding of public space as more accepting of war than of domestic symbolism. A preliminary version of the soldadera gave equal emphasis to her revolutionary roles, as a child appeared hugging her leg on the side opposite to the rifle.[12] The figure of the child was omitted from the final version, which reveals the intention of the monument makers and sponsors to leave the nurturing labor of the soldadera out of the narrative. As happened with the items used to configure the mobile dwellings of the war, the motherly reference disappeared from the built commemoration. It shared with the items a domestic connotation.[13] Conceivably, such domestic character of motherhood and the household objects did not fit the masculinist understandings of revolutionary geographies, and did not merit recognition in urban space. While it is important to acknowledge the soldaderas' brave role in actual fighting, the refusal to represent their nonfighting roles leaves untold the complexity of women's contributions to the nationwide transition of the early twentieth century.[14]

Whereas the final shape of the soldaderas' built commemorations told an incomplete story, this story is not final. Subjects whose voices were not considered in the original planning of the monuments have managed to open up a space for the roles of soldaderas that appeared too "domestic" or "feminine" to afford visibility in city spaces. As the second part of this chapter will show, the emerging narrative does not come from the "upper" level of stakeholders and art creators. The process described below renders the term "narrative" obsolete and invites its replacement by the term "dialogue."

Women Writing

FOR MORE THAN thirty years, a feminist collective led by local teachers has met on March 8 at the Monument to the Soldadera in Torreón.[15] They first started protesting against the 1988 election fraud that prevented a party from the left from winning the federal presidential election. The yearly meetings have gradually become opportunities for exchanges among workers fighting for gender equity, who engage with the monument by placing flowers in the hands of the soldadera.[16] They also attach a shawl onto her body, as this garment was at the center of the revolutionary work of camp followers.[17] The shawl, which enabled soldaderas to carry food, domestic items, children, and even weapons close to their bodies, functioned as a threshold between domestic and war spheres. It was key to countless missions that required these women to look like they were going about their "feminine" lives while participating in the secret operations of armies. The shawl sculpted onto the figure of the Torreón soldadera ignores this carrying function, as it merely veils her head and wraps around her neck. Contrastingly, the shawl that the feminist collective attaches to her body remains loose at the back. It reminds observers that the shawl was more than a garment and that it bore a crucial war function as a vessel for messages and items that ensured the survival of armies. Hence, this fabric shawl that the collective puts up every year tacitly recalls the domestic work that soldaderas performed in war spaces, rendered invisible by the scarf-like sculpted shawl.

The Adelita monument in Chihuahua has brought together feminist collectives such as Movimiento de Mujeres and Marea Verde. In 2015 Movimiento de Mujeres designated it as a stop in the route of a march protesting the censorship of journalist Carmen Aristegui, which culminated at the Plaza de Armas and made the monument part of a new symbolic axis by means of the movement of protesters across urban space.[18] In 2018 the group Marea Verde met around the soldadera and engaged the statue in the fight for safe and legal abortion by attaching a green handkerchief around her neck (figure 5).[19]

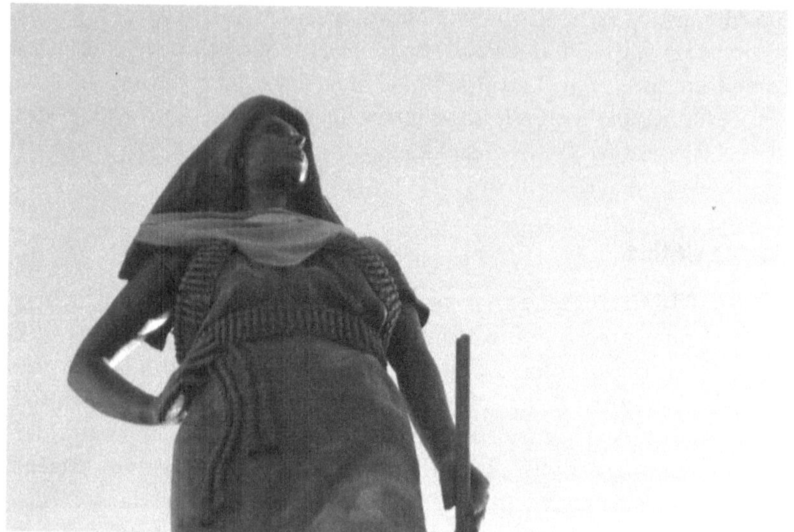

Figure 5. Chihuahua soldadera wearing green handkerchief, 2020. Photograph courtesy of Abril Martínez Villa.

The physical interventions to the sculptures resemble the work of Bolivian activists on the monument to Queen Isabella the Catholic. On October 12, 2020, they dressed the figure as a *chola*. The chola is an Indigenous or mestiza (mixed white and Indigenous) woman who wears traditional clothing and traverses urban space, often as a vendor. With her hair arranged in braids, the chola wears eighteenth-century Spanish garments and a borsalino hat.[20] The skirt, shawl, and hat of a chola put on the monument to Isabel the Catholic propose contesting the imposed European ideal of white femininity. Changing the queen's identity into that of a chola expresses the rejection of Euro-centered beauty and social standards. The intervention by these Bolivian activists transformed the entire place. The plaza, renamed Plaza of the Globalized Chola, lent its surfaces to broader messages of protest against the racism and inequality brought by the European conquest and global capitalism.[21]

It is crucial to note the emerging dialogue in this example as well as in the interventions upon the monuments to soldaderas. The performance of these women and the physical reshaping of the monuments activate the built form as the means of a communication that resonates in more than one way: it is no longer the case of a unidirectional history lesson "taught" by monument makers and authorities to city dwellers. Instead, the surfaces, which initially look mute and unchangeable, become a canvas for collectives and citizens to teach the lesson, to protest, and to contest.

Cultural memory scholar James E. Young states that monuments present themselves as originary, "even geological outcrops in a national landscape" and strive to "naturalize values, ideals, and laws of the land itself."[22] But often the physical gesture in which monuments emerge from below contrasts with the formal message that comes from "above." The message and ideology written by a sponsoring government and its selected artist are conveyed "downward" to a citizenry that is expected to take the history lesson. Engaging with built memorials at ground level, feminist and anticolonial collectives open up a space for contesting, a space to teach the lesson back to the makers.

In Mexico and around the world, these forms of agency create messages written on the monuments' surfaces as well as grassroots memorials that remind the government of the consequences of its inaction. In downtown Chihuahua, activists have built an altar in honor of Marisela Escobedo, who was killed right in front of the Government Palace after years of denouncing the state's inability to convict the murderer of her daughter. Since Escobedo's unsolved assassination, the site has become a place of protest to this and other cases of inaction by authorities—mostly cases of femicide.

The interventions of these groups encourage reflection on how the symbolic function of monuments extends beyond the footprint of the built piece. In the case of most official monuments, the design, location, and symbols chosen to reflect a "collective" memory strive for a supposed place of unity—both spatial and mnemonic. But the subtext of this imagined unity is often the legitimation of the state's authority, its power symbolized spatially on the hardware of the public realm.[23] Mass protests and interventions upon monuments—such as those mentioned here, the ones by Black Lives Matter in the United States, or by feminists in Mexico—have brought attention to the long-raised questions about memory, belonging, and (site) ownership in these spatial messages.

In the heart of Mexico City, the feminist collective Antimonumenta Vivas nos queremos installed the countermonument *Antimonumenta* on November 25, 2019 (figure 6).[24] Soon after, the piece was replicated in other cities across the country. Decidedly feminist in its name and agency, the *Antimonumenta* gives visibility to what is often excluded from public space for being too domestic and personal: the growing

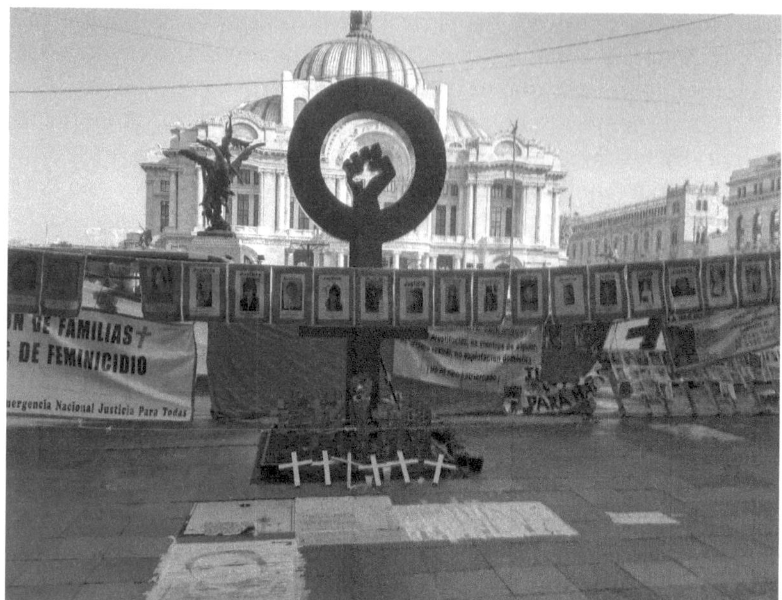

Figure 6. The *Antimonumenta* rises in front of the Palacio de Bellas Artes, 2021. Photograph by the author.

femicides behind closed, private doors.[25] The *Antimonumenta* raises the voice of the women who are gone, especially those whose race and class make them invisible to society.[26] Since its 2019 origin, the piece roots itself in strategic spaces to challenge the celebratory narrative of hegemonic monuments, yet it affirms its belonging everywhere in Mexico by allowing its many selves to carry the equity message far and wide.[27] In the words of writer and journalist Ana Buerón, it arises from the need to show a persistent, painful void:[28] the memorial is no longer a celebration; it is an urgent demand for justice.

Placed downtown on Avenida Juárez, the Mexico City *Antimonumenta* rises in front of the emblematic Palacio de Bellas Artes and of the sculpture of renowned revolutionary leader Francisco I. Madero. Having been the target of interventions during feminist protests, the latter is now barricaded and surveilled by the police.[29] Right across the street, the *Antimonumenta* emerges from the space freed by the removal of a square of quarry tiles. Its volume rises in the form of the feminist Venus symbol circumscribing a raised fist. The monument makers filled the square with dirt at the foot of the memorial in order to evoke a burial site. Smaller pink crosses around the *Antimonu-*

menta puncture the dirt carpet, which has slowly allowed the natural growth of plants in between. This countermonument has purposefully claimed a space larger than its footprint. The activists who have created and taken care of it have used ropes, banners, and canvases to create a rectangular perimeter. These surfaces show photographs of disappeared women and children, as well as texts sharing their stories and denouncing the inefficiency or direct involvement of authorities in the cases of femicide and disappearance. Some posters also demand the liberation of political prisoners such as activist Kenia Hernández.[30] A handmade plaque on the floor relates the origins of the piece:

> Two years ago, we, mothers of disappeared and murdered women, got together to organize the installation of the *Antimonumenta*. We reached out to Abraham Fraijo, father of one of the children of the ABC, [who had organized a previous antimonument] to ask for orientation.[31] After he contacted the artists and blacksmiths, the project kicked off. We worked for months until we finally set the 25N as a start date.[32] The installation ended on March 8th in Bellas Artes [the Fine Arts Museum].[33]

Having endured removal threats by authorities and city dwellers,[34] the *Antimonumenta* bravely rises while harnessing the spatial qualities of its form and placement: the piece communicates the protest in all directions but also at multiple scales. There are messages legible from afar as well as detailed texts inviting audiences to approach and read. There is no back or front, as the political messages face the street and sidewalk: drivers and pedestrians are equally responsible for answering to the crisis. Conscious of how monuments transform the surrounding landscape, the feminist creators of this piece have claimed the territory around it to gather and support each other, give workshops, collect funds, and raise awareness. The *Antimonumenta* becomes a place-making project.

Akin to the role of the Chihuahua and Torreón soldaderas, the *Antimonumenta* becomes a landmark for the route of feminist marches. It was a pivot for the 2020 International Women's Day March, which created a symbolic axis between historical and political sites. Lina Arias Saldaña examines the trajectory of this protest and the mark that it left upon the city. The feminist march traversed four sites with historical and social significance in Mexican culture, as well as the culture of the country's capital: the monument to the Revolution (historical value), Fine Arts Museum/Palace (heritage and cultural value), the Street Francisco I. Madero (economic and touristic value), and the Zócalo or main square (symbolic value for political and civic order).[35]

On September 25, 2021, the Antimonumenta Collective installed another monument, choosing an existing commemorative site that had recently stirred controversy: a roundabout where a Columbus sculpture stood since the late nineteenth century. Like other Columbus monuments in Latin America, this was to be the target of anticolonial marches. The organizers of one of these marches announced their intention to topple it on October 12, 2020, which prompted the city government to remove it a few days earlier under the pretext of planned restoration works.[36] A year later, the authorities announced that, instead of reinstalling the Columbus figure at the site, they would commission non-Indigenous male artist Pedro Reyes to create the sculpture of an Indigenous woman. The choice attracted heavy criticism; three hundred artists signed and sent a letter to Head of (City) Government Claudia Sheinbaum demanding the creation of a curatorial committee of women artists and art experts self-identified as Indigenous to select the creator(s) of the monument.[37] Sheinbaum's administration abandoned the plan to install the work of Pedro Reyes and delegated the decision of the future of the site to the Committee of Public Space Monuments and Artistic Works in Mexico City.[38]

In the meantime, the Antimonumenta Collective seized the opportunity to claim the space and resignify it. The new monument (figure 7) had to be:

> dedicated to the mothers looking for disappeared children, or looking for justice upon the femicide of their daughters, but also dedicated to the women survivors of acid attacks, the displaced Triqui women, the Zapatista women, the female political prisoners, the women who fought for the Independence, the Revolution, and female suffrage.[39]

On September 25, 2021, this new memorial emerged.[40] As with the first *Antimonumenta*, the creators remain anonymous while the piece invites the city residents to engage in the collective writing of the entire site. Its name is *Monument to the Women Who Fight*. The germinal element of what has become a new site of dialogue was the life-size outline of a woman raising her fist, made out of a wood board and supported by an easel back out of which the word "Justicia" has been cut. The monument creators jumped the barricades that the government had erected in previous attempts to protect the now absent Columbus

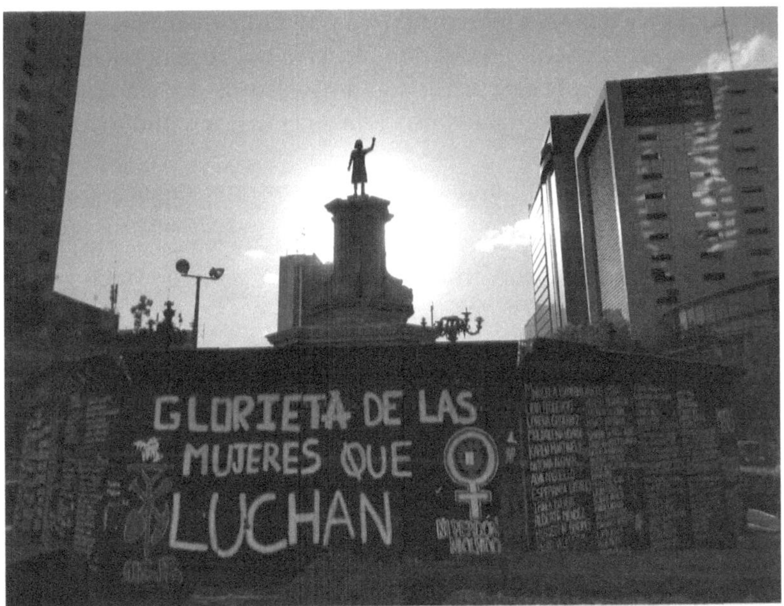

Figure 7. *Monument to the Women Who Fight*, 2022. Photograph by the author.

sculpture. These activists installed the purple figure of the woman on the plinth, overlooking Avenida Reforma, arguably the most iconic thoroughfare of the country's capital. Avenida Reforma branches off at Avenida Juárez (on which the first *Antimonumenta* rises) to lead to the Zócalo. Once positioned on the plinth, the monument brought about a setting for dialogue and collaboration. Its surrounding barricades have become surfaces for inscribing the names of the "women who fight." Rather than being sculpted and laid out, the monument and its landscape are written. Among the names, the Venus symbol circumscribing a raised fist reappears, and pink crosses that allude to the femicide crisis connect these inscriptions with the symbols of the first *Antimonumenta*. The monument writers have also drawn flowers, arguably in reference to those laid on the graves of femicide victims or to the plant-like growth of communities who grieve and protest together. In March 2022, the collective replaced the wood figure of the woman with an identical metal figure.[41]

Enacting its eponymous theme, the women writers of the monument have contested the government's attempts to regain control of it: when city authorities painted the barricades black to remove (erase) the names written on them, the activists rewrote them.[42] Reclaiming the entire site, these (re)inscriptions became spatial actions. Marisela Escobedo's name appears at the top of the list of women who have been killed in their search for justice. Women who continue the quest for justice appear below.

A member of the Antimonumenta Collective has stated:

> The decision to take over the [Columbus] roundabout was meant to tell them [the authorities]: "You cannot continue looking at the past while ignoring the present." . . . We are tired of being imposed things, forms, figures, ways of thinking. Looking at the past is an easy way of positioning oneself in a safe corner. Facing the challenges of the present, that would make it a true leftist government: attending to these women.[43]

The spokesperson of the collective pointed to the form in which Indigenous women become invisible and are used for political purposes at convenient times, "in a superficial way. But they are ignored when they are displaced by paramilitary groups."[44] She mentioned the Triqui women of Oaxaca who have installed a protest camp in front of the Palacio de Bellas Artes. Some of them participated in the appropriation of the roundabout. The Antimonumenta representative concludes: "One cannot think about women who fight without naming the Indigenous women. They are the foundation of this country."[45]

This mere "naming" of Indigenous women, however, raises a significant issue. Whereas several Indigenous women (such as the aforementioned Triqui women and poet and writer María Luisa Rivera Grijalva) have written their own names, others have been more frequently named by someone else; they were not present at the monument to name themselves.[46] Having seen the names of Yásnaya A. Gil, María de Jesús Patricio, Comandanta Esther, and the late Comandanta Ramona, I was unable to find any evidence that the first three did the inscriptions themselves. The high profile of María de Jesús Patricio (spokesperson for the Congreso Nacional Indígena) and Comandanta Esther (who belongs to the Ejército Zapatista de Liberación Nacional) would have made their visit attract significant attention. Arguably, their naming relates to other historically renowned women whom someone else decided to immortalize on the barricades, like Sor Juana Inés de la Cruz and Rosario Castellanos.

Head of City Government Claudia Sheinbaum has reiterated the importance of keeping the space centered on the voice of Indigenous women, who have been silenced even more than other Mexican women.[47] In the writing of the monument, Indigenous women are among a larger list of non-Indigenous Mexican women: this list obscures who has been self-named or named by others. Feminist (counter)monuments and their reshaping of urban landscapes are necessary, especially in a country where femicides and disappearances directly terrorize women's existence. The problem here, nonetheless, lies in the threat that the feminist narrative might engulf antiracist and anticolonial narratives. The feminist collective responsible for the takeover has "invited" Indigenous women but does not actually include Indigenous women members as organizers. Their whole action, especially when appropriating a site that called for reflection on race and historical symbols, would have occasioned a more careful questioning on whose voice is privileged.[48] María Luisa Rivera Grijalva, mentioned above, points to examples of urban spaces claimed by feminist collectives where Indigenous women remain invisible.[49] Whereas reflections on race can and must include gender, it is impossible not to see the voice of mestiza urban feminists leading the conversation, even if trying to remain inclusive by inviting Indigenous women. This leads to a missed opportunity for the creation of a space for discussions on racism and colonialism. Needless to say, the former site of a Columbus monument explicitly calls for such discussion.

This far from simple issue raises the questions that, in a different context, Indigenous communities rightfully asked to Canadian Occupy protestors, who sought to occupy and reclaim a territory from the hands of the 1 percent elite. Such Indigenous communities asked how much the protestors had reflected on the reality that Canada is already occupied land. The reclamation of the roundabout site by a feminist movement led by a mestiza majority should consider more carefully these issues of land "ownership" to avoid taking over the space that more rightfully belonged to an Indigenous presence and narrative.

The disproportionate number of mestiza women who wrote their names on the *Monument to the Women Who Fight*, as compared with Indigenous women, brings forth another issue on representation and belonging in a collective. As pointed out by postcolonial feminists for more than three decades, mainstream feminism would often claim to fight for all women, even naming specifically Black,

Brown, and Indigenous women.[50] Yet when analyzed closely, it is evident that mainstream feminist organizations kept the leadership of white women uncontested and their interests at the center— ignoring the oppression exerted by their own class and racial group. In many senses, the particular needs of women of color became subsumed by white feminist scholars.[51]

All of this problematizes the statement cited above, "You cannot continue looking at the past while ignoring the present," where the Antimonumenta Collective justified the placement of a woman (who absorbed the identity of the Indigenous woman, among others) in lieu of the figure of an Indigenous woman, as proposed by the government. As mentioned, the government's choice of artist needed serious reconsideration, but it is important to point out that the rationale of the Antimonumenta Collective seems rooted in an understanding of Indigeneity as a thing of the past.[52] This understanding, also legible in the denotation of Indigenous women as "the foundation of this country" (cited above), ends up freezing Indigenous personhood(s) in a historical, long-gone Mexico. This discussion elucidates the contingent nature of the landscapes of remembrance. Reinscription by the people is one of many stages of the lifetime of a monument. The *Monument to the Women Who Fight* is clearly at a stage that invites deeper reflection and more iterations of writing.[53]

In this chapter, I have discussed the transformation of the narratives of the landscape of memories into spatial dialogues. These dialogues, inscribed in built forms that at first sight remain immobile, open up other discursive and political spaces. I have examined how built memorials to revolutionary women have been reshaped and inserted into new narratives by feminist collectives and I have observed new forms of commemoration. These practices create a space of visibility for an everyday that calls for historical recognition (the homemaking work of soldaderas) and for political action at present (against the femicide crisis).

The transformations of urban and memorial landscapes outlined here politically activate sites and decenter prevalent historical understandings. By doing this, they revalue the margins, where the soldaderas were historically relegated as they marched with the revolutionary columns. Today, the actions of the collectives and grassroots artists discussed here transform the urban and monumental landscapes of Mexico by opening up new spatial dialogues. They counter the gendered histories that present a country only shaped by epic events. By unearthing the everyday in its history and politics as the very tissue of past and present Mexico, these new forms of commemoration and projection lay the groundwork for social justice paths. Even the reinscriptions that require further development have illustrated that surfaces that first appear unchangeable must remain in motion, changing alongside the narratives that shape the country.

Notes

1. My use of "the everyday" here draws from an architectural scholarship that engages the revalorization of the ordinary, influenced by Henri Lefebvre and Michel de Certeau, among others. Introducing *Architecture of the Everyday*, coeditor Steven Harris explains: "The everyday is that which remains after one has eliminated all specialized activities. It is anonymous, its anonymity derived from its undated and apparently insignificant quality" (3). See also Deborah Berke, "Thoughts on the Everyday," in *Architecture of the Everyday*, ed. Steven Harris and Deborah Berke (New York: Princeton Architectural Press, 1997), 222–26. Nonarchitects such as bell hooks had earlier brought attention to the everyday within architectural thinking, including a reassessment of the values of the profession. See her conversation with architect LaVerne Wells-Bowie, "Architecture in Black Life: Talking Space with LaVerne Wells-Bowie," in bell hooks, *Art on My Mind: Visual Politics* (New York: The New Press, 1995), 159. In other fields such as history, anthropology, literature, and film studies, postcolonial feminists have advanced the everyday as a key political and historical site. See Chandra Talpade Mohanty, Ann Russo, and Lourdes Torres, eds., *Third World Women and the Politics of Feminism*, Cultural Studies (Bloomington: Indiana University Press, 1991).

2. Susie Porter, "Working Women in the Mexican Revolution," in *Oxford Research Encyclopedia of Latin American History*, ed. William H Beezley (Oxford: Oxford University Press, 2016), 2.

3. See Elizabeth Salas, *Soldaderas in the Mexican Military: Myth and History* (Austin: University of Texas Press, 1990); Andrés Reséndez Fuentes, "Battleground Women: Soldaderas and Female Soldiers in the Mexican Revolution," *The Americas* 51, no. 4 (1995): 525–53; Christine Arce, *México's Nobodies: The Cultural Legacy of the Soldadera and Afro-Mexican Women* (Albany: State University of New York Press, 2017).

4. I explore these spaces in depth in Tania Gutiérrez-Monroy, "Bodies, Shawls, and Train Cars: Women and the Travelling Homes of the Mexican Revolution," *Buildings & Landscapes* 30, no. 1 (Fall 2023): 36–58.

5. To locate the Battle of Torreón: https://www.cultura.gob.mx/centenario-ejercito/batalla_torreon.php#prettyPhoto. See also Ilhuicamina Rico Maciel, *Efemérides de la Historia de Torreón* (Torreón: Archivo Municipal de Torreón, 2018), 62.

6. José Manuel García, "La Toma de Ciudad Juárez," *Noésis. Revista de Ciencias Sociales y Humanidades* 20, no. 39 (2011): 179–93; Miguel Sánchez Lamego, *Historia militar de la revolución constitucionalista* (Mexico City: INEHRM, 1960), 119.

7. Gustavo Ramos Becerril was the mayor who commissioned the *Chihuahua soldadera* to Ricardo Ponzanelli, and Homero del Bosque Villarreal was the mayor who commissioned the *Torreón soldadera* to Vladimir Alvarado. Juan Carlos Núñez, "El monumento a la Adelita," *El Diario de Chihuahua*, February 27, 2021; Segundo Informe de Gobierno Lic. Homero H. del Bosque Villarreal, 27 December 1980, Ficha 1, Caja 7, Mod. 14, Ent. 56, Biblioteca de escritores laguneros, Archivo Municipal de Torreón; Vladimir Alvarado, Esculturas laguneras, 1980, Ficha 48, Caja 1, Mod. 16, Ent. 64, Biblioteca de escritores laguneros, Archivo Municipal de Torreón.

8. See Salas, *Soldaderas in the Mexican Military*, 44.

9. Arguably, the idealized version of the female warrior attempted to place women on equal footing to men in war narratives. Yet such uncritical pursuit of images of equity both traces and represents female revolutionary activity through recognizable masculinity constructs, the most evident being war paraphernalia. This "add women and stir" approach (pointed out by Angel Kwolek-Folland with regard to vernacular architecture studies) misses the complex roles that women have played in this and in other wars. Angel Kwolek-Folland, "Gender as a Category of Analysis in Vernacular Architecture Studies," *Perspectives in Vernacular Architecture* 5 (1995): 3. Billie Melman points to the persistent study of the "female equivalent to the combatant man" when trying to unearth women's contributions. Billie Melman, introduction to *Borderlines: Genders and Identities in War and Peace 1870–1930*, ed. Billie Melman (New York: Routledge, 1998), 4. In the case of the soldadera monuments, the resistance to portray women's domestic roles during war reveals an adherence to the most comfortable and recognizable masculine figures of war, which in hegemonic narratives appear opposed to the feminized realm of the home.

10. These imagined boundaries, based on a binary understanding of a feminized private space and a masculinized public space, emerge within the separate-spheres theory, which proposes that men and women inhabit different realms. See Linda Kerber, "Separate Spheres, Female Worlds, Woman's Place: The Rhetoric of Women's History," *Journal of American History* 75, no. 1 (1988): 9–39.

11. The Puente Plateado in Torreón, for example, displays military cannons. Examples around the world include the Civil War cannons in the State of New York (Riverside Park and John Paul Jones Park), a World War I cannon in Connecticut (Norwalk), and the Soviet War Memorial in Berlin, among others.

12. Image available at the artist's website: http://www.vladimirs-foundry. com/english/ViewGallerya01f.html?PIC=1&SHOT=2&COUNT=4. It was first brought to my attention by Gerardo Güereca Hernández.

13. As Mark Wigley points out, the home is meant to shelter the reproductive function of women in patriarchal culture. Mark Wigley, "Untitled: The Housing of Gender," in *Sexuality & Space*, ed. Beatriz Colomina (New York: Princeton Architectural Press, 1992), 336–37.

14. Andrés Reséndez Fuentes argues for the need to differentiate between camp followers and women fighters as, he claims, women had diverse reasons to partake in the revolutionary struggle. Elizabeth Salas, however, points to the porosity of both identities in the actions of soldaderas, and it is with this broader understanding that my chapter aligns. Reséndez Fuentes, "Battleground Women," 525–53; Salas, *Soldaderas in the Mexican Military*, 44.

15. https://diariofemenino.com.ar/mexico-mujeres-en-homenaje-a-la-mujer-a-traves-de-la-adelita/.

16. https://diariofemenino.com.ar/mexico-mujeres-en-homenaje-a-la-mujer-a-traves-de-la-adelita/.

17. Arce, *México's Nobodies*, 74.

18. Though "flexible spine" might be a more suitable term than "axis." https://laopcion.com.mx/local/con-pancartas-marchan-en-apoyo-a-carmen-aristegui-20150322-86385.html.

19. https://entrelineas.com.mx/local/marea-verde-interviene-la-adelita-y-recuerda-a-mujeres-revolucionarias/.

20. Ximena Soruco Sologuren, "La chola boliviana en la primera mitad del siglo XX: De femme fatale a madre de la nación," *L'Âge d'or: Images dans le monde ibérique et ibéroaméricain*, Ville hispanique et paysage, no. 10 (2017): 13n2; Isabel Scarborough, "Two Generations of Bolivian Female Vendors," *Ethnology*, Markets, 49, no. 2 (Spring 2010): 1.

21. https://latinoamericapiensa.com/vistieron-de-chola-a-la-estatua-de-isabel-la-catolica-y-colon-aparecio-pintado-de-rojo-por-el-dia-de-la-conquista-en-bolivia/28268/.

22. James E. Young, "The Counter-Monument: Memory against Itself in Germany Today," *Critical Inquiry* 18, no. 2 (Winter 1992): 270.

23. See Kim Dovey, *Framing Places: Mediating Power in Built Form* (London: Routledge, 1999), 12; Susana Torre, "Claiming the Public Space: The Mothers of Plaza de Mayo," in *The Sex of Architecture*, ed. Patricia Conway, Leslie Weisman, and Diana Agrest (New York: Harry N. Abrams, 1996), 142–43.

24. https://www.elimparcial.com/mexico/Colocan-antimonumenta-en-Bellas-Artes-obstaculizan-avance-de-marcha-20191125-0155.html.

25. Legal definitions, scholarship, and media coverage refer to the homes of victims when talking about the "private spaces" where femicides take place: "at home" femicides accounted for 42 percent of the total in Puebla in 2021, for example. Here, however, I propose extending the use of the term "private spaces" to the closed doors behind which perpetrators assassinate women. Even if the abductions take place in public space, femicide perpetrators forcefully take their victims to a space that provides the privacy they need to follow through with their crime. Including secluded sites controlled by the killers, the "private sphere" where women are murdered encompasses more than their own homes, and it is important to consider that its privacy and invisibility provide excuses for authorities already unwilling to efficiently conduct the investigations. Saydi Núñez Cetina, "Violencia contra las mujeres y feminicidio íntimo a la sombra del covid-19: Los efectos perversos del confinamiento," *Cultura política*, El SARS CoV-2 y la covid-19: balances preliminares de una pandemia, no. 55 (June 2021): 99–119. See also https://genero.congresocdmx.gob.mx/wp-content/uploads/2020/10/2020.09.03-EspacioPubVioSexual.pdf; https://retodiario.com/educacion/2021/09/09/registra-ibero-puebla-66-probables-feminicidios-en-2020-42-ocurrio-en-espacios-privados/.

26. https://www.facebook.com/AntimonumentaVivasNosQueremos.

27. After the Mexico City "Antimonumenta," and in close collaboration with its creators, activists in other cities installed "Antimonumentas" in cities such as

Nezahualcóyotl, Guadalajara, Chetumal, Tuxtla Gutiérrez, etc. https://vocesfeministas.mx/cinco-estados-mexico-antimonumenta-feminicidios/

28. Ana Buerón, "La Antimonumenta: La Escultura Más Importante Para No Olvidar," Local.Mx, March 5, 2020, https://local.mx/ciudad-de-mexico/antimonumenta/.

29. Its author, Javier Marín, has expressed support for the interventions: https://www.milenio.com/estilo/marcha-8-marzo-artista-celebra-pintas-escultura-cdmx.

30. See also https://www.animalpolitico.com/2020/10/detienen-activista-kenia-hernandez-organizaciones-denuncian-montaje/.

31. ABC was a daycare in the northern city of Hermosillo (Sonora) that caught fire on June 9, 2009. Forty-nine children died and others suffered grave injuries. Investigations showed that despite the failure to adhere to the regulations (including safety regulations) dictated by the Instituto Mexicano del Seguro Social, the business had been allowed to continue operating. The owner was a relative of President Felipe Calderón's wife, who actively obstructed the pathway to justice. The report by the National Commission for Human Rights reads: "Arturo Zaldívar, President of the Supreme Court of Justice, declared that in 2011 he opened a file to hold public servants accountable [for the ABC case], yet he was subject to media lynching and pressure by the then President Felipe Calderón, who aimed at stopping him." Translation by author. See https://www.cndh.org.mx/noticia/incendio-en-la-guarderia-abc.

32. November 25 marks the celebration of the day for the elimination of violence against women. https://www.un.org/es/observances/ending-violence-against-women-day.

33. Handmade plaque on sidewalk in front of the *Antimonumenta*. Translation by author.

34. https://polemon.mx/gobierno-de-sheinbaum-amenaza-con-quitar-antimonumentos/. Other *Antimonumentas* have been effectively removed, though the feminist collectives have proven resilient and have reinstalled them. https://www.elsoldemexico.com.mx/republica/sociedad/feministas-de-michoacan-reinstalan-antimonumenta-en-morelia-6639651.html.

35. Lina M. Arias Saldaña, "Marca de lugar, espacio público y movimientos feministas en la Marcha del 8 de marzo de 2020 en Ciudad de México, México," *Revista Memória em Rede* 14, no. 26 (January 2022): 199.

36. https://elpais.com/mexico/2020-10-10/el-gobierno-de-ciudad-de-mexico-retira-la-estatua-de-colon-a-dos-dias-de-la-conmemoracion-de-su-arribo-a-america.html.

37. https://elpais.com/mexico/2021-09-14/mas-de-300-personas-del-mundo-de-la-cultura-firman-una-carta-contra-la-escultura-tlali-de-pedro-reyes.html.

38. Neldy San Martín, "'No Nos van a Borrar,'" *Revista Proceso* (November 3, 2021): 43.

39. Ibid., 44.

40. Ibid.

41. https://www.reforma.com/aplicacioneslibre/preacceso/articulo/default.aspx?__rval=1&urlredirect=https://www.reforma.com/colocan-figura-de-mujer-

hecha-de-metal-en-antimonumenta/ar2361961?referer=--7d616165662f3a3a-
6262623b727a7a7279703b767a783a--.

42. https://www.reforma.com/pintan-mujeres-valla-de-ex-glorieta-de-colon/.

43. San Martín, "'No Nos van a Borrar,'" 44. Translation by author.

44. Ibid.

45. Ibid.

46. On María Luisa Rivera Grijalva's inscription, see https://piedepagina.mx/
necesitamos-ser-escuchadas/?fbclid=IwAR1vN7DyzGCa6bVxwYqsLFkhVhXy7gd
1ZtOa5IlikuYYPNvt9zV_T-w3QCE.

47. My pointing to Sheinbaum's statement does not mean that the monument originally proposed by her administration was successfully representing the voices she claims to care for. https://www.infobae.com/america/
mexico/2021/09/27/mujeres-indigenas-no-han-tenido-voz-sheinbaum-volvio-a-
posicionarse-sobre-antimonumenta/.

48. While a monument hardly helps confront the material legacies of a colonial state, a more thoughtful representation would at least help bring visibility to
some of these legacies.

49. https://piedepagina.mx/necesitamos-ser-escuchadas/?fbclid=IwAR1vN7D
yzGCa6bVxwYqsLFkhVhXy7gd1ZtOa5IlikuYYPNvt9zV_T-w3QCE.

50. See Jacqui Alexander and Chandra Talpade Mohanty, eds., *Feminist
Genealogies, Colonial Legacies, Democratic Futures*, Thinking Gender (New York:
Routledge, 1997); Chandra Talpade Mohanty, Ann Russo, and Lourdes
Torres, eds., *Third World Women and the Politics of Feminism*, Cultural Studies
(Bloomington: Indiana University Press, 1991).

51. Of course, Black, Brown, and Indigenous feminists needed no permission
from hegemonic feminisms to create their own intellectual and activist circles,
and went ahead and did do so.

52. As Brenna Bhandar explains: "Indigencity becomes a space that is
traversed, and often rendered as an artifact of the past." Brenna Bhandar,
Colonial Lives of Property: Law, Land, and Racial Regimes of Ownership (Durham: Duke
University Press, 2018), 26.

53. Indigenous organizations belonging to the Congreso Nacional Indígena
have recently embraced the monument, making it a pivotal point in their protest
marches. Arguably, this involves a rewriting that takes the form of movement
in urban space: an ephemeral reshaping of the city flows and dynamics. In it,
Indigenous peoples and their allies resignify the site and the identities at its
center.

Dell Upton

Memorial to the South Carolina Women of the Confederacy (Frederick Wellington Ruckstuhl, 1909–1912), Columbia, South Carolina

THE PUBLICATION OF Jefferson Davis's *The Rise and Fall of the Confederate Government* (1881), with its lengthy dedication to Confederate women, spurred southerners to plan memorials to the "Women of the Sixties." As South Carolinian Sally Elmore Taylor wrote, the U.S. Civil War "cannot be shut into the records of military struggle."[1] White women on the home front "made the four years of fire and blood possible."[2] After the war, women assumed the leading role in commemorating the Confederate dead and undertook it in a way that (clandestinely at first) guarded the faith of Confederate nationalism and passed its values on to their children.[3]

The movement for women's monuments came to a head in the late 1890s when South Carolinian C. Irvine Walker headed a committee to propose a memorial to the annual convention of the United Confederate Veterans (UCV). The idea was that a common design would be commissioned by the UCV, castings of which would be provided to each southern state. The UCV rejected the Walker committee's first proposal, which depicted a robed, classicizing woman raising a furled

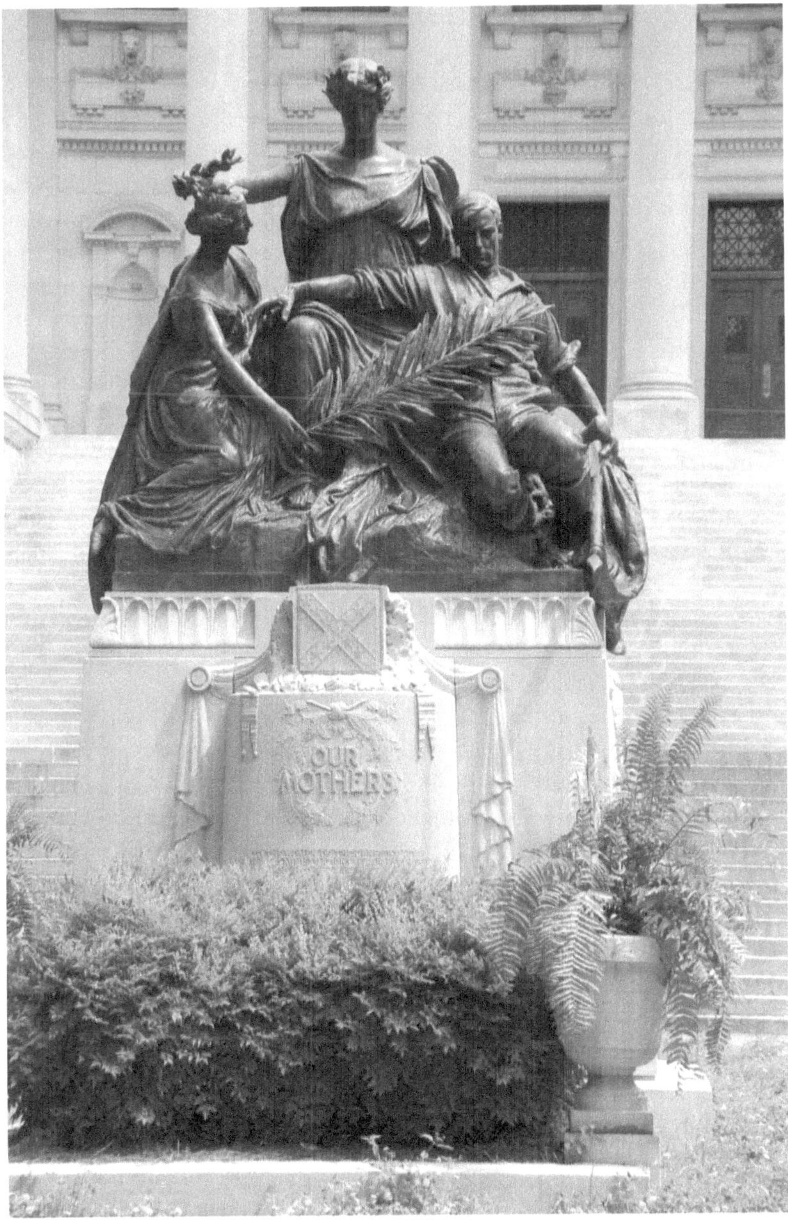

Figure 1. *Monument to the Women of the Confederacy* (Belle Kinney, 1917), New Capitol Grounds, Jackson, Mississippi. Another casting was erected in Nashville, Tennessee. The palm leaf is a traditional Christian symbol of martyrdom. Photograph by the author.

flag in one hand and a sword in the other. The veterans were offended by "the Amazonian proportions and warlike attitude of the figure," which did not embody their "ideals of a true Southern woman."[4] They opted instead for a proposal by twenty-three-year-old Belle Kinney, an accomplished sculptor despite her youth.[5] Kinney created a Pietà-like tableau in which a woman comforted a dying soldier, placing a palm branch of "love" on his chest. In her modesty she is "unconscious" that "Fame, the impartial judge" is crowning *her* (figure 1).[6] Eventually only two states, Mississippi and Tennessee, used Kinney's design. Five others, including South Carolina, used designs of their own choice.

The historians Cynthia Mills and Thomas J. Brown have shown that the memorial project ran aground on the changing gender norms of the late nineteenth-century South.[7] For male monumentalizers, women had been no more than supporting actors during the Civil War, however necessary and at however great a personal and economic cost. They "stood back of the thin gray lines of Lee and Jackson" and "made the campaigns and the hardships of the Confederate soldier lighter and easier."[8] When the war ended so did their public role.

To vocal southern white women, these monuments reduced women either to "the slave and drudge of men" or to "his plaything and mock divinity."[9] "Keep back your shaft of granite; we do not want or need it," these contemporaries of Freud announced; they "wanted no monuments."[10] By the late nineteenth century genteel white women had appointed themselves the agents of Confederate commemoration and of social progress in the New South. They promoted women's education and philanthropic institutions for needy Confederate veterans, widows, and orphans. If men wanted to memorialize women, they should support these projects. When the organizers of the South Carolina women's monument approached the legislature for support, they competed directly with women seeking funds for their own work. Nevertheless, the men persisted.

A mostly male committee selected Frederick Wellington Ruckstuhl, a student of the French sculptor Marius-Jean-Antonin Mercié, to create the new South Carolina memorial (figure 2). Ruckstuhl's product was distinctly different from other Confederate women's monuments. The central figure was a woman "about 40 years of age, but still handsome." She had "Southern eyes" and an "expression of that simple sphinx-like seriousness of one who has overcome past tragedies and sorrows and was equally to face the troubles, as well as the triumphs,

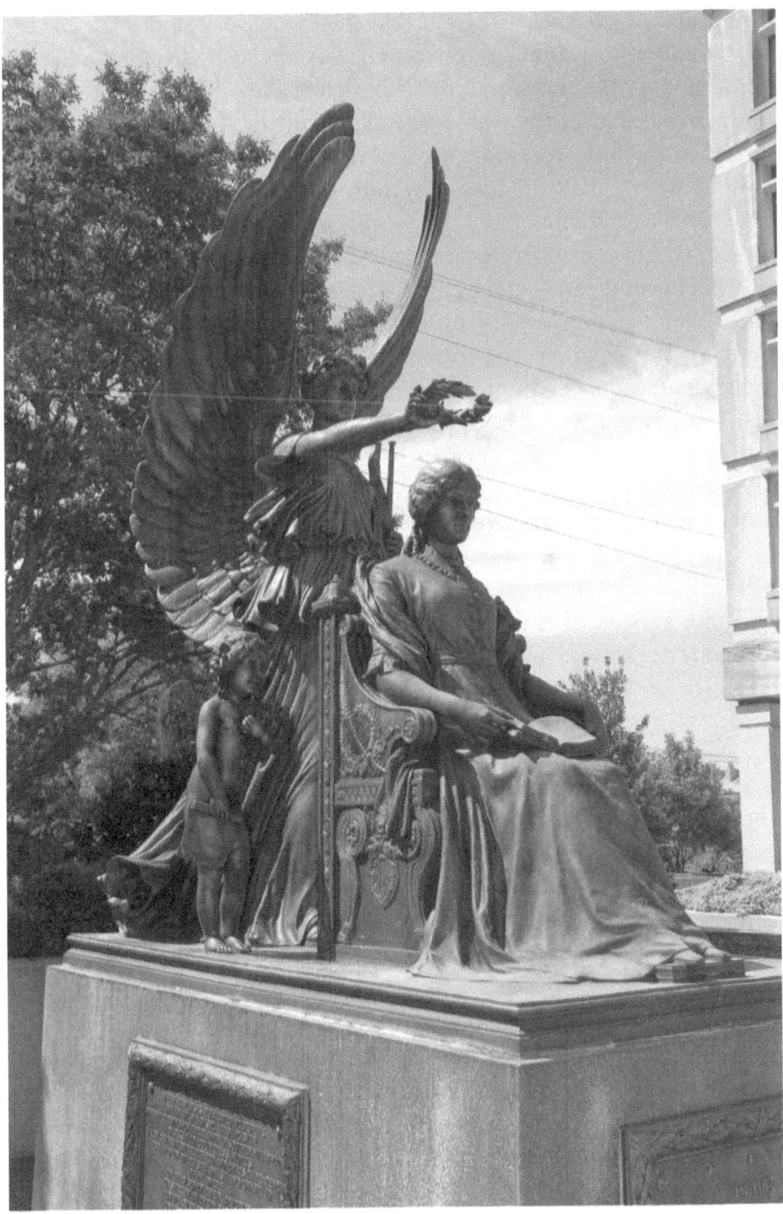

Figure 2. Memorial to the South Carolina Women of the Confederacy (Frederick Wellington Ruckstuhl, 1909–1912), State House Grounds, Columbia, S.C. Photograph by the author.

of the future." To Ruckstuhl, the practical war work that male admirers attributed to Confederate women was trivial. Instead, Ruckstuhl would honor "the most high of all her characteristic activities carried on during and after the war—that of consulting Holy Writ and losing herself in the lofty contemplation of her war-work, after it was done, and meditating over the past as well as the future of her country."[11]

Behind the woman, and seemingly unknown to her, "the ideal winged Genius of the State advance[d] with a royal stride and, with a feeling of proud satisfaction at the privilege of honoring this woman, holds over her a crown of immortality, while in her left hand she holds a palm of glory and a trumpet to announce to the world her great virtue and deed." Beside the seated woman, also outside her field of vision, a winged boy "full of enthusiasm and his arms filled with roses which, boy-like, he did not even stop to tie into a bouquet" rushed forward to give them to her. On the other side his "little winged sister, carrying a well-ordered bouquet," moved forward "timidly" to present them.

As Ruckstuhl reported his thinking, it all seemed consonant with the male version of the "war-woman." The central figure is passive, her modesty preventing her seeing the praise she has earned, her face placid, even "listless." But the monument itself is not so straightforward. The simple patriarchal hierarchies that southern men sought to celebrate and that southern women resisted became entangled in a welter of nineteenth-century nationalist ideologies and visual tropes familiar to Ruckstuhl from his European training. These often placed women on the front lines of nation-building, sometimes even as armed fighters, while, in their conservative iterations, the same women maintained traditionally feminine roles. Ruckstuhl's southern woman was a member of this tribe. She was "a fighting beauty and a beautiful fighter."[12]

The South Carolina memorial strongly evokes an ancient Roman triumph, a celebration of military victories and of the generals who won them (figure 3). Although Ruckstuhl never described the work as a triumph, he quoted approvingly the inscription composed by William E. Gonzales, editor of the Columbia *State* and the chief proponent of the project, that described the Confederate woman

> As the Supreme Citadel
> With Strong Towers of Faith and Hope
> Around Which Civilization Rallied
> and Triumphed.[13]

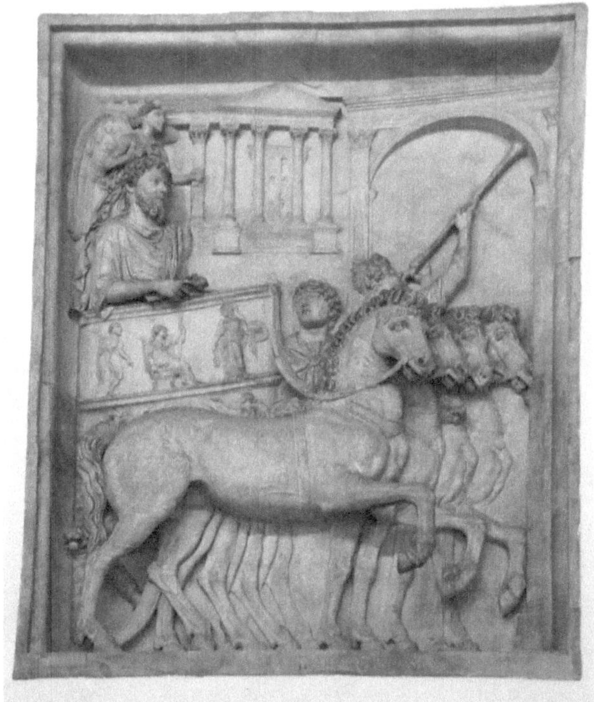

Figure 3. *Triumph of Marcus Aurelius* (ca. 176–180 CE), now in the Capitoline Museums, Rome. Photograph by the author.

This text is telling. Karl Marx and Friedrich Engels argued that the only reason for a nation to exist was to "advance historical evolution and progress," the very role that late nineteenth-century southern women claimed for themselves.[14]

The triumph has fascinated European American artists since the early modern period (figure 4). In the nineteenth century allusions to the triumph abounded both as images of historical figures such as, but not only, Napoleon and as allegories. Ruckstuhl incorporated one into his *Peace* on New York's Appellate Court.[15] However, the use of triumphal imagery here opens a particularly squirmy can of worms. In her authoritative study of the Roman triumph, Mary Beard has summarized the modern conception of the ancient ritual. These include a triumphator riding in a specially fitted-out chariot, wearing a laurel crown and holding an ivory scepter and a laurel branch. His children

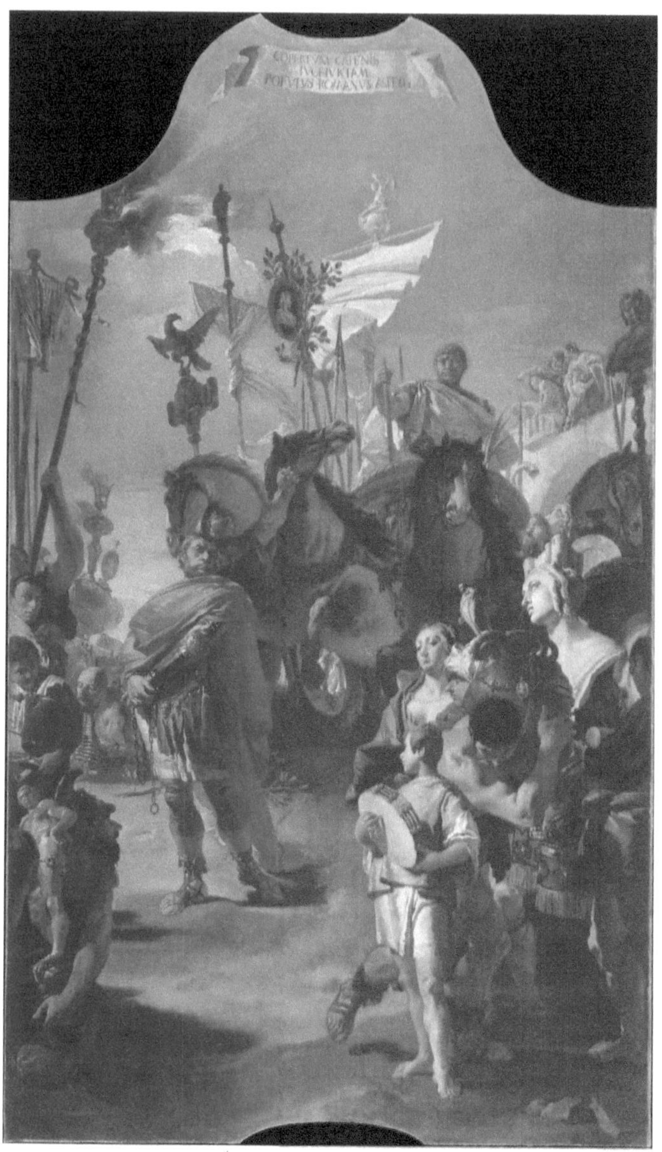

Figure 4. *The Triumph of Marius* (Giovanni Battista Tiepolo, 1729). The triumph celebrated the Roman general Marius's 104 BCE victory over Jugurtha, a North African king. The painting captures the violence and chaos of such events, as well as Jugurtha's defiant pose, which would have elicited admiration from his captors. Photo: Metropolitan Museum of Art, New York.

ride with him or beside him, and a slave stands behind him holding a golden crown over his head, all the while reminding him to "Remember, you are a man [not a god]."[16]

As Beard demonstrates, the individual elements of this widely accepted description are thinly documented and no ancient account includes all or even most of them, yet this synthesis has spurred the imagination of artists and scholars alike since the early modern period. At the same time, in modernity as in antiquity, the triumph's meanings and forms were ambiguous and multivalent. Rather than simply an orgy of domination and booty (although it was that), a triumph could serve as a warning against personal pride and national hubris. Captives' demeanor might gain them honor equal to or surpassing that of their captors.[17] In visual representations, the putative slave in the chariot might be replaced by the winged figure of Victory or Fame, flying above the triumphing general and holding the crown, emphasizing glory rather than humility.

Nineteenth-century nationalist artists made imaginative use of these ambiguities, but none more so than Ruckstuhl. What does it mean to place a woman in the victor's role? As a triumphator, why does she wear the sober countenance of resolution-in-defeat? Whom has she defeated and in what manner? What happens after the triumph is over? Why are her children semi-divine as opposed to the human children visible in other Confederate women's memorials? In the guise of a monument that, as Lydia Mattice Brandt summarizes it and as Ruckstuhl asserted, "commemorates White men's vision of White women's contributions to South Carolina during the Civil War," the sculptor created a visual work that twists truisms about gender and war into an intriguing Gordian knot.[18]

Notes

1. Taylor quoted in Thomas J. Brown, *Civil War Canon: Sites of Confederate Memory in South Carolina* (Chapel Hill: University of North Carolina Press, 2015), 207.

2. "Story of Monument Told by Ruckstuhl; Interesting Interview with Noted Sculptor, in St. Louis Paper of Last Sunday—First to Be Erected by a State to Women of the Confederacy," *The State* (Columbia, SC), March 15, 1912, 14.

3. Bridges Smith, "Woman's Monument Movement in Macon," *Confederate Veteran* [CV] 13, no. 6 (June 1905): 272; Caroline E. Janney, *Burying the Dead and Not the Past: Ladies' Memorial Associations and the Lost Cause* (Chapel Hill: University of North Carolina Press, 2008), 6–8, 40, 54–58.

4. "Review of the Memphis Reunion," *CV* 17, no. 7 (July 1909): 316. The sculptor was Louis Amateis.

5. "Concerning Monument to Our Women," *CV* 6, no. 2 (1898): 50.

6. "Southern Woman's Monument," *CV* 17, no. 7 (July 1909): 312; "Concerning Southern Woman's Monument," *CV* 17, no. 8 (August 1909): 372.

7. Cynthia Mills, "Gratitude and Gender Wars: Monuments to the Women of the Sixties," in *Monuments to the Lost Cause: Women, Art, and the Landscapes of Southern Memory*, ed. Cynthia Mills and Pamela H. Simpson (Knoxville: University of Tennessee Press, 2003), 183–200; Brown, *Civil War Canon*, 91–126. Brown's chapter is the fullest treatment of the South Carolina monument's history.

8. "Story of Monument Told by Ruckstuhl"; "Monument to Southern Women," *CV* 10, no. 10 (October 1902): 440.

9. Carolina, "The Problem of the Feminine," *The Keystone* 1 (1899); 5, quoted in Brown, *Civil War Canon*, 107.

10. Brown, *Civil War Canon*, 112; "Concerning Southern Women's Monument."

11. Unless otherwise indicated, these and succeeding descriptive passages are taken from F. Wellington Ruckstuhl, "Sculptor Interprets the Memorial," *The State*, April 12, 1912, 18. Ruckstuhl changed his name to the less-German-sounding Ruckstull during World War I.

12. Ibid.

13. Ibid.

14. Hobsbawm, *Nations and Nationalism*, 41; Brown, *Civil War Canon*, 107, 126.

15. Richard Ladegast, "A Notable American Sculptor," *Bay View Magazine* 15, no. 8 (May 1908): 539.

16. Mary Beard, *The Roman Triumph* (Cambridge, MA: Harvard University Press, 2007), 81–82. Beard's study is the source of my understanding of the triumph and its interpretation.

17. Ibid., 138, 157–58, 173.

18. Lydia Mattice Brandt, *The South Carolina State House Grounds: A Guidebook* (Columbia: University of South Carolina Press, 2021), 54.

Daniela Sandler

Memorial to the Black Mothers of the Periphery Fighting against State Terrorism, Rio de Janeiro

THE COLORFUL MURAL pops out from behind a soccer goal and a chain-link fence, flanking a field. On the left side, six profiles represent an array of Afro-Brazilian women—old, young, brown- and black-skinned, wearing braids and turbans. On the right side, a single, larger profile of a Black woman, donning a headband with the pan-African colors (red, gold, green), next to a raised fist and a green map of Africa. She is Mother Africa, ancestral, atemporal, and still present. The women's profiles face each other across the mural, eyes closed; behind them, a panorama of gray cubic houses. Over the skyline, scripted letters spell out: *Memorial to the Black Mothers of the Periphery Fighting against State Terrorism*. The memorial, built by three organizations (the Network of Mothers and Family Members against State Terrorism; the Inclusion Project; and the Initiative for the Right to Memory and Racial Justice), was unveiled in 2020, in the Baixada Fluminense, the most violent area of the Rio de Janeiro Metropolitan Region.[1] The "periphery" in the title alludes to the peripheral areas of Brazilian cities, precarious neighborhoods surrounding wealthier, whiter urban cores. This memorial sits at the margins of the city and

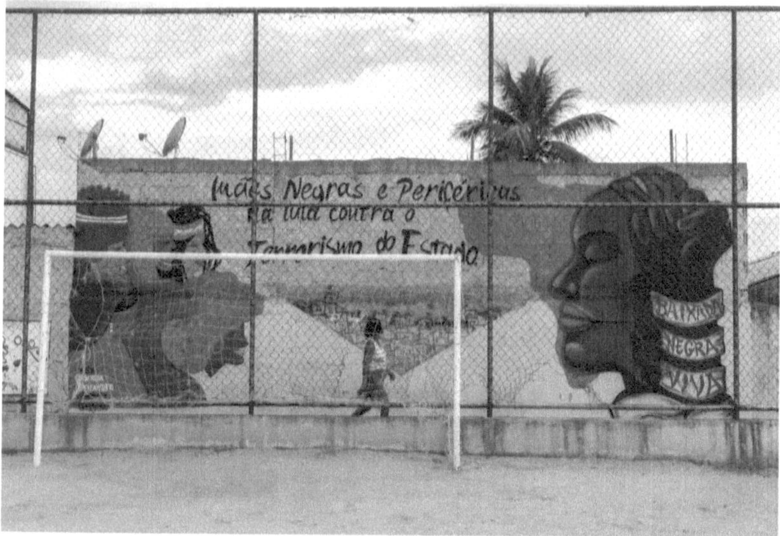

Figure 1. *Memorial to the Black Mothers of the Periphery Fighting against State Terrorism*, Rio de Janeiro. Tércio Teixeira.

of representation—a graffiti memorial by the soccer field, devoted to poor Black women.

The memorial fuses past and present, not only because of the fluidity of memory, which seeps into the present, but also because the events this memorial commemorates are ongoing. For over five hundred years, Black mothers in Brazil have been fighting the decimation of their children—first with slavery, then under structural racism and police violence. This memorial addresses two challenges: one, the sociocultural need to remember past traumas; two, the sociopolitical urgency to stop violence now. The memorial conjoins these impulses by building identity out of a history of resilience, a history that is not only represented by the women painted on the wall but embodied by the women who have organized themselves to fight police terror.

In 2020, Brazil had the most police killings in the world: 6,416 (301 per ten million people).[2] Of those killed by police, 79 percent were Black, whereas Blacks make up 56 percent of the population.[3] Most of the victims were young: 76 percent ranged in age from 0 to 29; and almost half (44.5 percent) from 18 to 24.[4] Police brutality also includes imprisonment without due process, stray bullets, torture, intimidation, extortion, and the disappearance of people taken from their communities without record. This violence forms a relentless backdrop in the life of Black Brazilians—as the memorial puts it: "state terrorism."

Mothers are prominent among those fighting this violence. They are organized in networks: Mothers, Relatives and Victims from Baixada Fluminense; Fighting Mothers; Mothers from Ceará; Mothers in Mourning from Zona Leste; and Mothers from Manguinhos, among many others. The role of mothers evokes other movements led by women whose children were killed or "disappeared" through state terror, such as the Madres of the Plaza de Mayo in Argentina.[5] The mothers are at the center of both this fight and the memorial, not only because most of the targets of violence are young but also because Black Brazilian women have long led and anchored their communities, as single mothers, heads of social movements, and spiritual figures in Afro-Brazilian traditions.

The memorial becomes heritage by entangling historical memory and contemporary action. Such action begins with the way the memorial portrays Black mothers. They are depicted in hieratic and solemn profiles, reclaiming the gravitas reserved for white men, who are the subject of most monuments in Brazil.[6] When monuments represent others, such as Indigenous Brazilians or Blacks, it is in an idealized manner that elides their oppression. Women are a minority, often represented submissively—for example, Júlio Guerra's *Black Mother*, in São Paulo, depicts an Afro-Brazilian slave who nursed the master's children.

The *Memorial to the Black Mothers* sits far from these cultural prejudices, centering Black women as agents of power who have the audacity to put their children first and the potential to humanize their communities. Despite its humble appearance, this memorial earnestly enacts monumental principles. It aggrandizes, celebrates, and reassures, but also transposes those principles to Black women. This is not another graffitied wall but a focal point for mourning, rallying, and community building.

This brings us to the quotidian but crucial soccer field—a poignant site, used by the very demographic that is the target of state terrorism. Soccer fields are a staple in low-income neighborhoods—spaces for leisure, sociability, and the play of socioeconomic aspirations (soccer is a ticket out of poverty for many young Brazilians). The memorial functions in symbiosis with this sociocultural potency, while at the same time subverting it. The memorial suggests the system is broken; one cannot wish to join it but only hope to change it and stop its terrors.

Notes

1. The memorial is in São João de Meriti, one of thirteen municipalities in the Baixada Fluminense.

2. "Police Killings by Country 2021," World Population Review, https://worldpopulationreview.com/country-rankings/police-killings-by-country.

3. In the United States, there were 1,126 killings in 2020 (34 per ten million people). Of the victims, 27 percent were Black, while Blacks are 13 percent of the population. "2020 Police Violence Report," Mapping Police Violence, https://policeviolencereport.org/.

4. *Anuário Brasileiro de Segurança Pública 2021* ([São Paulo: Fórum Brasileiro de Segurança Pública, 2021]), 40.

5. Abril Zarco, "Maternalismo, Identidad Colectiva y Participación Política: Las Madres de Plaza de Mayo," *Revista Punto Género*, no. 1 (2011): 229–47, https://adnz.uchile.cl/index.php/RPG/article/view/16883/17586.

6. Instituto Pólis, "Quais histórias as cidades nos contam? A presença negra nos espaços públicos de São Paulo," 2020, https://polis.org.br/estudos/presencanegra/; Louise Freire, "Monumentos do Rio que homenageiam a cultura negra ainda são minoria," *Notícia preta*, November 19, 2018; "Rio tem 2 mil monumentos, mas menos de 20 são de figuras femininas," G1, March 8, 2016, http://g1.globo.com/rio-de-janeiro/noticia/2016/03/rio-tem-2-mil-monumentos-mas-menos-de-20-sao-de-figuras-femininas.html.

Ana María León

Mujeres Creando, Plaza Chola Globalizada, La Paz, Bolivia

ON OCTOBER 12, 2020, a week before general elections, the anarcha-feminist queer collective Mujeres Creando (Women Creating) organized an action in La Paz, Bolivia.[1] In broad daylight, and surrounded by an encouraging crowd, Yolanda Mamani and Emiliana Quispe, members of Mujeres Creando, dressed up the monument of Isabella I of Castille (Isabel la Católica) with clothes of their own, characteristic of the Bolivian chola: an *aguayo* (a rectangular woven blanket used to carry items, in this case clearly full), a *pollera* (a skirt), and a wool hat (figure 1). The oval plaza is surrounded by police, military, and financial buildings, a five-star hotel, and a large shopping mall. In this inhospitable context, but surrounded by an encouraging crowd, the women stained the pedestal with red paint, dressed the statue with their own garb, and took over the microphone to narrate personal histories of struggle against racism and discrimination. Recast in this way, the monument took on a notion that Aymara and Bolivian scholar Silvia Rivera Cusicanqui describes as *ch'ixi*: a layered and nuanced assemblage of Indigenous identity.

The Bolivian chola is an ethnic denomination taken up by Indigenous women from the region who wear this traditional clothing.

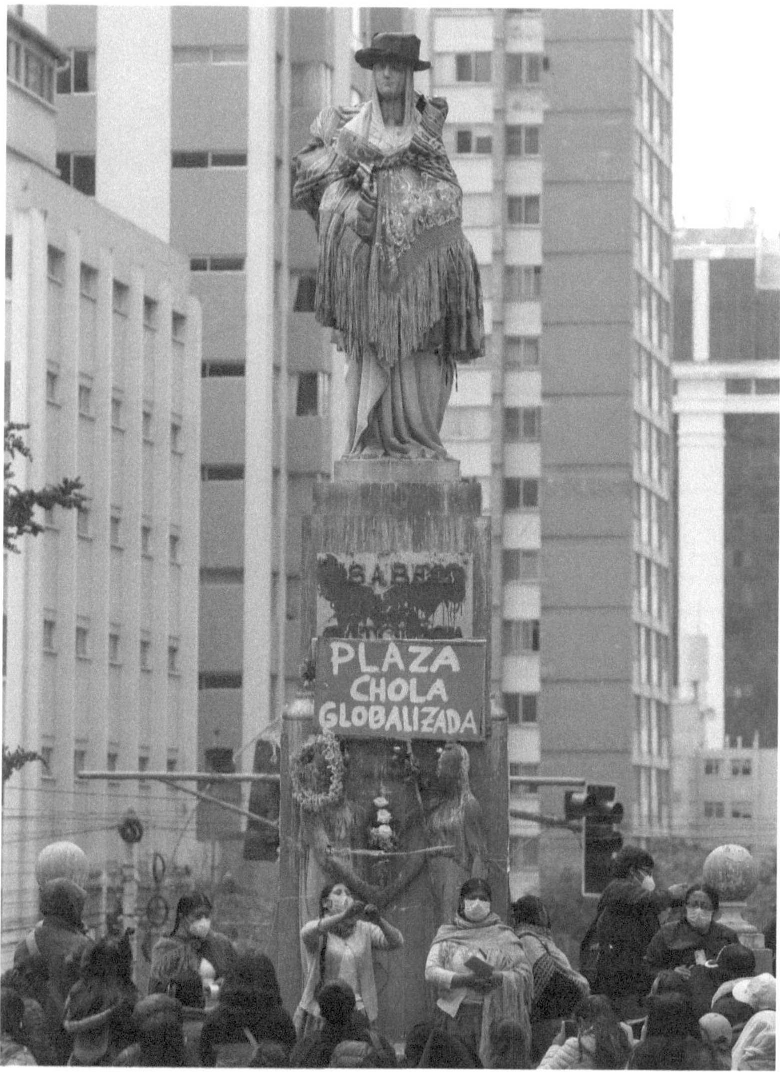

Figure 1. Mujeres Creando, Plaza Chola Globalizada, La Paz, Bolivia (October 12, 2020). Courtesy Martin Alipaz/EPA-EFE/Shutterstock.

This somewhat tautological definition points to the fact that in this identity construction, the clothes make the chola, and as such they are unique markers, coded and recognized throughout the Andes. These clothes forge an Indigenous identity through the manipulation of both European and Indigenous markers. Indigenous women in the Andes use the aguayo to carry their children or various items on their backs. The pollera, however, has more complicated origins. It was originally brought over from Spain, and eventually appropriated and transformed into traditional Indigenous garb in many countries in South and Central America. The wool hat, also initially European, was adopted by Indigenous folks and is now worn in the Andes primarily by these groups. In other words, while the aguayo is an Indigenous fabric, and connotes carrying a heavy burden, the pollera and the wool hat were initially European and were taken up by Indigenous peoples throughout the processes of colonization, to the degree that they are now read in the Andes as markers of Indigeneity. This network of crossed provenances and appropriations gives powerful significance to Mujeres Creando's action on the monument. By dressing up the Spanish monument with the traditional clothing of a Bolivian chola, Mujeres Creando appropriates and assimilates the European other into a triumphant Indigenous presence.

We can think about this activated monument through the Aymara notion of ch'ixi, a term derived from Indigenous textile production.[2] In opposition to Nestor García Canclini's understanding of hybridity, which to Rivera Cusicanqui ultimately connotes infertility, ch'ixi expresses "the parallel coexistence of multiple differences that do not extinguish but instead antagonize and complement each other."[3] Ch'ixi reflects the Aymara idea of something that is and is not at the same time: it is the logic of the included third, a way of combining the Indigenous and its purported opposite without mixing them. As Rivera Cusicanqui explains, ch'ixi is a color that is the juxtaposition, in small points or spots, of opposed or contrasting colors: black and white, red, and green, and so on. The processes of colonization that marked the region have led Latin American scholars to formulate how terms such as "mestizaje" have erased Indigeneity and to reflect critically on the implications of alternatives such as the term "hybridity."[4] Like the appropriation of European clothing to signify Indigeneity, ch'ixi points to the more nuanced and complicated ways in which Indigenous groups construct their identity and agency.

Mujeres Creando was founded in 1992 by María Galindo, Mónica Mendoza, and Julieta Paredes, and it has been led by Galindo since 2001 with a clear antipatriarchal and anticapitalist position. In Galindo's words, "there is no decolonization without depatriarchalization."[5] Galindo explains the action Plaza de la Chola Globalizada as a "travestir" (the verbal form of transvestite in Latin American Spanish) of the monument, responding to the racist practice of humiliating corrupt public functionaries by dressing them as cholas. If this practice assumes the chola dress as a form of divesting public authorities of their rank, Mujeres Creando's action elevates the monument precisely by dressing it as a Bolivian chola. Importantly, the clothes Mamani and Quispe use are not purchased: these are their own clothes, donated for the action. Galindo underlines the importance of the participation of Mamani and Quispe as Bolivian cholas, but also explains the action is not only a revindication of the chola but more broadly, "starting with the chola," seeks to bring together "all women in a complex array of belongings and social conditions."[6] In the transformed monument these identities relate to each other such that, thinking with Rivera Cusicanqui, "Each one reproduces itself from the depths of the past and relates to others in a contentious way."[7] The plaza of the globalized chola is a ch'ixi monument and points to the possibility of a ch'ixi futurity.

Notes

1. The action was done in collaboration with the Organization of Sex Workers in El Alto, the Organization of Women in Situation of Prostitution (OMESPRO, for Organización de Mujeres en situación de prostitución), the Organization of Women in Situation of Prostitution of La Paz, and several independent women. Maria Galindo, "De Reina de España a Chola globalizada," in La Acera de Enfrente, mujerescreando.org/de-reina-de-espana-a-chola-globalizada-la-acera-de-enfrente/.

2. While we may understand ch'ixi through aesthetics, Indigenous artist and curator Elvira Espejo Ayca has explained how Indigenous weavers never talk about form but rather focus on structure and technique. Espejo Ayca suggests that the aesthetics of Indigenous textiles are the result of the processes by which they are produced, in contrast to what she describes as the academic focus on iconography and form. Elvira Espejo Ayca, "Decoloniality and the Politics of History" (Columbia University, May 7, 2021).

3. Silvia Rivera Cusicanqui, *"Ch'ixinakax utxiwa*: A Reflection on the Practices and Discourses of Decolonization," *South Atlantic Quarterly* 111, no. 1 (2012): 95–109, at 105.

4. See Josefina Saldaña-Portillo, "Who's the Indian in Aztlán? Re-Writing Mestizaje, Indianism, and Chicanismo from the Lacandón," in *The Latin American Subaltern Studies Reader*, ed. Ileana Rodríguez and María Milagros López (Durham: Duke University Press, 2001), 402–23; Nestor García Canclini, *Hybrid Cultures: Strategies for Entering and Leaving Modernity* (Minneapolis: University of Minnesota Press, 1995); Carolyne Dean and Dana Leibsohn, "Hybridity and Its

Discontents: Considering Visual Culture in Spanish Colonial America," *Colonial Latin American Review* 12, no. 1 (2003): 5–35.

5. María Galindo, *No se puede descolonizar sin despatriarcalizar: Teoría y propuesta de la despatriarcalización* (La Paz, Bolivia: Mujeres Creando, 2013). For more of Galindo's writing see María Galindo, *Feminismo Bastardo* (La Paz, Bolivia: Mujeres Creando, 2021).

6. Galindo, "De Reina de España a Chola globalizada."

7. Rivera Cusicanqui, *"Ch'ixinakax utxiwa,"* 105.

PART IV
Allegorical Women

Daniel E. Coslett

7. The Colonial Marianne: Representing *Liberté* and France in Occupied North Africa

REPRESENTATIONS OF WOMEN were relatively rare in the public art of French colonial North Africa. In the Maghreb, which was far from immune to nineteenth-century European *statuomanie* (statuemania in English), statues of male politicians, soldiers, clerics—the so-called *grands hommes* (Great Men) of France—were common. Where women did appear, they were almost exclusively present in the form of allegorical images and sculptures intended to represent France, and thus the state, culture, and power of the colonizing authority (figure 1). The stoic Marianne figure—a woman typically dressed in classical garb (a chiton or stola) and liberty cap—was deployed in public squares and inside town halls for this inescapably political purpose, frequently as a secondary figure intended to lend her attributes or qualities to the male subject(s) being commemorated. Although some scholars have addressed the use of the female body in allegorical French art more broadly, the sociopolitical significance of this art form within the context of colonial built environments has escaped critical interrogation and remains a noteworthy lacuna in art and architectural scholarship.[1]

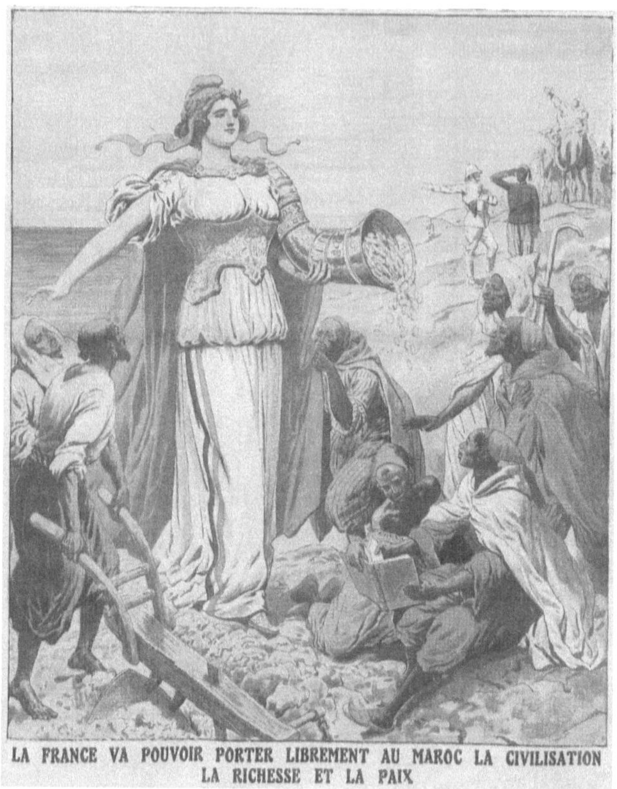

Figure 1. "La France va pouvoir porter librement au Maroc la civilisation[,] la richesse[,] et la paix" (France will be able to freely bring civilization, wealth, and peace to Morocco). *Le Petit Journal*, Sunday supplement, November 19, 1911, cover. Bibliothèque nationale de France.

Following a brief introduction to colonial monuments and the origin of La Marianne, this chapter presents a sampling of historic monuments and statues displayed in Tunisia and Algeria during the nineteenth and twentieth centuries by the colonial state. It concludes with a brief exploration of Tunisian appropriation of allegorical imagery as a form of resistance to colonialism. The chapter attends to compelling questions regarding sociopolitical symbolism in public spaces, aesthetic responsiveness to cultural norms, and the accommodation of various audiences in colonized settings. Within the colonial North African context, what did the installation of statues depicting women mean? In a time and place in which Europeans fetishized North African culture and female bodies, how did La Marianne function for both French and indigenous viewers? How were standard representations popular in Europe deployed in occupied North Africa? Assessing the degree to which imperialist intentions changed meanings and complicated matters is the aim of this chapter, which is far from a complete survey of this expansive topic.[2] This chapter explores historical issues that may inform ongoing debates regarding the suitability of highly visible monuments, representations of the past, and gender equity in public art and space.

La Marianne and France

PRIOR TO THE French Revolution, the French state was represented by images of the king's person, related paraphernalia such as the crown and scepter, or symbols like the monarch's coat of arms and the fleur-de-lis. A different image was needed to represent the nascent French republic after 1792 and to illustrate political power through a visual metaphor better suited to the liberal new era.[3] Consistent with the prevailing aesthetics of the time, artists turned toward the classical past for inspiration. As illustrated in works such as Gravelot and Cochin's influential 1791 compendium of allegorical imagery titled *Iconologie*, artists adopted *Liberté* (Liberty).[4] There one finds Liberty embodied as a young woman, dressed in white, wielding a liberty cap (*pileus*) and scepter (figure 2).

In addition to representing freedom—her cap was the type worn by freed slaves in ancient Rome—she exemplified the self-empowerment possible in the absence of tyranny.[5] Complex compositions of the active king surrounded by various supporting allegories such as Valor, Victory, and Abundance were replaced with this solitary figure that came to represent both freedom and the new French republican form of government.[6] As Walter Benjamin noted in 1928 and others have since confirmed, "allegories no longer told stories; they offered values to be admired."[7] The "narrated body" of the king performing acts of gallantry, bravery, and munificence gave way to the "embodied value" of Liberty—a fundamentally intrinsic attribute of the Republic.[8] She typically appeared alone as a young and active warrior, bare-breasted and dynamic, or as a solemn, seated, and more aloof goddess-like figure whose strength depended on her virtue rather than physical strength. Variations were many and suited the time and artists' intent.[9]

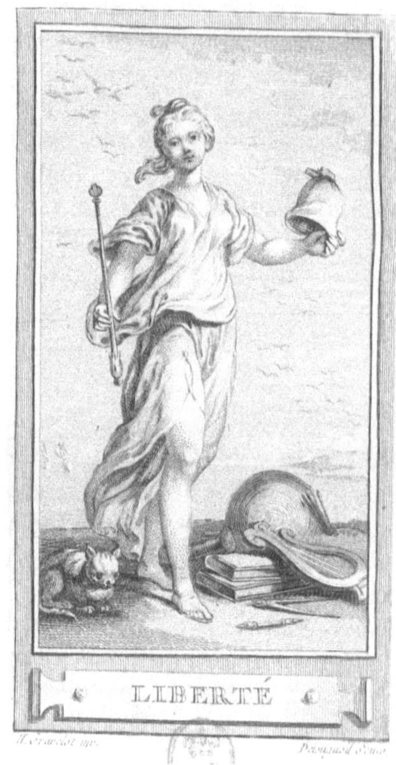

Figure 2. *Liberté* (Liberty) allegory (1791). *Iconologie* (Cochin et Gravelot, 1791), vol. 3, 31. Bibliothèque nationale de France.

With the establishment of the Third Republic in 1870 (at the dawn of France's colonial ascent), following the vicissitudes of various restorations, republics, and empires, Liberty took on her current form and was given a name—La Marianne. Eventually she lost her scepter and donned the cap, but the latter remained a controversial element for quite some time due to its association with the violence of the revolution and 1871 Commune.[10] As had been the case with the generic Liberty, her attributes and attitudes were inconsistently rendered; in some venues she appeared crowned, helmeted and in armor, calmy seated, or in a more active stance, as she does in Léopold and Charles Morice's iconic *Monument to the Republic* in Paris's Place de la République (1883).[11] Maurice Agulhon, who remains the preeminent scholar of La Marianne, has established a basic genealogy for the figure, noting that the goddess-like Liberty became "The (French) Republic," and then more generally "France."[12] By the twentieth century the bonneted rendition of Liberty/Republic/France—which

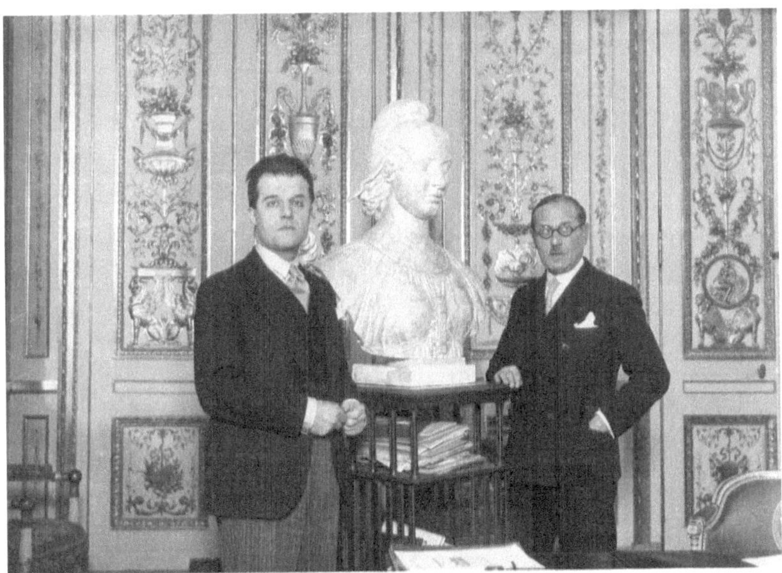

Figure 3. "La nouvelle Marianne avec M. Mistler et le sculpteur Poisson" (The new Marianne with Mr. Mistler and the sculptor Poisson) (Agence Meurisse, 1933). Bibliothèque nationale de France.

tends to be called La Marianne despite formal nuances—found its way onto coins, stamps, and banknotes, and into public squares and government buildings throughout France.[13] As the personification of both the nation and the state she has sat inside municipal buildings, in the form of official busts "of the Republic," since the 1870s (figure 3).[14] From these places she still today "proclaims the principles of the republic, in a didactic and pedagogical" fashion.[15]

In her antique costume, according to Joan Landes, Marianne represented a desire "to institute an ideal non-despotic Republic wherein personal liberty and communal togetherness would be reconciled" through an impersonal image, a metaphor for a universal post-revolutionary French society.[16] One ought not overestimate the symbolic status of women, deified as the Republic, according to Landes. Indeed, to her

> Marianne is *nothing but a picture.* She neither reflects nor authorizes the public actions of actually existing women in postrevolutionary society. Nor is she the only expression of nationhood. At a higher level of abstraction in the newly dominant symbolic

order of representation, the invisible fatherlands need not be and ought not be pictured. It is spoken and written. The nation's body is a discursive body. . . . Liberty, it will be recalled, was not figured as a mother, but as a virginal, chaste daughter. . . . She has a decidedly emotive force, but one purged of all unruliness and sexuality.[17]

The use of a woman as a revolutionary symbol of freedom at a time when actual women remained second-class citizens in France reveals both the complexity of artistic symbolism and contemporary gender relationships.[18]

Scholars have furthermore suggested that the female personification was not only the product of allegorical traditions and a desire to see a figure as unlike the ousted king as possible, but also because of the Catholic population's existing adoration of the Virgin Mary and willingness to accept a sacred female figurehead. In this case, the "idolisation of Marianne was a kind of inversion of the idolisation of Mary."[19] Furthermore, from a linguistic perspective, abstract nouns—such as *liberté*—are typically gendered feminine in Romance languages. The femininity of the figure thus perhaps follows this logic, further seen in the French word for "kingdom" (*un royaume*) being a masculine noun, while "republic" (*une république*) is a feminine one. Agulhon concludes that the use of a female figure may have been a manifestation of these various tendencies but was likely a product of male-dominated societies' normative deployments of the subjugated "woman-object."[20]

Statuomanie in France

STATUES HAD BECOME more than just commemorative installations after the revolution; they became charged political and "ideological signposts," as "public homage became a statement of national identity and an ideological weapon, both of which accelerated its popularity."[21] The statuemania years from 1870 to 1914 witnessed a major proliferation of statues as public monuments in France.[22] Elements of *décor urbain*, statues of politicians, artists, inventors, and "heroes in the arts and sciences" crowded cities' streets, squares, and parks so much so that in 1911 Paris's Municipal Council proposed a ten-year moratorium.[23] Linking the colonies to the metropole, colonialist figures were featured as well.[24] The choice of these personalities reflected the "pedagogically oriented, meritocratic system of democratic advancement and public honours" that emerged during the Third Republic (1870–1940).[25] As such, these monuments were collectively an important component of what Eric Hobsbawm identifies as the "invented tradition" of the Third Republic. Along with public education as a "secular equivalent to the Church" and civic ceremonies and holidays, such as July 14 (Bastille Day), public monuments (which were often dedicated during well-choreographed public events) bound together French citizens with their state and confirmed legitimacy upon this relationship and its continuity with its revolutionary past.[26] The celebration of particular individuals and events not only embellished public space in the modernizing city, but dominant factions of society claimed territory, incorporating physical space into shared communal memories and cultural identities.[27] Statuemania was thus not only an artistic and political phenomenon but also an implicitly ideological process wherein those empowered to erect monuments expressed ideas that both represented and, to some extent, shaped popular opinion.[28]

Members of the public and critics became increasingly displeased with the overabundance of commemorative installations cluttering increasingly congested streets, and at the turn of the twentieth century the general obsession with monuments yielded to "statuophobia—or plain weariness."[29] Sentiments and priorities shifted in light of World War I's devastation and the destabilizing sociocultural changes that came with it, further divorcing the public from its passion for monuments. Huge numbers of pieces were razed, their bronzes recycled during World War II in a fit of what might be called "extreme statuophobia" as the Vichy regime rejected the legacy of the Third Republic's meritocratic and democratic tendencies.[30] While new public monuments would continue to appear in subsequent decades, they never did so with the frequency they had prior to World War I.[31]

Statues in the Colonies

WITHIN THE CONTEXT of colonialism, this marking of space took on particular significance and authorities frequently paid tribute to celebrities of the metropole, as well as to colonialist individuals (politicians, military heroes, scientists, etc.) of more local significance.[32] Highly choreographed inaugurations and annual celebrations often revolved around such statues, which continued to appear in the colonies despite growing statuophobia in metropolitan France (figure 4). Accompanied

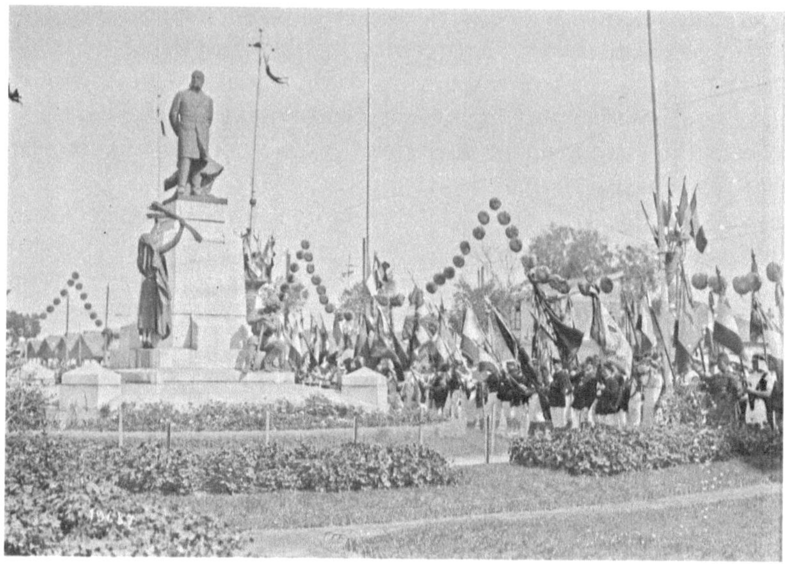

Figure 4. A ceremony at the Jules Ferry monument (Antonin Mercié, 1899), Tunis, Tunisia. Though described in the archives as the dedication of the monument, the photo is dated 1912. Bibliothèque nationale de France.

by military bands, choral performances, political speeches, and colorful parades, they were "opportunities to confirm and exhibit French domination" in occupied territories.[33] Occupation meant power, and imperial power was considered intrinsically masculine, and so statues of accomplished French men dominated, just as they had in France.

In colonial Algeria, soldiers and generals associated with the country's conquest were most repeatedly celebrated (in contrast to the situation in France where subjects were generally civilian and cultural). Among the more prominent monuments from the early decades of Algeria's colonization are those to the Duc d'Orléans (Carlo Morochetti, 1845) and Thomas Robert Bugeaud (Auguste Dumont, 1852) in Algiers.[34] Statues proliferated with statuemania. Statues known to have appeared in Tunis during the colonial period include those of statesman Jules Ferry (1899), geologist Philippe Thomas (1913), and Archbishop Charles Lavigerie (1925) (see figure 4).[35] The city of Sfax had monuments to Philippe Thomas (1913) and author and administrator Paul Bourde. Bizerte had prominent monuments to Justin Massicault (1908) and aviators Roland Garros (1924), who piloted the first trans-Mediterranean flight, which landed there in 1913, and Georges Madon.[36]

Such monuments to masculine French power were part of what Frantz Fanon referenced in noting that the colonist "refer[red] constantly to the history of his metropolis" and thus created spaces that seemed to be extensions of the metropole. Amid their buildings, colonizers created

> a world compartmentalized, Manichaean and petrified, a world of statues: the statue of the general who led the conquest, the statue of the engineer who built the bridge. A world cocksure of itself, crushing with its stoniness the backbones of those scarred by the whip.[37]

Fanon's assessment confirms that colonial statues operated on behalf of the state and their symbolism was recognized. Not surprisingly, they were therefore interpreted in different ways by different audiences. For some they were inescapable symbols of oppression, while for others they represented French "civilization" and linked the far-flung territories of the empire.

Statues of women were relatively scarce in colonial Tunisia and Algeria, undoubtedly a reflection of the normative masculinity brought by colonizers from Europe. Tunis's monument to Phillip Thomas (Jean-Baptiste Belloc, 1913) included an allegory of France at its base and was crowned with a strident figure of Ceres (ancient goddess of grain) in honor of the improvements to agriculture made possible by his discovery of phosphates. In Algeria as well, it would seem that no prominent portrait statues of actual women were erected during the French period, with the exception of equestrian monuments to Joan of Arc. One (by Joseph Ebstein, 1931) was installed outside Oran's cathedral in the midst of a prideful period during which France celebrated the centenary of Algeria's conquest. A similar statue (by Georges Halbout du Tanney, 1939), the plinth of which noted that it was dedicated by the public "to the glory of Joan of Arc, pure symbol of French heroism," was placed in central Algiers in 1951.[38] Elsewhere women appeared in abstract allegorical form. Winged victories inspired by ancient sculptures were found in war memorials across Algeria, and a togated figure representing the law dating to the Second Republic stood between the colonial-era gendarmerie and former cathedral in Oran as recently as 2017 (figure 5).[39] Elsewhere generic women appeared in the guise of France or La Marianne, often in sec-

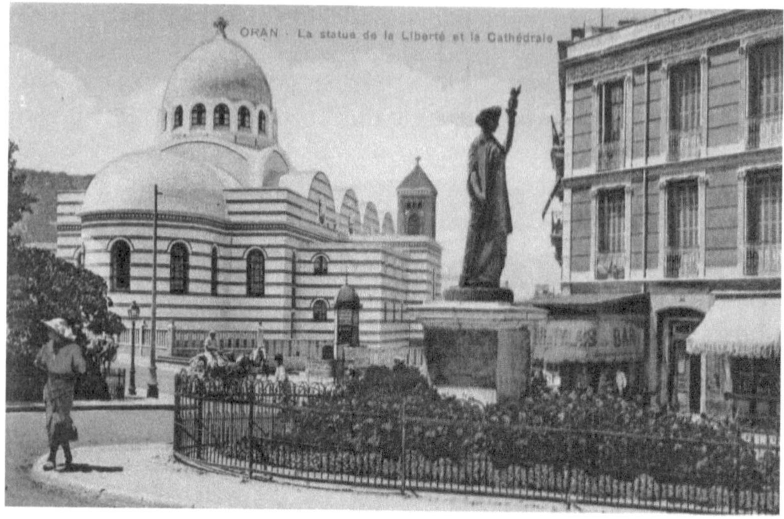

Figure 5. *The Law* statue (also known as *The Republic* and *Liberty*) (Bosio, 1849), Oran, Algeria. The crowned figure carries a tablet labeled "constitution" and a staff capped with the "hand of justice," a Gallic rooster, and RF (for *République française*). Author's collection.

ondary roles recalling the supportive thematic function of allegories in the monuments of the *ancien régime.*

La Marianne in North Africa

TWO IMAGES OF La Marianne in colonial Tunisia reveal her limited presence. A photo of Raphaël Guy's Arabesque city hall in Sfax, with its dome and minaret-like clocktower the epitome of what François Béguin would call the "style of the protector,"[40] illustrates the architect's skillful interpretation of indigenous architecture within the context of colonial administrative spaces (figure 6).[41]

Its council chamber—a rich Orientalist fantasy—is clad in carved and painted decoration. Barely visible against the far wall is La Marianne, an increasingly standard feature of French town halls after 1870, and presumably colonial ones as well.[42] Sfax, through this act, was brought into the French symbolic sphere. Its primary political space was designed to represent the local context through the lens of the French architect, and the presence of La Marianne signified the presence of France, but also the incorporation of territory into France's jurisdiction.

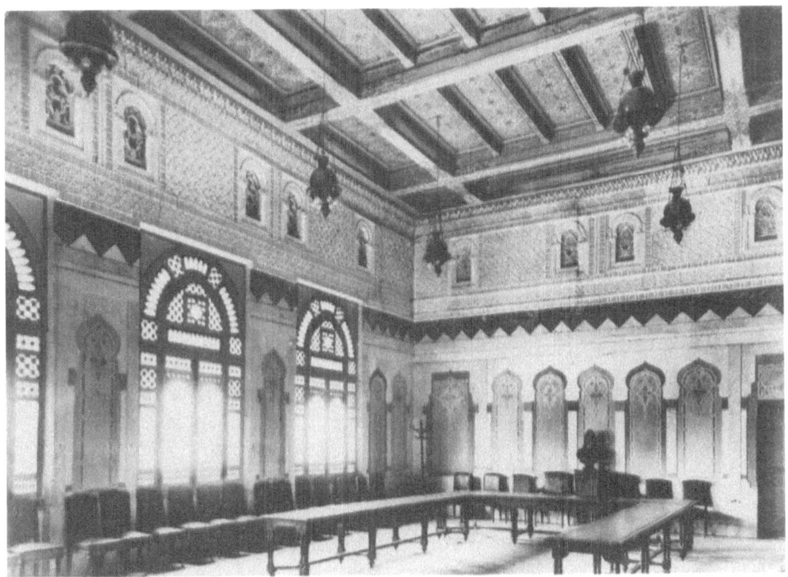

Figure 6. Council chamber at the Hôtel de Ville, Sfax, Tunisia (Raphaël Guy, 1905) featuring a bust of Marianne. Author's collection.

La Marianne might have been much more prominent in Tunis had the city adopted a 1903 proposal for a bronze monument "to the glory of France and the Protectorate" on Tunis's main square between the French headquarters and the Catholic cathedral. Jean-Baptiste Belloc's piece would have centered La Marianne in a way similar to the Marianne-focused installations by Jules Dalou and the Morice brothers in Paris.[43] Though openly supported by the editorial staff at the *Dépêche tunisienne*,[44] many were skeptical and deemed the expenditure of the allocated 140,000 francs to be wasteful. Such a commemoration seemed inappropriate after only twenty-two years of colonial rule, particularly when far more important issues (e.g., paving streets, reducing odors emanating from the polluted lake, etc.) warranted the administration's attention and resources, protested at least one Municipal Council member.[45] According to an article in the *Revue nord africaine*, two different monuments were being deliberated in early 1903 in advance of a planned visit by French president Émile Loubet.[46] Reminiscent of Dalou's dynamic *Triumph of the Republic* (1899), the preferred iteration was arranged in typical triangular or pyramidal composition. It was to depict "the arrival of France in Tunisia" through an image of a "pretty and robust peasant girl" (*paysanne*) riding an

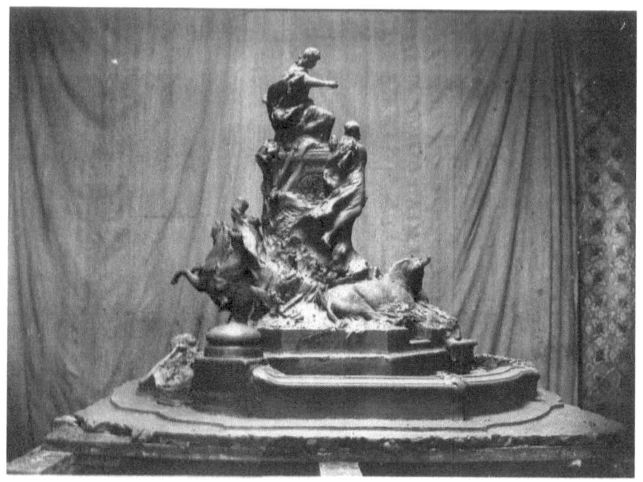

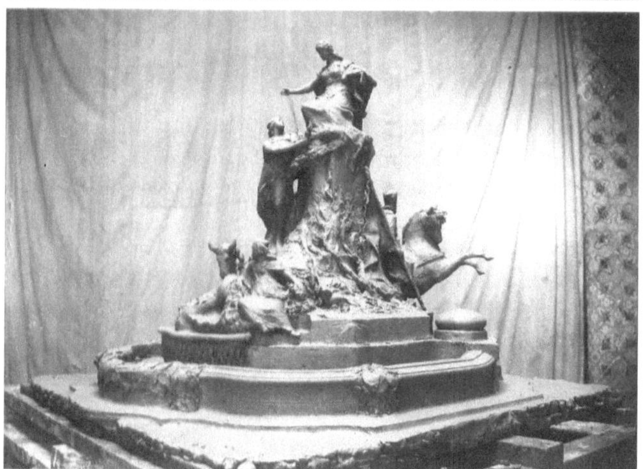

Figure 7. Model for a monument "to the glory of France and the Protectorate" for Tunis, Tunisia (Jean-Baptiste Belloc, 1903). Source: National Archives of Tunisia.

"ancient chariot" pulled by four Percheron horses. With the reins in her left hand, she controlled the rearing beasts, thereby demonstrating "strength and moderation."[47] Reaching down with her right hand, she beckoned toward another female figure, this one dressed in tattered clothes and representing a destitute Tunisia, it was said. Through this gesture, "France" or "the Protectorate" symbolically invited Tunisia to accompany her on a journey toward civilization and prosperity.[48] Note that in this iteration the female representing France appears not to have been rendered as the bonneted Marianne but nonetheless continues the idea of an allegorical female representing France in the colonial context.

Models for a simpler version—likely the second of the two monuments said to be under consideration—survive in Tunisia's national archives (figure 7).[49] This one, which incorporated a water fountain at its base, included an enthroned France or Marianne in Roman armor (it is unclear if she wears a helmet or Phrygian cap), reaching down from high above on a plinth of verdant landscape and swirling waves, an ox, a horse, and Tunisian people. Here, the personified Protectorate/France appeared in an attitude of beneficence and generosity, gesturing toward another female figure cowering below. Though photographs of the models prepared by Belloc are a bit unclear,[50] a report submitted to the Municipal Council describes the monument's appearance in detail and assesses its representation of the French Protectorate and colonization:

> On a high pedestal, in which one sees fragments of Roman monuments recalling the glory of the past, is seated France dressed in Roman attire. She offers a helping hand to Tunisia. The latter stands at the foot of the pedestal, rising like a woman invoking assistance. In the left foreground is a reposing cow, symbolizing agriculture, and to the right is a seated woman representing viticulture. Behind France, a little to the right, is a Tunisian cavalryman on a spirited horse. . . . The female characters are dressed in the Roman style. None of them will wear the indigenous costume. Nothing in the attitudes, or in the expressions of the figures, nor in the clothing will displease any part of the Tunisian population. The impression given by the monumental ensemble is one of homage to France and to the establishment of the Protectorate. The proud posture of the Tunisian cavalier indicates that France has not come to enslave the indigenous people, but that she intends, on the contrary, to maintain in them the sentiments of personal dignity that suit free people.[51]

Hinting at the perceived universality of Rome and references to it, the report's authors suggested that members of the "non-French part of the [European] population" (i.e., Italian nationals) would draw from the apparently noncontroversial and modestly rendered Roman costumes memories of their own past in Tunisia (i.e., ancient Roman) and identify with their shared civilization.[52] References to the clothing

may also be addressing the issue of modesty considered appropriate
for Tunisian viewers. That is to say that the statue did not accentuate
maternal aspects of the personified France figure through the depiction of the woman bare-breasted, as was often the case in post-revo-
lution France (but less so by the end of the nineteenth century).[53] It
was hoped that the monument would "satisfy the moral needs" of the
city's residents, act as an homage to France, and represent concord
among all its inhabitants.[54] Attempts by earlier revolution-era artists
to "resacralize the present by way of a primitive model of Greek and
Roman antiquity" via such imagery seem compatible with the hubris-
tic claims made by nostalgic colonialists in North Africa who pursued a modern corollary to Rome's "civilizing" empire using a similar
symbolic language.[55] This unbuilt monument survives only through
archived documents, published descriptions, and a few images of the
sculptor's rudimentary model.[56]

Completed Marianne-like figures seem to have appeared in colonial Algeria more frequently. This is perhaps not surprising, since
Algeria endured colonial occupation for far longer (1830–1962) than
Tunisia (1881–1956) and was declared an integral part of France in
1848. A prominent example was dedicated to commemorating war
dead in Oran. Erected in 1898 outside the city's grandiose *hôtel de
ville*, the obelisk honored soldiers who had died during the Battle of
Sidi Brahim (1845), which was part of France's bloody conquest of
the country. Dominating the Place d'Armes here in Algeria's second
city, Dalou's winged victory alights at its pinnacle, and at its base his
youthful (and bare-headed) bronze Marianne-like figure, identified
as "La France," on bended knee inscribes the last of many soldiers'
names upon the monument. Her back to the viewer, she defiantly
clutches the tricolor in this unambiguous monument to conquest.[57]

Antoine Bourdelle's 1922 *La France*, a copy of which was erected
outside the Algiers Fine Arts Museum, represented the nation not in
the traditional form of La Marianne but rather as Athena or Minerva,
goddess of wisdom and strategic warfare.[58] Gazing across the city
toward the Mediterranean Sea, spear in hand, this particular representation adds explicit references to knowledge, civilization, and,
again, military prowess. This would have been appropriate for the
colonial context and its ultimate placement outside the city's premier
cultural institution. Rather than an entirely distinct form of representation of France, one might read this monument as an alternate
or enhanced personality for La Marianne, as Agulhon does in his
description of this typology as a "La Marianne des lettrès" that might

have appealed more to elites.[59] There was some flexibility to her more active depiction here, but she remains within the confines of Greco-Roman iconography. In searching for the potential reason for the figural shift seen in the Algiers case, one might turn to Paris in 1931 for an illustrative corollary. There a similar France/Marianne-as-Minerva was used in a statue by Léon-Ernest Drivier variously referred to as *La France de la Paix* (France of Peace) and *La France apportant la paix et la prospérité aux colonies* (France Bringing Peace and Prosperity to the Colonies) erected for the 1931 International Colonial Exposition outside the Museum of the Colonies.[60] Perhaps something appearing more authoritative or academic (but not bellicose) was deemed appropriate for this triumphalist colonial context at that time. Indeed, the awkwardness of celebrating empire with a figure of liberty may have been increasingly felt and could have contributed to the failure of Belloc's proposal for Tunis.

Based on the limited selection of works presented here, it would seem that the colonial context elicited a particularly militaristic aura for La Marianne, whether fighting, mourning, or preening. In Tunisia and Algeria, when she appeared, it was often as a figure representing wisdom and martial strength—both essential elements within the so-called French "civilizing mission." The emphasis was on a strong, active, forceful figure, particularly when contrasted with the rare representation of the North African woman, who appears weak and submissive. With such effect, La Marianne was placed in public spaces generally intended for European use and audiences—war memorials within "European" districts and administrative centers and inside city halls. Colonial authorities seem to have had little concern for causing offense to indigenous people when erecting monuments, at times within zones reserved for Tunisians and Algerians, but female forms were absent.[61] Men still dominated public spaces and zones of contact between "French" and indigenous quarters. Was the abstention from placing La Marianne in closer proximity to indigenous people and places reflective of a sensitivity to cultural difference and North African objections to representations of human forms? Was she deployed here not as a "civilizing missionary" but rather an indicator of France's presence intended to communicate with European audiences who would have been fluent in the symbolism of Western allegory?

La Marianne, Al-Kahina, and Resistance

THE USE OF allegorical representations of the nation and state, though clearly a major part of European artistic traditions, was not limited to the French in the Maghreb. Indeed, North Africans have at various times also represented themselves in the guise of a single mythological female figure. Al-Kahina ("the Diviner," also known as Dihya), a late seventh-century Berber (Amazigh) queen known to have valiantly fought against the Arab invasions that swept across the region during her lifetime, has been an essential figure in much of the historiography of North Africa from both the indigenous and colonial perspectives.[62] The details of her ambiguous identity and accomplishments have been debated—was she Jewish, of mixed race, Semitic in origin, truly hostile to Islam, an effective indigenous leader?—but her role as a powerful female resistance figure remains consistent. Whereas French colonial writers presented her as a Berber of European origin and thus a character in their Roman North African mythology—that is, in support of the anti-Arab Western "civilizing mission" ideology pursued through Roman and then French interventions—many of North Africa's Arab Muslims came to view her as an indigenous opponent of Byzantine/Roman rule and ultimately a champion of Islam. More precisely, Tunisians came to view her as the personification of "the myth of revolutionary Tunisia."[63] For them, the Kahina resisted the oppression of the region's Christian Byzantine rulers and the invasion of Tunisia by Arab outsiders, rather than Islam itself. She ultimately embraced Islam, according to this line of thinking, because it brought order and justice to the region. In this way the Maghrebi discourse inverted the colonial one; the French saw the Romans as sources of civilization and themselves as their descendants, while Tunisians viewed Islam as the civilizing factor and the Kahina as the embodiment of their open, justice-seeking, and rebellious nature as a nation.[64] The parallels between La Marianne as a popular opponent of the unjust *ancien régime* and al-Kahina as a personification of justice and national strength are compelling.

Within the archives one finds a few images of a Kahina-like allegorical figure. The Tunisian nationalist and anticolonial Destour Party published within their propaganda several personifications of Tunisia during the mid-1920s that make use of recognizable iconography drawn from European traditions, suggesting that both allegorical and Roman imagery resonated with Tunisian audiences. In one drawing from 1924, the Destour (Constitutional Liberal) Party rides in a char-

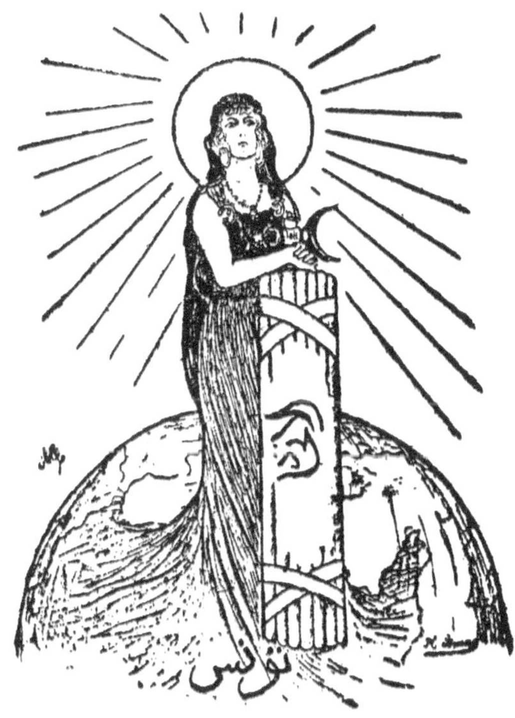

Figure 8. Destourian allegory featuring a
personification of Tunisia (1925). Source: "L'Afrique
française," *Chronique de Tunisie: Août 1922–Août 1928*
(Tunis, 1928), 286. Bibliothèque nationale de France.

iot with fasces representing unity and power. She raises a torch in a
manner recalling New York's iconic *Statue of Liberty* (Liberty Enlight-
ening the World, Frédéric Bartholdi, 1885).[65] Completing a narrative
allegorical scene reminiscent of ancient Roman relief sculptures, a
winged Tunisia in what appears to be Berber attire hovers with a laurel crown of victory overhead. In a drawing from 1925, a similarly
dressed figure representing Tunisia stands proudly, the flowing drapery of her clothing extending from the Tunisian landscape and globe
below (figure 8).

The figure clutches the Roman fasces (a symbol of state power)
topped with a crescent moon.[66] A similar figure appears on the inaugural front page of *Ech-Chabab*, a short-lived satirical Tunisian newspaper, in 1936 (figure 9). There the figure wears a star and crescent

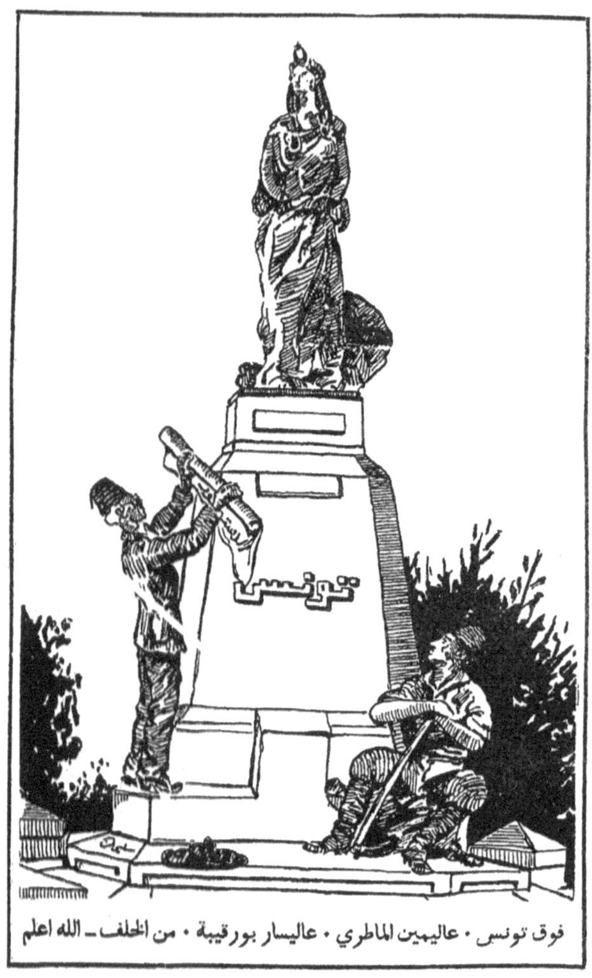

Figure 9. Mercié's Jules Ferry monument reinterpreted in *Ech-Chabab* (October 29, 1936), 1. Source: Beit el Bennani, Tunis.

moon crown (emblems representing Islam taken from the Tunisian flag) and stands at the apex of a tall pedestal labeled Tunisia. Her hands are behind her back (are they bound?); she is being offered plans—a constitution—for the country's future by Habib Bourguiba, a prominent member of the country's nationalist Neo Destour (New Constitutional Liberal) Party and eventually the country's first president. Mahmoud El Materi (the Neo Destour Party's leader at the time) is seated opposite and looks on in the tall *tarbouche* hat of the nationalist.

The full effect of this reimagined piece becomes clearer with a closer look at the referenced monument in Tunis and its origin. The *Ech-Chabab* drawing reconceives the 1899 monument to Jules Ferry, an ardent colonialist and administrator, that had lorded over Tunis's premier tree-lined boulevard (which had since 1900 borne his name) and would through independence in 1956 (see figures 4 and 9).[67] The figure swapping in the drawing is particularly noteworthy, given the composition of Antonin Mercié's first Ferry monument that had been installed in Ferry's hometown, Saint-Dié-des-Vosges, in 1896 and the changes made for the Tunis version referenced in the illustration. In Mercié's original piece, a bronze grouping at the base included a flag-wielding and bonneted Marianne "in a proud and noble posture."[68] Dressed in armor, she gazes up at Ferry while her hand rests on the shoulder of a Vietnamese child conferring with a French boy holding a book. The ensemble commemorates Ferry's staunch republicanism, his advocacy for empire, and his work in education. When erected in Tunis in 1899, however, an identical Ferry stood atop a taller stone pedestal, designed by architect Emile Resplandy, upon which was placed a cast of characters more suited to the North African context. Here the modified statue grouping constituted a "living translation" (*une vive traduction*) of the regionally specific colonial "civilizing mission" through a tableau of submissive Tunisians and benevolent colonists.[69] A "young Arab woman," who has replaced La Marianne, offers a sheaf of wheat to "the regenerator of Tunisia" above, while a colonist farmer watches.[70] A pair of children are also present, as in Saint-Dié, though in Tunis they are relegated to the back of the monument. Unsupervised, the French boy here gestures to the open book while a Tunisian boy, hunched over the page, learns to read.[71] The substitution of a generic Tunisian woman for La Marianne suggests that the latter was deemed less appropriate for the more explicitly colonialist Tunis installation where agriculture and alleged imperial benevolence were paramount.

Bourguiba has replaced the Tunisian woman in the satirical image from 1936, filling the place originally occupied by La Marianne in the original work. Al-Kahina/Tunisia has replaced the subservient Tunisian character. She has been physically elevated and symbolically promoted through her displacement of Ferry. Here one sees Tunisians imagining—at least in a drawing—an alternative form of public commemoration that was impossible at the time but that drew from a representation mode and particular piece with complex histories.[72] The story of this drawn monument and its built antecedents fills out the larger story of commemorative dynamics in the colonial context.

While the Kahina-like figure served as the theoretical and visual embodiment of the Tunisian nation during the final decades of the French Protectorate, several examples of sculptural projects intended to represent the Tunisian Republic in very Marianne- or Liberty-like personas can be found in Tunisian newspapers from the years after its independence in 1956. For example, a project by Jean Bota called the Tunisian Republic depicts a woman crowned in a star and crescent moon diadem carrying the Tunisian flag in her left hand, while in her right she holds aloft a torch in the manner of the *Statue of Liberty*—a reference noted by the author of the article and appropriate given the transition of Tunisia from independent kingdom to republic that had just occurred.[73] Hédi Selmi's torch-wielding Tunisian Liberty strides forward boldly. Her exaggerated form recalls the traditional allegorical image of Liberty popularized by the New York icon and betrays the twenty-three-year-old Tunisois sculptor's enthusiasm for Rodin, which was acknowledged in a published interview.[74] Though looking less like Bartholdi's Liberty, a figure from 1965/66 was described as "La Marianne tunisienne" (Tunisian Marianne) in a 2016 newspaper article announcing its discovery inside a farm building in rural Menzel Bouzelfa.[75] This woman in flowing classical garb and sash wields a sword with its blade downturned, reminiscent of some French republican imagery.[76] The crescent and star that appear in the flag she clutches and on the diadem she wears, however, indicate that the otherwise generic figure represents Tunisia.

Given the fundamentally hybrid nature of the North African nationalist tradition, which "conjoins the French colonial mythology and the Salafi [i.e., Islamicist] one," as well as Tunisia's tendency to see itself as a "land of migration for both men and ideas and an arena of struggle against any unjust system," it is not a surprise to see such intersections among opposing allegorical representations.[77] While the particular attributes suited different identities, the shared idea of representing the nation and state in the form of a female body, within the public realm, is noteworthy. Although al-Kahina has her origin in a historical figure, rather than an abstract personification as seen in the case of La Marianne, the former's ambiguity has allowed her to take on multiple meanings in becoming an allegory, the actual identity of which has become less important.[78]

Conclusion

STATUES OF ACCOMPLISHED Frenchmen dominated the public realm in colonial North Africa, much as they did in France itself. They existed not in isolation but in prominent, central public spaces in Tunis, Algiers, Oran, and elsewhere. A politicized artform blending sculpture, architecture, and urbanism, these monuments were unavoidable landmarks within the colonial city's fabric. Busy roads wrapped around them, landscaped spaces and buildings framed them, and elaborate pedestals held them aloft. Women, however, were represented in abstraction as the personification of the French nation and state. Sometimes they symbolically commanded attention as active conquerors of space, while in other sites they played secondary roles on statue bases and in other media. This of course does not mean that women were appropriately represented, nor should one necessarily see in statues of La Marianne a serious interest in honoring women. A complete indexing of the figure's placement, attributes, and symbolism in colonial contexts remains necessary in order to fully understand the phenomenon. The sampling presented here, however, reveals the potential of such a study that would deepen our understanding of historic statuemania, nineteenth- and twentieth-century allegory, and colonial and postcolonial built environments.

The particular intent of the politicians, sculptors, and architects who participated in the commissioning, design, and installation of these monuments remains somewhat unclear. Within the colonial context, however, one might interpret through these acts not just the extension of Metropolitan practices overseas—where familiar European architectures and cultural norms were often maintained—but also the subjugation of women to the colonial state. Unlike the prominent monuments of Paris that centered La Marianne, she appears in North Africa most often as an ancillary figure whose attributes were intended to aggrandize the men at the core of commemorative discourses. Stepping beyond the age's endemic sexism, the celebration of the female form and freedom in the colonial context may have been deemed inappropriate, given the inherent contradictions of empire. Tunisians, however, in their appropriation of allegory and use of al-Kahina/"La Marianne tunisienne" as a form of resistance, elevate a female form to primary status, albeit still an impersonal one.[79] Such consideration allows one to further see how female bodies were typically celebrated and deployed within patriarchal societies—colonizing, colonized, and postcolonial—in both France and North Africa.

Although the Kahina's fame predates European occupation of North Africa, French and indigenous populations used similar methods to communicate opposing ideas in visual and sculptural languages ultimately drawn from gendered European allegorical traditions. Thus, one may view these conflicting or ambiguous personifications of both victory and liberty as statements of competing sovereignty and compelling evidence of postcolonial cultural hybridity.

Notes

Special thanks are owed to Susan Slyomovics and Abdelmajid Hannoum for their helpful comments on earlier drafts of this chapter. I am also grateful to Valentina Rozas-Krause and Andrew Shanken for their inclusion of this work in their 2020 Society of Architectural Historians conference panel, as well as their supportive feedback on this chapter since then.

1. See, for example, Joan Landes, *Visualizing the Nation: Gender, Representation, and Revolution in Eighteenth-Century France* (Ithaca: Cornell University Press, 2001); Marina Warner, *Monuments and Maidens: The Allegory of the Female Form* (New York: Atheneum, 1985); Anne Dymond, "Embodying the Nation: Art, Fashion, and Allegorical Women at the 1900 Exposition Universelle," *RACAR: Revue d'Art Canadienne/Canadian Art Review* 36, no. 2 (2011): 1–14.

2. The considerable variation seen in La Marianne's representation and the different ways in which French artists rendered her and related personifications of Liberty, France, and the Republic are addressed throughout this chapter as appropriate, but this is not the venue for a detailed interrogation of all the nuanced meanings.

3. On La Marianne in general, see Maurice Agulhon, *Marianne au combat: L'Imagerie et la symbolique républicaine de 1789 à 1880* (Paris: Flammarion, 1979), republished as *Marianne into Battle: Republican Imagery and Symbolism in France, 1789–1880*, trans. Janet Lloyd (Cambridge: Cambridge University Press, 1981); Maurice Agulhon, *Marianne au pouvoir: L'Imagerie et la symbolique républicaine de 1880 à 1914* (Paris: Flammarion, 1989); Maurice Agulhon, *Les métamorphoses de Marianne: L'Imagerie et la symbolique républicaine de 1914 à nos jours* (Paris: Flammarion, 2001); Bertrand Tillier, "Le corps de Marianne," in *La Républicature: La caricature politique en France, 1870–1914* (Paris: CNRS, 1997), 34–39; Richard Sennett, "Freedom in Body and Space," in *Flesh and Stone: The Body and the City in Western Civilization* (New York: W. W. Norton, 1994), 285–96; Lynn Hunt, *Politics, Culture, and Class in the French Revolution* (Berkeley: University of California Press, 2004).

4. Charles-Étienne Gaucher, *Iconologie, ou Traité de la science des allegories*, vol. 3 (Paris: Lattré, 1796), 31.

5. Agulhon, *Marianne into Battle*, 11–13; Yvonne Korshak, "The Liberty Cap as a Revolutionary Symbol in America and France," *Smithsonian Studies in American Art* 1, no. 2 (1987): 53. The cap is frequently referred to as a "Phrygian cap." Although this floppy type, which was used by ancient Greeks to represent

Phrygia (in Asia Minor) as well as generic "exotic" others, resembles the Roman *pileus* (which was not always peaked), it was not the same thing. The Phrygian cap was not initially a symbol of manumission, but it came to be regarded as one because it was confused with the *pileus*. This peaked "Phrygian" type was the standard form used in France. Korshak, "The Liberty Cap," 58–59. See also Richard Wrigley, "Liberty Caps: From Roman Emblem to Radical Headgear," in *The Politics of Appearances: Representations of Dress in Revolutionary France* (New York: Berg, 2002), 136–43.

6. Agulhon, *Marianne into Battle*, 18.

7. Antoine de Baecque, "The Allegorical Image of France, 1750–1800: A Political Crisis of Representation," *Representations* 47 (1994): 127. Benjamin's 1928 thesis was titled *The Origin of German Tragic Drama*. See de Baecque, "Allegorical Image," 112–13.

8. Ibid., 127. "The function of the sign was totally reversed. The monarchical sign was a face, a ubiquitous portrait that signified a nation and a principle—the France of traditional values. The sign of the Republic was a value, a principle that signified a body and an emblematic face—the figure of Liberty, soon to be Marianne" (ibid., 128). See also Agulhon, *Marianne into Battle*, 20–21.

9. Heidi E. Kraus, "Looking to the Past: Street Art Public Spaces, and Contemporary French Identity," in *Social Practice Art in Turbulent Times: The Revolution Will Be Live*, ed. Kristina Olson and Eric J. Schruers (New York: Routledge, 2019), 121–22; Marina Warner, "The Slipped Chiton," in *Monuments and Maidens*, 267–93; Agulhon, *Marianne into Battle*, 186–90.

10. Agulhon, *Les métamorphoses*; Tillier, "Le corps," 34–39; Agulhon, *Marianne into Battle*, 136–61; Maurice Agulhon, "Un usage de la femme au XIXe siècle: L'allégorie de la République," *Romantisme* 13–14 (1976): 149–50; Wrigley, "Liberty Caps," 150–68. Though largely forgotten today, the cap as a symbol of liberty was used in the American revolutionary context (initially by Paul Revere) before it became popular in French iconography. See Korshak, "The Liberty Cap," 53–58.

11. Janice Best, *Les monuments de Paris sous la Troisième République: Contestation et commémoration du passé* (Paris: L'Harmattan, 2010), 61–94.

12. Agulhon, *Les métamorphoses*, 9.

13. On coinage, banknotes, and stamps featuring such representations, see Patrick Laurens, "La Figure officielle de la République française: Monnaies et timbres," in *La France démocratique: Combats, mentalités, symboles*, ed. Christophe Charle et al. (Paris: La Sorbonne, 1998), 421–29; Laura Anne Kalba, "Beautiful Money: Looking at La Semeuse in Fin-de-Siècle France," *Art Bulletin* 102, no. 1 (2020): 55–78; Alain Chatriot, "L'impossible 'Marianne': La politique philatélique colonial française (1849–1962)," in *La République et ses symbols*, ed. Évelyne Cohen and Gérard Monnier (Paris: Éditions de la Sorbonne, 2013), 193–203, http://books.openedition.org/psorbonne/58312. On later manifestations of La Marianne and French identity, see Kraus, "Looking."

14. Sergiusz Michalski, "Democratic 'Statuomania' in Paris," in *Public Monuments: Art in Political Bondage 1870–1997* (London: Reaktion, 1998), 16. On the early use of Marianne busts in French government buildings in France (and statues in public spaces), see Agulhon, *Marianne into Battle*, 168–76; Charlotte Pon-Willemsen, "Les premiers bustes de la République: *Marianne n'est pas fille de*

Paris," in *La République,* ed. Cohen and Monnier, 135–42; Yvan Boude, "Marianne et le Président: Socio-histoire du décor municipal sous la Troisième République," in *La République,* ed. Cohen and Monnier, 237–46.

15. Tillier, "Le corps," n.p.

16. Landes, *Visualizing,* 76.

17. Joan Landes, "Representing the Body Politic: The Paradox of Gender in the Graphic Politic of the French Revolution," in *Rebel Daughters: Women and the French Revolution,* ed. Sara E. Melzer and Leslie W. Rabine (New York: Oxford University Press, 1992), 31, 32 (emphasis original).

18. See Joan Landes, *Women in the Public Sphere in the Age of the French Revolution* (Ithaca: Cornell University Press, 1988).

19. Agulhon, *Marianne into Battle,* 183–85. Mary's significance notwithstanding, she remains secondary to her divine son and thus Marianne would find herself on unequal footing with the supreme state. Although the precise origin of the Marianne name remains unclear, it may be a portmanteau of Mary and Anne (the Virgin and her mother). Ibid., 30–34. See also Agulhon, *Marianne au pouvoir,* 175–81.

20. Agulhon, "Un usage de la femme," 151.

21. June Hargrove, *The Statues of Paris: An Open-air Pantheon* (New York: Vendome Press, 1989), 7.

22. For a general account of *statuomanie,* see Michalski, "Democratic," 13–55; Hargrove, *The Statues,* 105–261. Precise statistics are elusive, but June Hargrove states that more than 150 statues were erected outdoors in the capital during those years, amounting to a sixfold increase from the preceding sixty years. Hargrove, *The Statues,* 105. Michalski estimates that the total number of public monuments erected in Paris during the Third Republic was approximately 200. See Michalski, "Democratic," 44, 45.

23. Hargrove, *The Statues,* 111; "To Stop Statue Mania," *New York Times,* July 23, 1911, 1. The proposed ban was not enacted. In 1913 alone, thirty completed statues awaited pedestals and sites in Paris. Michalski, "Democratic," 44. See also Maurice Agulhon, "La 'statuomanie' et l'histoire," *Ethnologie française* 8, no. 2/3 (1978): 145–72. Agulhon attributed the major increase in monumental statuary in France to that country's defeat during the Franco-Prussian War of 1870–71. Despite the claims by some that *statuomanie*'s origin lay in France, Read contends that it began in Britain twenty years earlier, following the death of Robert Peel and several other notable public figures. See Benedict Read, "The British Contribution to Statuemania in the 19th Century," in *La sculpture au XIXe siècle,* ed. Aurore de Neuville (Paris: Chaudun, 2008), 370–77. War heroes were less celebrated in the republican context than they had been during the earlier eras. On the placement of statues in Paris, see Michalski, "Democratic," 28–31; Hargrove, *The Statues,* 185–95.

24. Robert Aldrich, "Of Men and Monuments," in *Vestiges of the Colonial Empire in France: Monuments, Museums, and Colonial Memories* (New York: Palgrave Macmillan, 2005), 157–95; Robert Aldrich, "On Colonial Sites and New Uses in Contemporary Paris," in *Neocolonialism and Built Heritage: Echoes of Empire in Africa, Asia, and Europe,* ed. Daniel E. Coslett (New York: Routledge, 2020), 23–41.

25. Michalski, "Democratic," 27. See also Hargrove, *The Statues,* 105.

26. Eric Hobsbawm, "Mass-Producing Traditions: Europe, 1870–1914," in *The Invention of Tradition*, ed. Eric Hobsbawm and Terrance Ranger (Cambridge: Cambridge University Press, 1983), 270–73; Isabelle Rouge-Ducos, "Les 14 Juillet à l'arc de triomphe de l'Étoile, de la IIIᵉ République à la Libération," in *La République*, ed. Cohen and Monnier, 75–86.

27. Marianne was of course a part of this too. For more on this during the revolutionary period in public spaces, see Agulhon, *Marianne into Battle*, 25–27.

28. Agulhon, "La 'statuomanie,'" 146.

29. Michalski, "Democratic," 49.

30. Though many statues were melted down across Europe during the war, the process in France was particularly robust and ideologically motivated. Surveys indicate that 1,527–1,750 statues were taken from the public domain (which excludes war memorials and monuments on Church property) during the Nazi occupation of France (October 1941 to August 1944). Kirrily Freeman, *Bronzes to Bullets: Vichy and the Destruction of French Public Statuary, 1941–1944* (Stanford: Stanford University Press, 2008), 1–2; Michalski, "Democratic," 49–55. See also Hargrove, *The Statues*, 302–6; Jean Cocteau and Pierre Jahan, *La mort et les statues* (Paris: Editions du Compas, 1946).

31. Hargrove, *The Statues*, 254–61.

32. Zeynep Çelik, *Empire, Architecture, and the City: French-Ottoman Encounters, 1830–1914* (Seattle: University of Washington Press, 2008), 132–34; Zeynep Çelik, "Colonial Statues and Their Afterlives," *Journal of North African Studies* 25, no. 5 (2020): 711–26; Claire Garcia, "Migrations, transferts et réécritures: Le destin des monuments publics d'Algérie après l'Indépendance," *Les Cahiers de l'école du Louvre* 12 (2018), https://journals.openedition.org/cel/920.

33. Çelik, *Empire*, 235. Explicit references to the French Revolution that were essential to Bastille Day events in France were generally less apparent in colonial contexts. On the appropriation of Bastille Day among indigenous Algerians during the 1930s as an act of resistance and appeal to the universalist claims of the French Revolution, see Jan Jansen, "Celebrating the 'Nation' in a Colonial Context: 'Bastille Day' and the Contested Public Space in Algeria, 1880–1939," *Journal of Modern History* 85, no. 1 (2013): 36–68.

34. Çelik, "Colonial Statues"; Alison McQueen, "Politics and Public Sculpture in Nineteenth-Century Colonial French Algeria," *Sculpture Journal* 28, no. 1 (2019): 7–34.

35. The Tunisian National Archives contains correspondence on erecting monuments in Tunis to Paul Cambon, Jean-Baptiste Curtelin, Massicault, Maréchal Pétain, and World War I dead, as well. Lavigerie statues were also installed in both Biskara and Algiers, Algeria.

36. Bizerte also had a statue in honor of dead soldiers and the city's *Contrôle Civil*. A monument in memory of those killed in the sensational *Farfadet* (submarine) accident near Ferryville was installed there in 1909. This listing, which may be incomplete, is based on available photographs and postcards observed by the author. Jan Jansen has identified at least thirty-four monument dedications in Algeria from 1884 to 1914. Jan Jansen, "1880–1914: Une 'statuomanie' à l'algérienne," in *Histoire de l'Algérie à la période coloniale (1830–1962)*, ed. Abderrahmane Bouchène et al. (Paris: Découverte, 2012), 263. No such total

has yet been calculated for neighboring Tunisia, but based on the relatively few known monuments to have been installed in central Tunis, it seems fair to assume a far smaller nationwide total. When the prominent statue of Jules Ferry was inaugurated in 1889, it was said to have been the first since the fall of the Roman Empire (and thus the city's only public statue). René Millet, "Discours de M. René Millet," in *A Jules Ferry, Tunis, 24 avril 1899*, ed. Gaston Deschamps (Paris: Chaix, 1899), 15.

37. Frantz Fanon, *The Wretched of the Earth*, trans. Richard Philcox (New York: Grove Press, 2004), 15.

38. Garcia, "Migrations." A statue of Joan of Arc by Emmanuel Fremiet was installed in Paris in 1874. It was the first public moment erected by the Third Republic. Joan of Arc (c. 1412–31), though a historical figure, was in many ways an allegorical entity that symbolized "hope and reconciliation" in a divided country at that time. Hargrove, *The Statues*, 106. The "masculinity" of her accomplishments set her apart from the abstract, typically maternal, Marianne. Michalski, "Democratic," 14–16. On statues of her in Paris, see Best, *Les monuments*, 127–40.

39. The statue by Bosio, known variously as *The Law*, *The Republic*, and *Liberty*, bears the date 1849. On winged victories, see the chapter by Susan Slyomovics in the present volume. On the imagery of the Second Republic, see Agulhon, *Marianne into Battle*, 100–121.

40. François Béguin, *Arabisances: Décor architectural et tracé urbain en Afrique du nord, 1830–1950* (Paris: Dunod, 1983). Béguin contrasts this style with the generally neoclassical "style of the conqueror" more associated with earlier colonial assimilationist policies.

41. Guy worked in Tunisia from 1900 to 1918 and was the chief proponent of the Arabesque aesthetic—what he called "modern architecture in the Arab style" during that time. He primarily built in Tunis and Sfax. In the latter his works defined the visual identity of the city center. See Fabienne Crouzet, "L'Orientalisme architectural en Tunisie: Œuvre et carrière de Raphaël Guy (1869–1918)," *ABE Journal* 13 (2018), http://journals.openedition.org/abe/4593.

42. On municipal busts, see Agulhon, *Marianne au pouvoir*, 37–68; Agulhon, *Marianne into Battle*, 168–70.

43. Belloc (1863–1919) was a French sculptor trained at the École des beaux-arts in Paris whose works were installed in cities across France and in several cities in Algeria and Tunisia. His dismantled *Monument to the Glory of French Colonial Expansion* (1913) can still be seen, in pieces, in Paris's Tropical Garden park. On the park and its colonial relics, see Aldrich, "Old Colonial Sites," 25–28. On Dalou's iconic Paris monument, see Richard Thomson, *The Troubled Republic: Visual Culture and Social Debate in France, 1889–1900* (New Haven: Yale University Press, 2004), 1–7; Best, *Les monuments*, 61–94; Michalski, "Democratic," 17–24.

44. *La Dépêche tunisienne*, January 25, 1903, n.p., in National Archives of Tunisia (ANT) FPC/M5/0011/0004. The short piece mentions the existence of two different monuments being considered but attributes to this one a "special character of originality and artistic cachet."

45. Ibid. Some maintained that waiting until the twenty-fifth anniversary of the Protectorate (1906) made more sense. See Conseil Municipal, Tunis, "Extrait

du registre des délibérations: Exercice 1903, session ordinaire (1er trimestre), séance du 23 janvier 1903," 7, in ANT FPC/M5/0011/0004.

46. "Nos échos: Les gloires africaines," *La Revue nord africaine*, February 5, 1903, n.p., in ANT FPC/M5/0011/0004. To the monument being described here, the article attributes a "special character of originality and artistic cachet." No mention of the second type's form is made. Ibid.

47. Ibid.

48. Ibid.

49. The second proposed monument was said in ibid. to depict a woman in antique attire reaching down from a tall pedestal to take the hand of a female representing Tunisia. As there is no mention of a chariot or horses, it is likely that the monument being discussed here is the one for which photographs of the models survive.

50. Photographs without attribution found in "Correspondances, notes. . . relatifs de l'érection d'un monument commémoratif à la gloire de la France et de la colonisation. . . . ," in ANT FPC/M5/0011/0004.

51. Conseil Municipal, "Extrait. . . 23 janvier 1903," 4. Note that there is no mention of a second proposed monument including a chariot, as discussed in "Nos échos," leading one to question the validity of their assertion that there were two types. A third description found in a 1903 issue of *La Croix* reveals subtle differences yet again. The statue grouping is described in this case as a mound decorated in shallow reliefs of Tunisian agricultural products—including date palms, wheat, olive trees, and vines—surmounted by a flag-wielding France. Tunisia is represented below her by "an Arab woman of the country." France places her hand on the Tunisia's shoulder. The latter turns toward her and "in a gesture of gratitude" offers her an olive branch and wheat sheath. Elsewhere, an armed Zouave "in an attitude of rest"—representing a vigilant and confident Army of Africa—watches guard over France and Tunisia. "Beaux projets," *La Croix*, February 15/16, 1903, 3.

52. Conseil Municipal, "Extrait. . . 23 janvier 1903," 4.

53. See Landes, *Visualizing*.

54. Conseil Municipal, "Extrait. . . 23 janvier 1903," 6.

55. Landes, *Visualizing*, 76.

56. In 1943 the landscaped square would become the site of an unknown World War II soldier's tomb, which was relocated at independence. Daniel E. Coslett, "(Re)branding a (Post)colonial Streetscape: Tunis's Avenue Bourguiba and the Road Ahead," *International Journal of Islamic Architecture* 6, no. 1 (2017): 67, 71.

57. Maurice Dreyfous, *Dalou: Sa vie et sa œuvre* (Paris: Renouard-Laurens, 1903), 194–96. See also the chapter by Susan Slyomovics in the present volume. On the postcolonial life of the monument (and historic preservation in Algeria more broadly), see Diana Wylie, "The Importance of Being at-Home: A Defense of Historic Preservation in Algeria," *Change Over Time* 2, no. 2 (2012): 172–87.

58. Various copies of this work were installed in different locations in France. The Algiers version was initially placed at the entry of the Foire d'Alger in 1935 before it was installed outside the art museum. It was destroyed by members of the Algerian resistance in 1961. A copy can be seen today outside the Palais de

Tokyo in Paris. Théophile Bruand, "La 'France' de Bourdelle," *Mémoire Vive* 45 (2010), available at Centre de documentation historique sur l'Algérie, https://www.cdha.fr/la-france-de-bourdelle.

59. Agulhon, *Marianne au pouvoir*, n.p. See also ibid., 184–86.

60. "The Colonial Exposition of 1931," Palais de la Porte Dorée, https://www.palais-portedoree.fr/en/colonial-exposition-1931.

61. See, for example, the highly provocative installation of the Duc d'Orléans in Algiers and a Bible-wielding statue of Cardinal Lavigerie set inside the Tunis medina in 1925. Zeynep Çelik, "Historic Intersections: The Center of Algiers," in *Walls of Algiers*, ed. Zeynep Çelik, Julia Clancy-Smith, and Francis Terpak (Seattle: University of Washington Press, 2009), 198–226; Daniel E. Coslett, "Broadening the Study of North Africa's Planning History: Urban Development and Heritage Preservation in Protectorate-era and Postcolonial Tunis," in *Urban Planning in North Africa*, ed. Carlos Nunes Silva (New York: Ashgate, 2016), 115–32.

62. Benjamin Hendrickx, "Al-Kahina: The Last Ally of the Roman-Byzantines in the Maghreb against the Muslim Arab Conquest?" *Journal of Early Christian History* 3, no. 2 (2013): 47–61; Abdelmajid Hannoum, *Colonial Histories, Postcolonial Memories: The Legend of the Kahina, a North African Heroine* (Portsmouth, NH: Heinemann, 2001). On al-Kahina within colonial and postcolonial historiographies across North Africa, see Hannoum, *Colonial Histories*, 29–69, 111–60.

63. Hannoum, *Colonial Histories*, 118.

64. She would also come to represent different elements of Berber nationalism, the Jewish nation, and women more broadly, often in conflicting ways. Her being a woman is, in fact, the most consistent element of her mythological identity. See ibid., 135–50. In this way she represented the unique Tunisian nation rather than an eastern Arab one. Similar claims about Tunisia's hybrid identity and rejection of unjust systems have persisted since independence and gained additional currency in light of the 2011 revolution.

65. A gift from France to the United States, the *Statue of Liberty* was the product of ongoing debates about representing the concept of freedom. The use of a radiant crown here can be seen in the Great Seal of the (Second) French Republic (1848). Light, as a common allegorical reference to enlightenment and liberty, was also symbolized as the sun, a torch and star hovering over the figure's head. Agulhon, *Marianne into Battle*, 94–95.

66. Images reproduced in "L'Afrique française," *Chronique de Tunisie: Août 1922–Août 1928* (Tunis: n.p., 1928), 256, 286.

67. On the avenue, see Coslett, "(Re)branding."

68. "Inauguration du monument élevé à Jules Ferry à Saint-Dié," *Mémorial des Vosges*, July 28, 1896, 1. An exact copy of this monument was also installed in Haiphong, in French colonial Vietnam. Paris installed a different Ferry monument in the Tuileries gardens in 1910 that included a Marianne figure guiding a child toward a teacher and book on its base. Hargrove, *The Statues*, 123. Mercié (1845–1916) was a prolific sculptor. His monumental equestrian statue of the Confederate general Robert E. Lee was unveiled in Richmond, Virginia, in 1890 (and taken down in 2021).

69. Georges Perrot, "7 mai," in *A Jules Ferry*, 38.

70. Ibid. See also Çelik, *Empire*, 134.

71. Also on the reverse was a portrait medallion of Jules Barthélemy-Saint Hilaire (1805–95), France's foreign minister under Ferry and an ardent supporter of Tunisia's annexation. Perrot, "7 mai," 38.

72. No such substitution was made here, although a statue of al-Kahina has been erected in Baghai, Algeria (presumed to be her hometown). Tunis's Ferry monument was razed after independence. An equestrian statue of Bourguiba (Hachemi Marzouk, 1978) now stands on the former Place Jules-Ferry, having been installed there in 2016. Originally located just east of the spot in 1978, it was sent to suburban La Goulette in 1987 before its recent return to the avenue. Coslett, "(Re)branding," 71–73, 83. On the fate of colonial monuments in Algeria and Tunisia, see also Alain Amato, *Monuments en exil* (Paris: Atlanthrope, 1979); Susan Slyomovics, "Dismantling a World: France's Monumental Military Heritage in Sidi-Bel-Abbès, Algeria," *Journal of North African Studies* 25, no. 5 (2020): 772–96; Çelik, "Colonial Statues"; Garcia, "Migrations."

73. "La République Tunisienne de M. Bota a un mois et pèse une tonne," *La Presse*, August 8, 1957, 3.

74. "Selmi Hédi: Sculpteur des symboles," *La Presse*, August 28, 1957, 3. Selmi, who was trained in Tunis and Paris, would go on to become an official sculptor of the Tunisian state and complete numerous works installed across the country for the government.

75. Abdel Aziz Hali, "La Marianne tunisienne tient compagnie à Bourguiba," *La Presse Magazine*, no. 1520, December 11, 2016, 12–13. A matching painting of Bourguiba appears nearby.

76. See *The Republic* of Jean-François Soitoux (1850), which was the first official portrait statue of the new republic, commissioned by the state in 1848.

77. Hannoum, *Colonial Histories*, 149.

78. Some French authors during the colonial period equated al-Kahina with Joan of Arc. On the problematic nature of such equations, see ibid., 47–49.

79. The relatively high social and political status of women in postcolonial Tunisia is noteworthy, although the culture remains an essentially patriarchal one. The way in which this intersects with the production of these artforms remains a potential relationship worth considering.

Susan Slyomovics

8. Female Winged Victory Statues in French Algeria

ON JUNE 15, 1858, M. Ribot, a colonel in the French Engineering Corps (*Génie militaire*) stationed in Constantine, Algeria's third city, discovered a well-preserved bronze Winged Victory statuette in the foundations of the town's medieval-era mosque. The context of his find is more than a curiosity and helps open up a complex reading of this female figure in particular, and in general, female allegorical statues depicting victory (as well as liberty and war) in French Algeria (1830–1962). Such allegorical female statues of victory were part of a widespread phenomenon exported from France to conquered Algeria. The ways that gender might or might not shape these allegories are reminders that gender does not equal women. Rather, gender is the concept for socially constructed associations and experiences that present particular bodies saturated with power relations. In France's Algerian provinces, a Winged Victory statue represents foremost the vastly unequal relations between settlers and military colonizers overseeing the native colonized populations. Analyzing where the statue was found, who found it, and why it lives in the colonial-built Constantine Cirta Museum lends weight to this proposition: like other female allegorical representations in French Algeria, commemorative allegories silence gender in the interest of conveying the meanings and structures of settler colonialism through personified imagery.

Even Winged Victory, a Greco-Roman symbol of purity and perfection, was transfigured into a symbol closely identified with racialized forms of French colonial supremacy. Frantz Fanon's depiction of the clear cause-and-effect relationship between form and function, signifier and signified aptly configures frameworks of remembering by the colonized:

> A world of statues, the statue of the general who carried out the conquest, the statue of the engineer who built the bridge; a world which is sure of itself, which crushed with its stones the backs flayed by whips.[1]

Ribot found Constantine's Winged Victory in the mosque of the Qasbah (citadel) quarter built during the Hafsid dynasty (1230–1514), rulers over Tunis and Algeria's eastern regions. After 1514, Constantine and its extended environs became attached to the Regency of Algiers as the Ottoman Beylik of the East for over three centuries until the French invasion of Algiers in July 1830 ended Ottoman sovereignty. After the capitulation of Algiers, the French turned to Constantine, a much more difficult, lengthy expedition that called for the combined French naval and land forces in two prolonged sieges. Despite heroic resistance by Constantine's city dwellers, seven years later the city walls were breached in 1837.

As with other urban areas in Algeria, France's military occupation led to the demolition of three of Constantine's precolonial Ottoman quarters, including the ramparts of the Qasbah. The Winged Victory statuette was unearthed after sections of the Ottoman fortress walls were razed.[2] Military *percement* ("piercing") penetrated and destroyed the urban fabric of many walled North African towns. Such engineering practices preceded and overlapped with bulldozing the central streets of Paris, a vast public works program known as "Haussmannization" undertaken by Georges-Eugène Haussmann (1809–1891).[3] Algeria's cities became an early laboratory to test modern ideas about urban design implemented through authoritarian measures. The Winged Victory statuette is material evidence that for North Africa, the French army of invasion and occupation remade Constantine through the creation of a new colonial European sector characterized by linear streets, wide boulevards, open squares, and military barracks. After Algeria's Islamic-era ramparts were bulldozed, the region's pre-Ottoman past as a flourishing Roman province with abundant Greco-Roman statuary was appropriated, effaced, or stored in museums in order to serve as a foundational colonial myth: the statuette was proof of a Roman legacy, which in turn was deployed to justify colonization by associating imperial France with Roman and Christianized Africa.[4]

Ribot, the acknowledged claimant to the Winged Victory archaeological find, belonged to the nineteenth-century class of French officers in Algeria who considered themselves direct inheritors of Rome in Africa. They asserted affiliations with the Roman legions, the exemplary military units in French eyes, and they also evoked ties to a Latin past (*latinité*) to connect themselves to the conquered Algerian lands and Greco-Roman antiquity through archaeological digs.[5] French scholars of the time conjectured that Roman vestiges in the statuette's vicinity belonged to a temple and fountain complex.[6] These archaeological findings, which produced extensive museum holdings in Algeria and France from the early decades of colonization, owed much to these amateur French army expeditions. Otherwise, artifact discoveries often came about from settler agricultural dispossession of native lands, for example, when a European colonist's plow rooted out another Winged Victory female statue in El-Meridj, Algeria, for deposit in another newly created local museum.[7] By the same token, after dismantling the precolonial Ottoman walled city and exhuming Winged Victory, the *Génie militaire* at the behest of Colonel Ribot gifted the statuette to the commune of Constantine. From there, it joined the collection of the colonial-era Museum of Constantine, currently Algeria's Cirta Constantine Museum, where it is on display even now.

The soldier, engineer, archaeologist, epigrapher, and museum curator each in turn immediately recognized the value and beauty of the Winged Victory statuette. Auguste Cherbonneau (1813–1882), a French professor of Arabic based in eastern Algeria and founder of the Archaeological Society of Constantine, in 1862 noted for the museum catalog:

> This figurine is considered to be the most important piece (*la pièce capitale*) of the museum. . . ravishing and airy. The features have an ideal purity: the head responding to other parts with distinction stands proudly; and the limbs, light in size, seem to act and glide into ethereal regions impelled by the wings. It is something above human nature, a celestial being, a goddess.[8]

Figure 1 is a first sketch, reproduced for Cherbonneau's 1882 album of the Museum of Constantine's holdings and illustrated by Laurent-

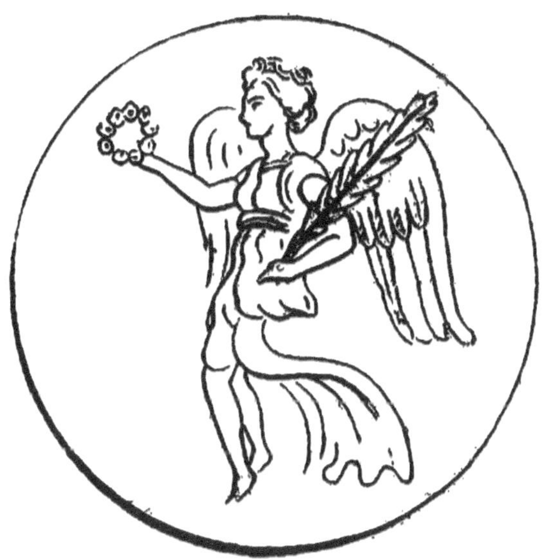

Figure 1. Laurent-Charles Féraud, sepia original in
Cherbonneau (1882), Plate III.

Charles Féraud (1829–1888), a distinguished career army interpreter,
painter, and erudite author of numerous historical descriptions of
colonial Algeria.[9]

A second image of the statuette (figure 2) is a sepia-tone, double-
sided photograph from 1890 which accompanied a scholarly article
by August Audollent (1864–1943), an archaeologist and epigrapher of
Roman North Africa. Audollent preferred accurate photos and criti-
cized Féraud's sketch in figure 1 for his insertion of imagined sheaves
and the laurel wreath that her hands traditionally held out.[10] Nonetheless, Féraud's reimagined Winged Victory sketch reveals prevailing
ideas concerning her associated iconographic accessories.

Both Féraud and Audollent relied on scholarly research about cult
statues to the goddess Victory from ancient Carthage, Rome, and
Pompeii. At the turn of the century, available publications circulated
about Winged Victory statues enshrined in temples or gracing span-
drels above Rome's central Arch of Constantine the Great, dedicated
in 315 CE to mark his military victory.[11] Scholars concluded that
Rome had assimilated the Greek goddess Nike and renamed her the
equivalent Victoria. Both personified victory in war and sport and

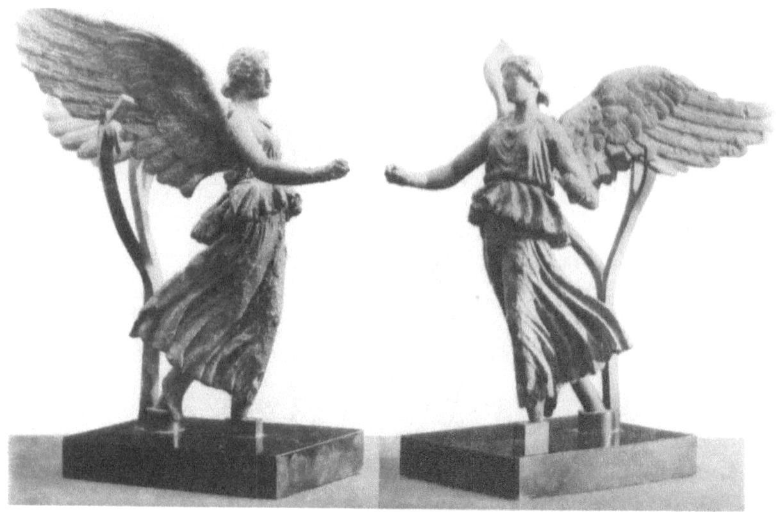
Figure 2. Photographs in Audollent (1890).

both were often described as messengers whose large wings in flight helped deliver news of victory. Sometimes Victory held a trumpet in her right hand and a scepter in her left or proffered the insignia of victory such as a laurel, fillet, palm, or a trophy. Extant collections attest to her widespread appearance on coins, reliefs, statues, columns of victory monuments, and temple and vase decorations beginning in the sixth century BCE (labeled by art historians as the Archaic period) and well into the Roman era. Her image appears on coins found in Algeria, both Punic and Roman ones (solidus), the latter issued by Constantine I.[12] For French colonial scholars of the antique world, it was not surprising that Winged Victory was to be found in the city of Cirta, which had been razed during an uprising against Rome, rebuilt in 313 CE, renamed to honor Constantine, and transformed into the most Romanized urban center of North Africa. Arising in the Greco-Roman Mediterranean region, the Winged Victory motif that arrived in Roman North Africa had signified empire, the emperor Constantine who had converted to Christianity, and Roman military victories. Centuries later, this motif signified French military victories.

The gender of an allegorical statue such as Victory is brought out by comparing the Winged Victory of Constantine with the well-known Victory of Samothrace, a statue of Nike. The Constantine Victory discovered by the French military in 1858 is dated to the fourth century CE. It measures nine inches (23 mm) and is relatively intact. In contrast, the Victory of Samothrace statue (ca. 220–185 BCE) was discovered in 1863 (or five years after Constantine's statuette) by Charles Champoiseau (1830–1909), an amateur archaeologist and French vice-consul in Greece. Today, the iconic white marble Nike, also a relic from the antique world, is dramatically displayed in the Louvre Museum at the top of the Daru Staircase. Standing nine feet tall and appearing to helm the prow of a ship, the statue continues to inspire artists to this day despite its famously fragmentary nature: it is missing its head, parts of its torso, portions of drapery, and one wing.[13] Although both the Constantine and Samothrace versions were thought to be sited in public spaces—presumably in sanctuaries devoted to deities—currently both artworks inhabit Algerian and French museums, respectively, far removed from their original ritual public functions. In contrast to the Nike of the Louvre, the embodiment of material ruin and a vision of sensual motion and feminine beauty, instead the Winged Victory statues in Algeria's public spaces embody the abstract virtues of the French nation. This is because Winged Victory, according to Marina Warner, is that rare figure to persevere in sculptural form across centuries with no known associated myths, despite moving uninterruptedly from Greece to Rome to Christian Europe. Warner insists that Winged Victory stands as:

> pure personification, first of desire, the desire for success, and then of its realization, success itself. By the side of Athena or Zeus, she personifies the power they have to change human fortunes, and when she crosses the barrier from the divine universe into the human, she signifies that those fortunes have been changed for the best, for the person at whose side she stands or whose head she crowns, for the state on whose beaked ships she alights. . . . Nike has no children, no lovers; she exists outside human suffering, as success.[14]

Warner attributes little female sexuality to Winged Victory, a conclusion underscored by Simone de Beauvoir, who did not count her among female statues. French gender divides in sculpture distinguish between a figural tradition of *aux grands hommes* ("to great men") which led to the placement of heroic, historically attested male statuary as opposed to idealized allegorical women with no reality beyond their form and the virtues they represent. This lack of great women was acknowledged as late as 1949 by de Beauvoir, who lamented that "it is remarkable that in Paris out of one thousand statues (excepting the queens who form the corbel of the Luxembourg for purely architectural reasons), there are only ten raised to women. Three are dedicated to Joan of Arc."[15] Instead, monumental sculpted female allegories in public spaces represented national sovereign qualities or purportedly universal values such as the Law, Nation, Liberty, Equality, Justice, Nature, and, from 1792, the French Republic herself.[16]

From Christian France across the Mediterranean to Muslim-majority French colonial Algeria, Winged Victory transformed again. Allegorical sculptures decorated the Paris Panthéon, according to art historian Erika Naginski, as "the Enlightenment dream of finding, somewhere between language and image, a universal sign accessible to all."[17] The "universal sign" of Winged Victory statues that emerged from an interwar *statuomanie* was rooted in wars and subsidized by a vast French state-supported program.[18] Statuary intended for durability, permanence, and immobility was an ideal way to memorialize the French nation's colonial troops, equal only in death and then on war memorial commemorations. At the same time, this French "mania" for memorializing their World War I dead in sculpture demonstrated the ways in which Roman North African artifacts such as Winged Victory were appropriated in the service of an allegorical demotic figure to stand for legitimating the French conquest of Algeria. Exported from the metropole to France's North African prize colony, memorializing war was a project that continued nineteenth-century statuemania by making and erecting statues throughout Algeria's cities and villages.

After World War I, public art commemorations intensified to honor the elevated death rates of European settler soldiers of Algeria who served with the forcibly conscripted so-called Algerian Muslim "native" troops. Universal military conscription was enforced in France by the law of March 21, 1905. Seven years after France's conscription law, the decree of February 3, 1912, added France's overseas colonies to mass conscription. Algeria's three bureaucratically constituted communities—to resort to colonial categorizations—were the European settler (*colon*) who was a French citizen, the "native" Muslim (*indigene*) who was a subject but not a citizen, and the "native" Algerian Jew enfranchised as a French citizen (*Français Israélites d'Algérie* or Français Algériens de religion juive) by France's Crémieux Decree of October 24, 1870. Although all three communities provided soldiers for two world wars and other battlefields, unlike European settlers and enfranchised Algerian Jews, there was no modification to military service for the Muslim population despite their legal status as subjects, not citizens.[19]

Some 26,000 Algerian Muslim soldiers were killed in the Great War and thousands wounded. For French citizens of Algeria (European settlers and enfranchised native Algerian Jews), the numbers of the dead ranged between 12,000 and 22,000 soldiers. In the interwar period in the colony, the ubiquity and preeminence of Winged Victory among several possible female allegorical figures attest to her legibility as a neoclassical representation of France's victory in World War I. French sculptors in the Algerian colony imagined her sentimentally as a female presence who promotes and mediates a fraternal colonizer-colonized cohesion through the "sacred union" (*union sacrée*) of military service by disparate religious communities united in defense of France. Even more for native Algerian Muslim troops, war memorials in the heart of each settler town referenced their debt of blood (*impôt de sang*), an unrequited tax paid in corpses to defend *la patrie*. This remained an unacknowledged price even when colonizers confronted returning Algerian Muslim combat veterans who unsuccessfully advocated for enfranchisement and equality. The brotherhood of dead soldiers never translated into equal rights or citizenship for Indigenous veterans but remained at the level of representation.

On behalf of the large numbers of colonial conscripts, the allegorical female figure of Algeria's Winged Victory statues adorned North African war memorials (*monuments aux morts*) and served to condense imagined overseas colonial histories. This came about when, in addition to memorializing the war dead, significant numbers of sculptures in cities and villages throughout French Algeria were commissioned between the two world wars to mark two overlapping commemorations: World War I and the colonial occupation of Algeria. Iconography commemorating the centenary of 1930 that celebrated one hundred years of French colonization in Algeria was added to the two-decade frenzy of post–World War I war monument building as sites of citizen-soldier memory and mourning.[20] The staggering losses of French and Algerian lives in a century of French military pacification campaigns against Algeria was conflated with the dead of two world wars. World War I's gendered allegorical representation contrasted with the commemorative silence of the former wars of colonial expansion. To put it another way, the colonial European male body was employed for public statues dedicated to colonial and continental wars, while the stereotypical allegorical female figure of Winged Victory was used to commemorate victory in World War I and II, borne by the colony's Algerian Muslims, European settlers, and Algerian Jews (listed proportionally from greater to lower deaths). This entailed purchasing some war memorials of a Winged Victory inexpensively from French catalogues that marketed readymade molds, while other statues, the topic of this chapter, were commissioned for the colony from renowned French sculptors.[21]

In 1962, the end of French Algeria and Algerian independence led to different outcomes for numerous Winged Victory sculptures in decolonized Algeria—they went missing, were spoliated to France, and destroyed or preserved in Algeria. Still others were replaced or repurposed for Algerian monuments rededicated to commemorating the country's hard-won independence and freedom from French colonialism. A notable example is the spectacular Algiers interwar memorial by Paul Landowski (1875–1961) and Charles Bigonet (1877–1931). Currently their monument is both preserved intact and missing because it is enveloped and built over by the 1978 post-independence monument of Mohammed Issiakhem (1928–1985). Postcards of the underlying Landowski-Bigonet interwar sculpture gender the Winged Victory statue as a mediator whose wings hover over a dead soldier borne on a shield upheld by an Algerian spahi and French cavalryman, two didactic figures of colonial wartime fraternity identifiable by their very different uniforms.[22] In Oran, Algeria's second city, two Winged Victory statues still stand: one in the main square by Jules Dalou (1838–1902) preserves a bronze Winged Victory atop a column and a second by Charles Bigonet on the grounds of the French consulate commemorates mainly students from the European settler community killed in war from Oran's Lycée Lamoricière.[23]

Examples of French Algeria's missing Winged Victories can be tracked through postcards and websites that circulate among former European settler communities and associations in Europe. For the agricultural settler village of Er Rahel near Oran, an image depicts the war memorial of 1934 in the form of an elaborate dark marble relief of Winged Victory. Sculpted by François-Émile Popineau (1887–1951), it is one of two memorials he completed for Algeria (a second was for the town of Biskra).[24] A Winged Victory once perched atop the war memorial of colonial Saint-Cloud (currently Gdyel). Removed at independence, the remaining war column was repurposed to commemorate the nineteenth-century Algerian resistance hero, the Emir 'Abd Al-Qadir, as well as the losses of the War of Independence. The town of Blida's 1925 bronze Winged Victory war memorial by Émile Oscar Guillaume (1867–1954) has also disappeared.[25] Statues still standing in place in post-independence Algeria mark the ways in which the hegemonic public cultural memory of French colonialism was weakened if not forgotten over time because a preserved war memorial with a Winged Victory figure was taken to represent the deaths of Algerian Muslim soldiers as cannon fodder fighting for France in two world wars.

Colonial Allegories by Joseph Ebstein

THE LIFE AND works of Joseph Ebstein (1881–1961), an Algerian Jewish sculptor noted for his Winged Victory war monuments in the French colony, present more possibilities for studying the provenance and destiny of French colonial statuary after Algerian independence in 1962. Because native Algerians Jews were enfranchised as French after 1870, they provide a contrast to the status of the Muslim population. They are also the rare legal example of an entire native community granted rights by an empire.[26] Algerian Jews turned to military service, patriotism, and bravery in World War I to prove they too had paid the debt of blood by acknowledging the duties and price of French citizenship that they shared with their coreligionists in the metropole.[27] Not surprisingly, these French values also took the form of public statuary. Sculptors Joseph Ebstein and Camille Alaphilippe (1874–1934?) used large-scale Winged Victory monuments to represent the assimilation of Algerian Jews to French colonial projects in the interwar period. Both Ebstein and Alaphilippe were celebrated for integrating the female form of victory into the iconography of war memorials, often including the omnipresent *poilu* (the mustachioed French infantryman) or more rarely a mourning female figure.[28] While Ebstein was born in Algeria and moved to Paris, Alaphilippe journeyed in the opposite direction across the Mediterranean Sea. Born in Tours, France, he arrived to Algeria after World War I with his wife, Avog-Alaphilippe, a sculptor and ceramicist in her own right. A wounded war veteran in search of sun and distance from the battlefields of Europe, Alaphilippe was welcomed to Algeria and immediately received municipal commissions for war memorials for the towns of Tipasa, Aïn-Temouchent, Saïda, Mostaganem, Bou-Arréridj, Bougie, Philippeville (the Winged Victory from 1926 removed to Toulouse in 1969), Tébessa, Guelma, and Fedj Mzala. He even sculpted the Winged Victory war memorial in Batna, Ebstein's hometown.[29] Inaugurated in 1925, it was moved to the town's Christian cemetery for safekeeping

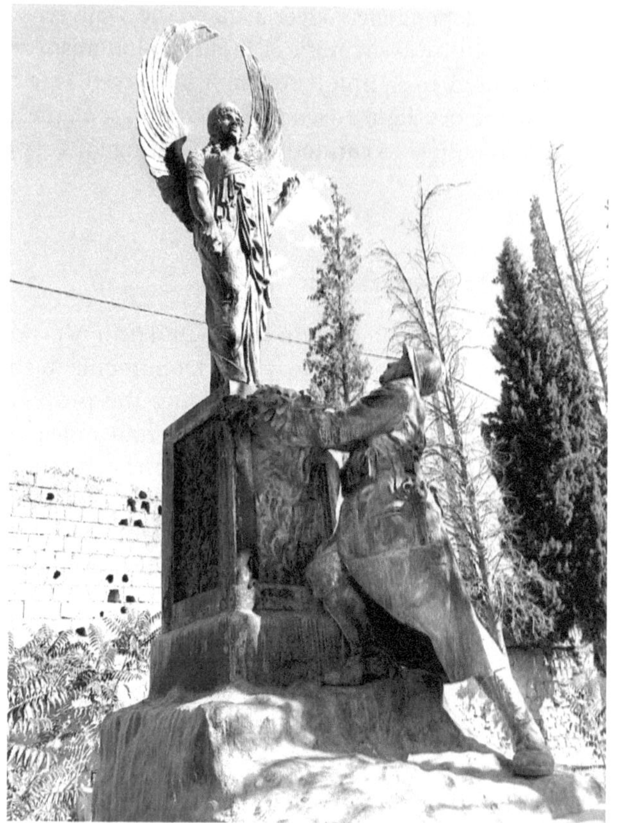

Figure 3. Camille Alaphilippe, war memorial currently in the Christian cemetery of Batna. Photograph by A. F. Chenni, June 10, 2021. Reproduced by permission.

after Algerian independence, where it still stands. A monument dedicated in the 1990s to the local Algerian resistance leader Mostefa Ben Boulaid (1917–1956) killed during the Algerian War of independence stands as a replacement for the removed but preserved Alaphilippe Winged Victory war memorial.[30]

Ebstein was born in Batna, French Algeria, on May 12, 1881. He was one of six children of Louis Ebstein, a businessman of Alsatian Jewish origin (b. 1841 in Quingey, eastern France), who left France in 1871 and moved to Algeria where he married Turkia Barkatz, a local Algerian Jewish woman from Batna. Joseph Ebstein studied at the Algiers School of Fine Arts with Victor Fulconis (1851–1913) and

   ■■■■■   SUSAN SLYOMOVICS

Léon Fourquet (1841–1938), sculptors of French Algeria, followed by
a stint at the École de Beaux Arts in Paris under Louis-Ernest Bar-
rias (1841–1905) and Jules Coutan (1848–1939), among the preeminent academic monument-makers of the Second Empire.[31] In 1910 he
received the Prix de Rome and in 1932 he was made a "Chevalier de
la Légion d'Honneur."[32] He maintained ateliers in Algiers (see figure
6) and Paris.[33] He contributed artwork to important salons organized
by the Society of Algerian and Orientalist Artists (Société des artistes
algériens et orientalistes) whose annual exhibitions were held
between 1897 and 1960.[34] Although Algeria's colonial-era art salons
are described by Roger Benjamin as being "like a visual propaganda
development wing of the Ministry of the Colonies, which helped fund
its annual Salons," Ebstein's artworks solidified his reputation as a
master sculptor trained in the tradition of French metropolitan fine
art objects.[35] As a native Algerian Jewish artist remade into a European settler and French citizen, he shared their privileges and benefits, such as study in Paris, prizes and honors, and salon exhibitions
denied Algerian Muslim artists.[36] He is mentioned as a sculptor who
exhibited in various salons such as the 25th and 27th Algiers salons
where his two sculptures, *Eve* and *En famille arabe* were displayed.[37]
Nonetheless, it was noted that he lost commissions in France because
he was "Algerian" and not authentically French, notwithstanding his
citizenship status.[38] Despite prizes and Paris art school credentials
and teachers, Ebstein's lack of work may have been due to metropolitan antisemitism or possibly part of a worldview that saw "colonial"
as imitative and degraded. Not much more is known about his life or
how he fared under Vichy laws of World War II that discriminated
against Jews in Algeria and France. Commentators mentioned that
he was deaf to account for the anomaly of his artistic success:

> It has been said that "it is an ill wind that blows no good," and
> this may be applied to the circumstance that, being deprived of
> his sense of hearing, Mr. Ebstain [*sic*] is cut off from all extra-
> neous stimuli of sound and is able to view his subjects with
> more intense concentration and without the distraction of the
> "tumult of words." When one enters his studio, one cannot help
> but feel the intense perceptive powers of the man and his sym-
> pathetic sensitivity to his subjects. Moreover, he has portrayed
> these living forms in their most harmonious attitudes. He has
> literally created melodies in marble.

He never married and died in Paris at the age of eighty on December 5, 1961, seven months before Algeria became independent on July 5, 1962. After his death, Ebstein's family donated his sculptures to the Paris Museum of Modern Art.[39]

Like Alaphilippe, Ebstein's Algerian oeuvre is divided between monuments spoliated to France by the French military after independence in 1962 and those remaining in post-independence Algeria. Famously, Ebstein's equestrian statue of Joan of Arc of 1931, erected at the entrance to Oran's Catholic cathedral to mark centennial celebrations of Algerian colonization, was removed by the French military and installed in Caen, France.[40] This displacement of large numbers of French colonial statues to France after Algerian independence is classified as "repatriation," confounding removed objects with people. This terminological confusion relies on the legal term "repatriate" that categorized former European settlers who departed Algeria at independence for their so-called homeland in France. Although the majority of Algeria's settler population came from the surrounding Mediterranean countries of Spain, Italy, Corsica, or Malta, the French law of 1961 named those settlers *rapatrié*: they were departing a country that had granted them French citizenship in Algeria.[41] At the same time, "repatriated" was bestowed on objects and statues of French Algeria, rather than the more accurate "spoliation" which involved taking artifacts illegally from Algeria, a widespread practice of the military, the Catholic Church, and European former inhabitants of North Africa.[42]

Among Ebstein's elaborate Winged Victory statues no longer in Algeria is an allegorical female Liberty supporting a French infantryman sculpted for the town of Marengo (currently Hadjout) in Algeria. It was removed to France by the military, then relocated for installation in Avirons, Île de la Réunion, a French overseas department in the Indian Ocean.[43] Ebstein's Sétif war memorial was inaugurated on Armistice Day, November 11, 1922. Local journalists wrote: "the talent of the artist shows us a magnificent soldier supporting a France stricken and battered" (*le talent de l'artiste [Ebstein] nous montre un magnifique poilu soutenant la France accablée et meurtrie*).[44] The swooning female statue representing France and the valiant soldier were also dismantled for transfer to France but disappeared en route. However, the names of the war dead on the Sétif plaques were reconstituted and attached to the cemetery wall of Béziers, France.[45] Relocating war memorial plaques from Algeria and recopying names served as partial replacement in French cemeteries for lost French Algerian memorials with their lists of the war dead. Ebstein's Tlemcen monument of 1924 was not lost but rather illegally removed from the town after independence by Gaston Montamat, a World War II war veteran who relocated to western Algeria. According to Alain Amato, the chronicler of "repatriated" statues from Algeria to France, Montamat was the presiding force behind at least three monument removals from Algeria to France. Ebstein's Tlemcen war memorial depicts a female Winged Victory leading two men: a helmeted French *poilu* and a colonial soldier wearing the *chéchia*, the soft red wool tasseled cap of the Army of Africa. At the dedication, the monument was parsed as Winged Victory allegorically safeguarding the army: "with outstretched wing, Victory protects the Army: French soldier, native infantryman advance with gusto [*de son aile deployée, la Victoire protège l'Armée: poilu français, tirailleur indigene avance avec entrain*]."[46] Large-scale transfers of war memorials such as Ebstein's from Tlemcen, Algeria, to the metropole after independence fit art historian June Hargove's observation that "the shuffling of monuments was a gentle form of iconoclasm."[47]

Ebstein's Two Constantine Monuments

COLONIAL MONUMENT PRESERVATION and destruction chronicle Algeria's relationships to its layered Roman artifacts as well as to France's colonial patrimony of allegorical female statues. At independence, many statues and busts representing generals and France's occupation vanished from sight. For example, Ebstein's Winged Victory statue of 1938 that surrounds a sculpture of General Charles-Marie Denys de Damrémont (1783–1837), a French officer and military governor of French Algeria, disappeared (figure 4). Damrémont was killed while leading the siege of the city of Constantine during the first decade of the French conquest. Ebstein's heroic sculpture of the general leading the battle charge immortalized the place where he reputedly fell in battle. His heroism was commemorated by French authorities through street names. The abstract obelisk-like column remains in Constantine, but the general's name and his statues were removed.

Algeria's most spectacular colonial war memorial, Ebstein's second statue for the town, stands on top of a grandiose arch overlooking the gorges of Constantine. The ambitious project began in 1918 and was finally completed twelve years later in 1930 in time for centenary celebrations of France's conquest of Algeria. The Algeria-based archi-

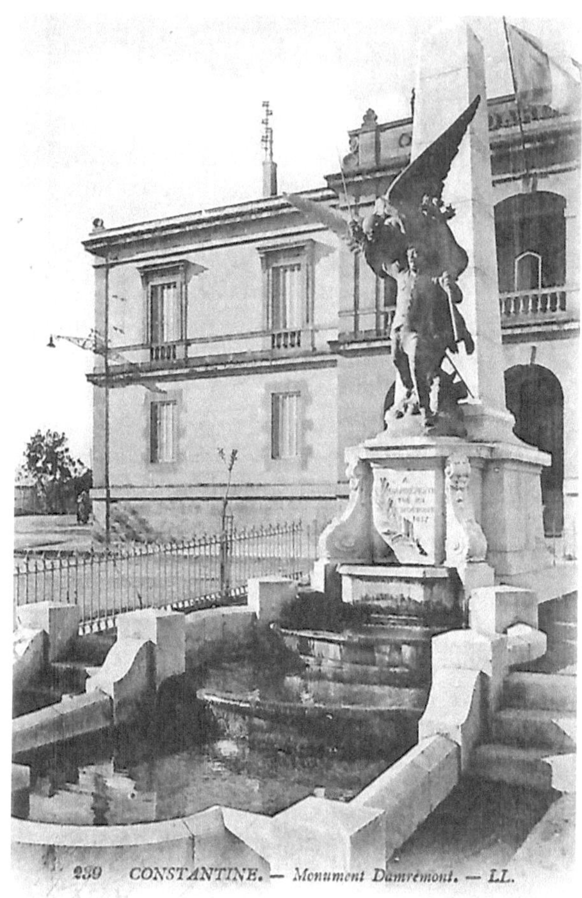

Figure 4. Winged Victory and General Damrémont
by Joseph Ebstein. LL (Léon et Lévy, no. 239),
undated. Author's collection.

tects Marcel Dumoulin and Maurice de La Chapelle conceived a base
inspired by the Roman triumphal arch of Trajan in nearby Timgad,
appropriated as a symbol of the French conquest of North Africa (figure 5).[48]

The arch is crowned by Ebstein's replica of the Roman statuette of
1858. The statuette had been reproduced in descriptions and drawings, as in figures 1 and 2, once on display in Constantine's newly
created museum where the antique object was separated from its original ritual context.[49] A series of decontextualizations for Constantine's

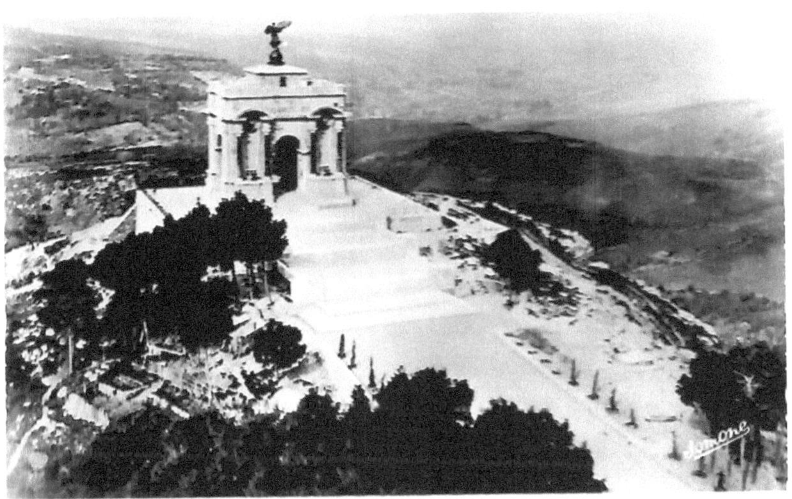

Figure 5. "Constantine: Le monument aux morts." Postcard of Constantine's war memorial, Edition Jomone, no. 10, undated, Algiers. Author's collection.

Winged Victory statuette resulted: antique Roman placement led to Ottoman immurement, followed by discovery by the French army, and finally to a nineteenth-century museum vitrine. Ebstein's oversized version restores the Winged Victory statue to public space, reimagining it on a much grander scale than the Victory of Samothrace. Given that Algeria's native Jewish community benefited from the 1870 decree of French citizenship before this status came to the European settlers, it is possible to conjecture that he sought to fuse conventional French sculptural symbols of war commemoration with the specificity of Constantine's native antique Roman Winged Victory statuette. In this way, he manifested materially the colony's native troops and their contributions to France's hard-fought victory in World War I to be shared among the three racialized religious communities of predominantly Catholic settlers and native Algerian Jews and Muslims.

Monumental Afterlives

WHEN SO MANY war memorials were dismantled by the retreating French colonial bureaucracy or repurposed by post-independent Algeria, how did Constantine's monument and Winged Victory statue remain in place? Much is owed to Algerian artist Ahmed Benyahia (b.

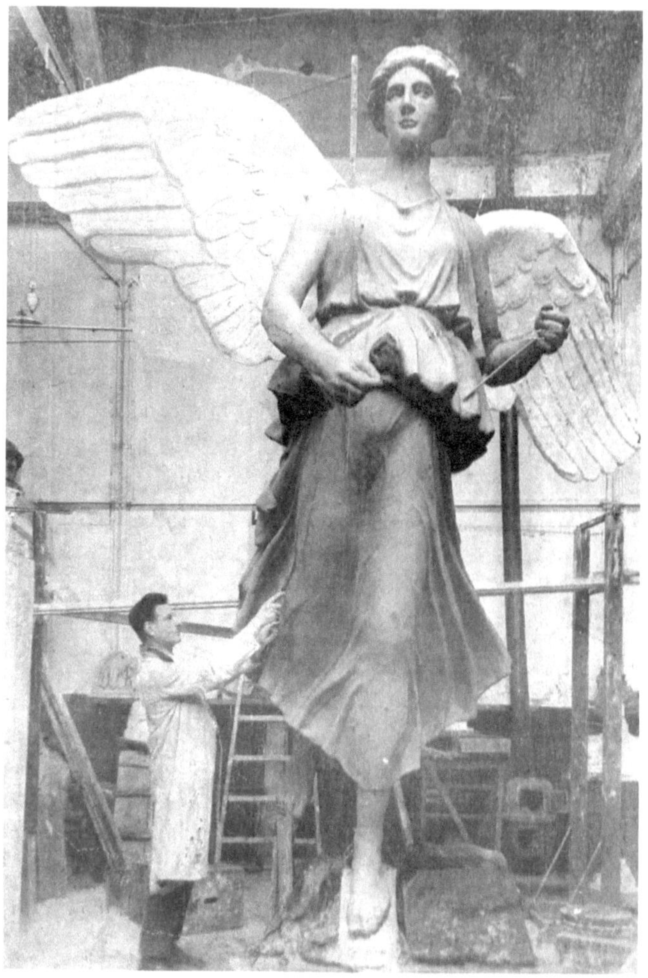

Figure 6. Ebstein sculpting the Winged Victory statue, ca. 1929. "Le Monument aux morts de Constantine," *L'Afrique du Nord Illustrée* 443 (October 26, 1929): 5.

1945), a key player in sixty years of efforts to preserve Constantine's interwar colonial monument. His heritage projects bring into focus post-independent Algeria's relation to French Algeria's colonial statues and war memorials. Benyahia belongs to the first generation of artists who studied in an independent Algeria's School of Fine Arts before furthering his education in Paris at the School of Fine Arts. The story he recounted to me is a variant of one I've heard all over

Algeria during fieldwork, albeit studying a different statue, different cast of municipal actors, and often a different outcome. Benyahia's version occurred in 1968 when a group of European settlers from Constantine, who had formed a mutual aid hometown association once they resettled in Marseilles, approached Constantine's first post-independence elected mayor. Hacène Boudjenana (mayor 1967–69) was a revolutionary fighter, a member of the PPA (Algerian Peoples Party), and local head of the union of railway workers. The former European settlers from Constantine made a formal request for what they deemed to be their war memorial. Advised by Benyahia in 1968 that this was not only Algerian heritage but also material proof that native Algerians went to their death as cannon fodder in two world wars to defend France, Boudjenana refused even though his municipal council approved of the transfer request. Benyahia had argued persuasively that the monumental arch with Winged Victory statue were affective city landmarks for locals no different than taking away the Eiffel Tower from Parisians. Finally, the men in his own family were conscripted, fought, and died for France, and their names were inscribed on the monument's inner archway. Decades later, as president of an association to preserve Constantine's heritage, Benyahia was instrumental in organizing funding for the war memorial's renovation and repair.[50] In 2015, to mark the centennial of the outbreak of World War I, diplomatic representatives from France and Germany, the two former enemy nations, participated in laying wreaths for the first time in Algeria.

The history of Algerian conscription and army service during two world wars is reflected in allegiances to France's aesthetic objects that dot the Algerian landscape. War memorials possess an aura and emotional intensity that is national and local, colonial and postcolonial. On this occasion, they are shared by natives and former settlers in dialogue with time and suffering. Constantine's war memorial enacts more than its temporal association with World War I. The dynamic shifts and exchanges among a succession of societies—Roman, Ottoman, colonial French, independent Algerian—uphold and maintain the visibility of an allegorical statue more expressive of victory in war rather than a representation of gender in the national consciousness. This is because gendered allegorical representations in the colony were easily subsumed by other powerful understandings about the meaning of statues. The twinned and intertwined historical sources for Winged Victory statues in Algeria are rooted in the country's Roman archaeological heritage or arrived via French classical sculpture's capacity to reshape Greco-Roman artistic practices for Algerian public spaces. At least in the colony, Winged Victory reduced gender to other impacts, namely the appropriation of the history of an oppressed people as merely male cannon fodder in imperial wars, while cultural and economic struggles against French colonial supremacy were made invisible. In the end, the female allegorical representation of victory in war was employed to represent political concepts in which the native population was denied being written through stone into history.

Notes

1. Fanon, *The Wretched of the Earth,* trans. Constance Farrington (New York: Grove Press, 1963), 51–52.

2. The large literature by colonial French historians and archaeologists reconstructing the precolonial Beylik of Constantine is summarized in Raymond André, "Les caractéristiques d'une ville arabe 'moyenne' au XVIIIe siècle: Le cas de Constantine," *Revue de l'Occident musulman et de la Méditerranée* 44 (1987): 134–47.

3. For these French urban colonial practices in Algeria and Tunisia, see Zeynep Çelik, *Empire, Architecture, and the City: French-Ottoman Encounters, 1830–1914* (Seattle: University of Washington Press, 2008), 75–79, 121–25. On French colonial destruction and repurposing of structures such as mosques and souks in Constantine, see Bernard Pagand, *La Médina de Constantine (Algérie): De la ville traditionnelle au centre de l'agglomération contemporaine* (Poitiers: Editions du Centre Inter-universitaire d'Études Méditerranéennes, 1989); Yasmina Boudjada, "L'église catholique de Constantine de 1839 à 1859: Cas de l'appropriation de la mosquée Souk el Ghzel par les Français," in *Villes rattachées, villes reconfigurées: Xvie–xxe siècles,* ed. Denise Turrel (Tours: Presses Universitaires François-Rabelais, 2003), 285–303; and Abdelkrim Badjadja, *La Bataille de Constantine 1836–1837* (Saint-Denis: Éditions Édilivre Aparis, 2011).

4. Patricia M. E. Lorcin, "Rome and France in Africa: Recovering Colonial Algeria's Latin Past," *French Historical Studies* 25, no. 2 (2002): 295–329.

5. Bonnie Effros, *Incidental Archaeologist: French Officers and the Rediscovery of Roman North Africa* (Ithaca: Cornell University Press, 2018); Monique Dondin-Payre, "Les auxiliaires militaires de l'armée d'Afrique héritiers de l'*exercitus Africae*?" *Antiquités africaines* 56 (2020), http://journals.openedition.org/antafr/1458.

6. Nicolas Lamare, "Le nymphée disparu du capitole de Cirta: À propos de ILAlg, II, 1, 483," in *L'eau dans les villes du Maghreb et leur territoire époque romaine,* ed. Véronique Brouquier-Reddé and Frédéric Hurlet (Bordeaux: Ausonius éditions, 2018), 311–27.

7. See figure 6 in André Berthier and Alexis Truillot, "Douilles et bronzes d'époque romaine découverts à El-Meridj," *Revue Archéologique* 8 (1936): 164–75.

8. Auguste Cherbonneau, *Album du Musée de Constantine* (Constantine: Alessi et Arnolet Libraires, 1862), 7. See also Cherbonneau's obituary in the *Bulletin*

d'académie d'Hippone (January 1, 1882): 85–87: "Ravissante et aérienne. Les traits ont une pureté idéale: la tête qui répond aux autres parties pour la distinction se dresse avec fierté; et les membres, volume impondérable, semblent agir et se laissent glisser dans les régions éthérées, sous l'impulsion des ailes. C'est quelque chose au-dessus de la nature humaine, un être céleste, une déesse." For a recent appreciation, drawn from memory by a former European settler, see Alain Amato, "Un matin au musée," *Mémoire plurielle: Les cahiers d'Afrique du Nord* 69 (2012): 43–54.

9. Nora Lafi, "Laurent-Charles Féraud entre le renseignement militaire et l'histoire," *Annales Tripolitaines* (2005): 7–17.

10. August Audollent, "Victoire Ailée du musée de Constantine," *Revue Archéologique* 16 (1890): 66–75, http://www.jstor.org/stable/41729873. On Audollent, see Auguste Diès, "Notice sur la vie et les travaux de M. Auguste Audollent, membre de l'Académie," *Comptes rendus des séances de l'Académie des Inscriptions et Belles-Lettres* 97, no. 3 (1953): 334–50.

11. H. A. Pohlsander, "Victory: The Story of a Statue," *Historia: Zeitschrift für Alte Geschichte* 18, no. 5 (1969): 588–97. A digital image is available at http://www.digital-images.net/Gallery/Scenic/Rome/Forum/Arches/arches.html#Severus-WingedVictory.

12. For Winged Victory motifs found on Punic coins, see Joseph Cantineau and Louis Leschi, "Monnaies puniques d'Alger," *Comptes rendus des séances de l'Académie des Inscriptions et Belles-Lettres*, 85, no. 4 (1941): 263–72 and on Roman coins, see David Sears, *Roman Coins and Their Values* (London: Seaby, 1964), 231–79.

13. "Victoire de Samothrace," Musée Louvre: https://collections.louvre.fr/en/ark:/53355/cl010252531. Since its restoration by the Louvre in 2013–14, see Kevin Clinton, Ludovic Laugier, Andrew Stewart, and Bonna D. Wescoat, "The Nike of Samothrace: Setting the Record Straight," *American Journal of Archaeology* 124, no. 4 (2020): 551–73. Élise Pampanay, "The Nike of Samothrace's Presences during the XX and XXI Centuries: Mysteries and Victories," *Thersites* 13 (2021): 71–83, includes a discussion of Beyoncé and Jay-Z's video "Apeshit" in front of Nike.

14. Marina Warner, *Monuments and Maidens: The Allegory of the Female Form* (Berkeley: University of California Press, 1985), 130–31. See Warner's chapter devoted to permutations of the Greco-Roman goddess of success and victory (127–45).

15. Simone de Beauvoir, *Le deuxième sexe* (Paris: Gallimard, 1949), 148: "Il est remarquable qu'à Paris, sur un millier de statues (si l'on excepte les reines qui forment pour une raison purement architecturale la corbeille du Luxembourg), il n'y en ait que dix élevées à des femmes. Trois sont consacrées à Jeanne d'Arc." Joan of Arc is also the favorite U.S. female statue; see Monument Lab, *National Monument Audit* (Philadelphia: Monument Lab, 2021), 17.

16. Although inspired by classical antiquity and Renaissance codes of iconography, according to Agulhon, a subliminal influence for abstractions of allegorical victory is inflected through feminine grammatical forms of *la victoire* in French and *victoria* in Latin; see Maurice Agulhon, "Un usage de la femme au XIXe siècle: L'allégorie de la République," *Romantisme* 13–14 (1976): 144 [143–52].

See the chapter in this volume on representations of France and La Marianne in France and North Africa by Daniel E. Coslett.

17. Erika Naginski, *Sculpture and Enlightenment* (Los Angeles: Getty, 2009), 275.

18. The term *statuomanie* is deployed in Maurice Agulhon, "La 'statuomanie et l'histoire," *Ethnologie française* 8, no. 2/3 (1978): 145–72. For histories of war memorials in France from France's defeat in the Franco-Prussian War of 1870 to World War I, see June Hargrove, "Qui vive? France! War Monuments from the Defense to the Revanche," in *Nationalism and French Visual Culture, 1870–1914*, ed. June Hargrove and Neil McWilliam (Washington, DC: National Gallery of Art, 2005), 55–81. On French *statuomanie* exported to Algeria, see Jan C. Jansen, *Erobern und Erinnern. Symbolpolitik, öffentlicher Raum und französischer Kolonialismus in Algerien, 1830–1950* (Munich: Oldenbourg, 2013) and Jansen, "1880–1914; une statuomanie à l'algérienne," in *Histoire de l'Algérie à la période colonial: (1830–1962)*, ed. Abderrahmane Bouchène (Paris: Découverte, 2012), 261–65.

19. Adolphe Messimy, "Le service militaire des indigènes algériens," *Bulletin de la réunion d'études algériennes* 10, nos. 2–3 (1908): 79–93.

20. Antoine Prost, "Monuments to the Dead," in Pierre Nora, *Realms of Memory: Rethinking the French Past* (New York: Columbia University Press, 1996), 3:307–30, appeared in *Les Lieux de mémoire*, ed. Pierre Nora (Paris: Gallimard, 1984–92), 7 vols.; Jan C. Jansen, "Une autre 'Union Sacrée'? Commémorer la Grande Guerre dans l'Algérie colonisée (1918–1939)," *Revue d'histoire moderne & contemporaine* 2, no. 2 (2014): 32–60; Claire Eldridge, "'The Forgotten of This Tribute: Settler Soldiers, Colonial Categories and the Centenary of the First World War," *History and Memory* 31, no. 2 (2019): 3–44; and Dónal Hassett, *Mobilizing Memory: The Great War and the Language of Politics in Colonial Algeria, 1918–39* (Oxford: Oxford University Press, 2019), 156–62.

21. Annette Becker, *Les monuments au morts: Patrimoine et mémoire de la Grande Guerre* (Paris: Errance, [1988]), 59–64, 73–75.

22. A photograph of the hidden monument is at the Paul Landowski site: http://www.paul-landowski.com/en/portfolio/monument-aux-morts-dalger-ou-le-pavois/.

23. Images of Dalou's Winged Victory are at https://e-monumen.net/patrimoine-monumental/monument-de-sidi-brahim-ou-a-abd-el-kader-oran/ and Bigonnet: http://www.les-anciens-du-lycee-lamoriciere-d-oran.com/pages/rejoindre-l-association.html.

24. For Popineau's Algerian corpus, see Élisabeth Cazenave, *La décoration monumentale peinte et sculptée en Algérie (1830–1962)* (N.p: Éditions Abd-el-Tif, 2013), 187. Photos of two successive Er Rahel monuments are at the Pied-Noir website of Amicale de Ro Salado, "Monument aux Morts d'Er Rahel": http://amicaledurio-salado.com/monument-aux-morts-der-rahel.

25. Roland Biguenet, *Émile Guillaume (1867–1954): Le sculpteur de la IIIème République* (Orthez: Publishroom Factory, 2020). For images of Guillaume's corpus of war memorials, see the website "Monuments aux morts: France-Belgique-Autre pays": https://monumentsmorts.univ-lille.fr/auteur/91/guil-laumeemileoscar/. In addition to Blida he sculpted a war memorial of several

infantrymen for the Algerian coastal town of Cherchell in 1937 and returned to the theme of the *poilu.*

26. Susan Slyomovics, "'False Friends'?: On Algeria, the Algerian Jewish Question, and Settler Colonial Studies," in *Race, Place, Trace: Essays in Honour of Patrick Wolfe*, ed. Lorenzo Veracini and Susan Slyomovics (London: Verso, 2022).

27. Jacques Fremeaux, "Les colonies dans la Grande Guerre: Combats et épreuves des peoples d'outre-mer" (Paris: Éditions 14-18); Philippe E. Landau, *Les Juifs de France et la Grande Guerre: Un patriotism républicain* (Paris: CNRS, 1999).

28. Élisabeth Cazenave, *Les artistes de l'Algérie: Dictionnaire des peintres, sculpteurs, graveurs, 1830–1962* (Paris: Association Abd-el-Tif, 2001), 232.

29. M. Michel, "Camille Alaphilippe," *Notre rive: Revue nord-africaine illustrée* (January 1, 1927): 20.

30. On new post-independent statuary such as the Ben Boulaid sculpture, see Emmanuel Alcaraz, "Les monuments aux martyrs de la guerre d'indépendance algérienne: Monumentalité, enjeux de mémoire et commemorations," *Guerres Mondiales et Conflits Contemporains* 237 (2010): 125–46. In most examples, Algerian male heroes of the revolution replace female allegorical statues.

31. On Ebstein's teachers, see June Hargrove, *The Statues of Paris: An Open-Air Pantheon* (Belgium: Mercatorfonds, 1989), 169.

32. See documentation at Archives Nationales, Ministry of Culture: http://www2.culture.gouv.fr/LH/LH204/PG/FRDAFAN84_O19800035v0942442.htm.

33. *Encyclopedia of Disability*, ed. Gary L Albrecht (London: Sage, 2006), 1:355.

34. La Société des peintres orientalistes was established in Paris in 1893 and the Algerian salon was cofounded by Charles Cordier; see Susan Slyomovics, "The Algerian Jewish Woman (*La Juive d'Alger*): Charles Cordier and Ethnographic Sculpture," *Hespéris-Tamuda* 56, no. 1 (2021): 133–59.

35. Roger Benjamin, *Orientalist Aesthetics: Art, Colonialism, and French North Africa, 1880–1930* (Berkeley: University of California Press, 2003), 66.

36. For letters to French authorities by Algerian artists Omar Racim in 1923 and Yahia Bahmed in 1952 in protest of their exclusion from colonial art world participation, see *Modern Art in the Contemporary World: Primary Documents*, ed. Anneka Lenssen, Sarah Rogers, and Nada Shabout (New York: MOMA, 2018), 57, 155. On the complexities of this exclusion from salons, see Nancy Demerdash-Fatemi, "The Aesthetics of Taste Making in (and out of) the Colonial Algerian Salon," in *The Art Salon in the Arab Region: Politics of Taste Making*, ed. Nadia von Maltzahn and Monique Bellan (Beirut: Orient-Institut, 2018), 75–89.

37. Paul de Bouvray, "Le XXVIIe salon official des artistes algériens et orien-talists," *L'Afrique du nord illustré* 230 (February 13, 1926): 6–7. These were deemed inferior to his previous submissions; "Pour le reste nous eussions aimé plus de diversité dans l'expression plastique. Combien supérieur était l'envoi de l'an passé de ce sculpteur!"

38. Edmond Gojon, "Les grands artistes algériens: Le sculpteur Ebstain [*sic*]," *L'Afrique du Nord illustrée* (November 6, 1920): 11.

39. "Who's Who Abroad: Joseph Ebstain [*sic*]," *Chicago Tribune* (Paris edition, August 17, 1928): 4.

40. Service historique de défense (SHD), 1962. 1R 368-1: "Rapatriement des souvenirs militaires," 1962. 1R 368 lists the successful removal of Joan of Arc

spoliated from Oran to Marseille in November 1962, five months after Algerian independence; see Alain Amato, *Monuments en exil* (Paris: Atlanthrope, 1979), 64–68. A current image is available at https://equestrianstatue.org/jeanne-d-arc-3/.

41. "La loi francaise du 26 décembre 1961": http://www.legifrance.gouv.fr/affichTexte.do?cidTexte=JORFTEXT000000508788.

42. For examples of military and religious spoliation of statuary, see Susan Slyomovics, "The Virgin Mary of Algeria: French Mediterraneans *En Miroir*," *History and Anthropology* 31 (2020): 22–42 and Susan Slyomovics, "Dismantling a World: France's Monumental Military Heritage in Sidi-Bel-Abbès, Algeria," *Journal of North African Studies* 25, no. 5 (2020): 772–96.

43. Séverine Laborie, "Les monuments aux morts de la Guerre de 14–18 en Guadeloupe avant 1945," *In Situ*, 25 (2014), https://doi.org/10.4000/insitu.11721, see Figure 28.prix.

44. "Inauguration à Sétif du monument aux morts de la grande guerre," *Le Progrès de Sétif* (November 18, 1922): 1. See also Andrea Smith, "Settler Sites of Memory and the Work of Mourning," *French Politics, Culture & Society* 31, no. 3 (2013): 65–92.

45. Paul Sermaize, "Le monument aux morts de Sétif," *L'Afrique du Nord Illustrée* 78 (28 octobre 1922): 4. See also Amato, *Monuments en exil*, 46–47.

46. "Inauguration du Monument aux morts," *L'Avenir de Tlemcen* (October 9, 1935): 1–2. See also Jan C. Jansen, *Erobern und Erinnern: Symbolpolitik, öffentlicher Raum und französischer Kolonialismus in Algerien 1830–1950* (Munich: Oldenbourg, 2013), 357–70; and Amato, *Monuments en exil*, 107–9, 177–79.

47. June Hargrove, *The Statues of Paris: An Open-Air Pantheon* (Antwerp: Mercatorfonds, 1989), 194.

48. Bonnie Effros, *Incidental Archaeologists: French Officers and the Rediscovery of Roman North Africa* (Ithaca: Cornell University Press, 2018); Nabila Oulebsir, *Les usage du patrimoine: Monuments, musées et politique coloniale en Algéria, 1830–1930* (Paris: Hyper Articles en Ligne and Centre pour la Communication Scientifique Direct, 2004).

49. Pascal Griener, *La république de l'oeuil: L'expérience de l'art au siècle des Lumières* (Paris: O. Jacob, 2010).

50. On Algerian artist Ahmed Benyahia and his crucial role to preserve Constantine's colonial heritage, see Susan Slyomovics, "On the Wings of the Gallic Cockerel: Ahmed Benyahia and the Provenance of an Algerian Public Sculpture," in *Reframing Postcolonial Studies: Concepts—Methodologies—Scholarly Activisms*, ed. David D. Kim (London: Palgrave Macmillan, 2021), 69–92.

Fernando Luis Martínez Nespral

The Argentine Marianne

IN SPANISH, THE nouns *republic, nation, land,* and *homeland* are feminine. For this reason, the adjective *argentina*[1] (which means made of silver) that is used to name my country is also expressed in feminine in Spanish, that is, ending with an "a."

In this way, the connection between Argentina and the feminine can be traced back to the origins of the European colonization of these lands, as revealed by its use in the historical poem *La Argentina o la Conquista del Río de la Plata* published in 1602 by Martín del Barco Centenera, a Spanish cleric who participated in the conquest.[2]

Starting in the eighteenth and even more in the nineteenth century, this identification with the feminine was reinforced through the appearance of another feminine nation, La France as the main reference for the enlightened local intellectuals who played a key role in the process of independence from Spain and the constitution of a new autonomous nation.

In this context, the symbolic representation of the Argentine Confederation, Republic, or Nation (all three names used in the Argentine Constitution) was established from the beginning as a female figure, dressed in a Greco-Roman tunic and wearing a Phrygian cap, almost identical to the French Marianne that Richard Sennett describes in his book *Flesh and Stone*, and which paradoxically owes its name to the Spanish Jesuit Juan de Mariana.[3]

The "Argentine Marianne" took form in multiple pictorial and sculptural representations of independence from Spain (1810–16) and remained consolidated as an allegory of the nation until the first decades of the twentieth century.

The Plaza de Mayo serves as a case study to examine how the idea of an Argentine Marianne occupied and still occupies a prominent role in a central public space that constitutes the foundational nucleus of Buenos Aires. In 1811, to celebrate the first anniversary of the revolution, even though, paradoxically, independence had not been officially declared yet, the ruling Junta grande (Big Junta) decided to build a so-called pyramid, or rather obelisk based on its shape, on Plaza de Mayo.

This first pyramid was small and simple, but in 1856 it was enlarged and centered in the square that had been remodeled. During this process, the monument was modified to include a statue on its top titled *Liberty*. A work of the French sculptor Joseph Dubourdieu, the sculpture represents a woman dressed in a tunic, with a Phrygian cap, holding a spear and a shield, showing clear references to the French Marianne model. Located in front of this monument is the Argentine presidential palace, Casa Rosada. In the main hall of this building, where presidential inaugurations and important government events take place, is an Argentine Marianne. In front of the main wall of the hall sits a sculpture made in 1890 by the Sicilian Ettore Ximenes titled *Bust of the Homeland*, a Marianne-like figure wearing a Phrygian cap. On the ceiling of the same room, there is a pictorial representation of the revolution showing a woman very similar to the previous ones, in this case holding in one of its hands a broken chain symbolizing the freedom acquired by independence. It is a work made in 1884 by the Italian painter Luigi de Servi, who at that time was very active in the region.

Also located around Plaza de Mayo is the Cathedral of Buenos Aires. Inside the temple sits another female sculpture, almost identical to those described above. It belongs to a sculpture group (designed by French artist Henry Dasson), which crowns a mausoleum (built between 1878 and 1880) for General José de San Martín, the leader of the independence revolution and so-called "Father of the Nation."

All of these cases reveal that the representations of the Argentine Marianne are concentrated in the second half of the nineteenth century. Until the celebrations of the first centenary of Independence in

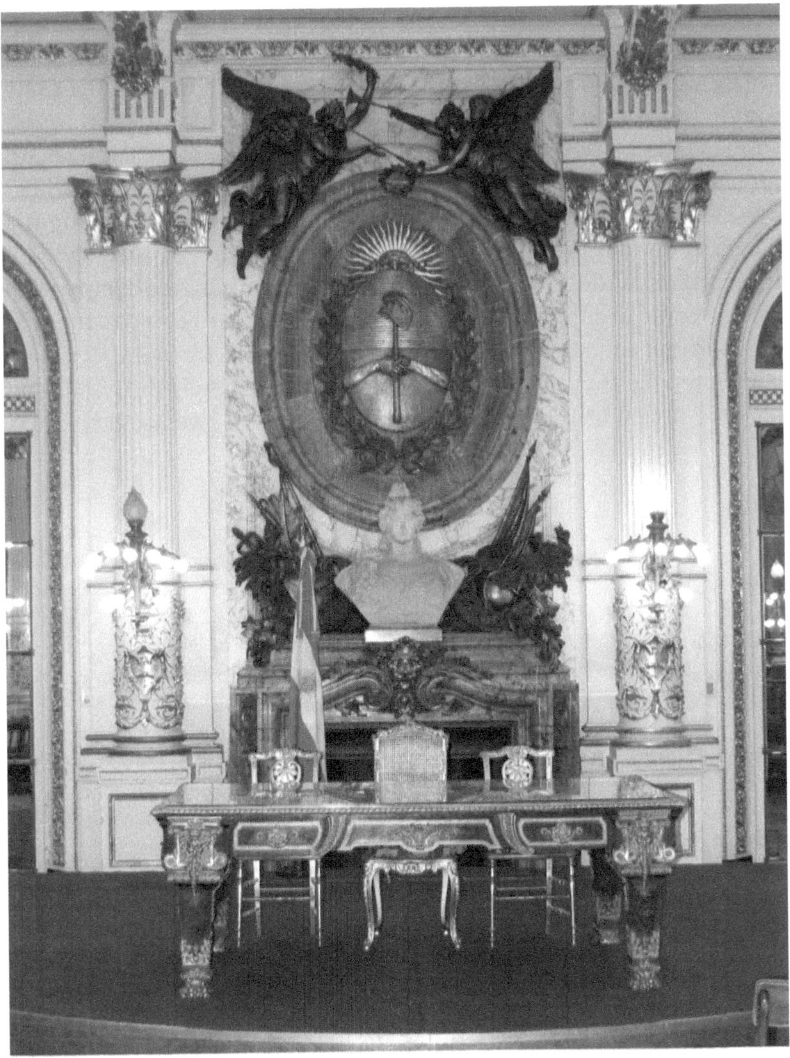

Figure 1. White Hall at the Casa Rosada. By Gustavo Facci, CC BY-SA 2.0. Courtesy of Gustavo Facci, photographer.

1910, her image was almost ubiquitous. The dominance of the Argentine Marianne as national symbol started to shift in the 1930s in the context of the suppression of freedoms after a military coup, and later during President Juan Perón's industrialization efforts. Alternative images to represent the nation started to emerge, while the influence of France was weakened. In particular, in the mid-twentieth century, a woman, Eva Perón, became a symbol of the popular claims for social justice based on her public appearances in front of the same square, on the balcony of Casa Rosada. Closer to the present, other women, the Mothers of Plaza de Mayo, became known to the world for marching around the same pyramid monument dedicated to Marianne demanding justice for the murder of their children during the dictatorship that ruled in Argentina between 1976 and 1983. Despite these changes, the Argentine Marianne did not disappear completely.[4]

One could argue that Mariannes sculpted in marble and painted in oil from the nineteenth century and the ideas of freedom, equality, and fraternity they represent are still present, embodied in flesh and blood in actual historical Argentine women of the twentieth century.

Notes

1. *Argentina* is a Spanish word, derived from the Latin *argentum* (silver in Spanish), projecting unfulfilled fantasies of the European conquerors about finding a lot of silver in this land.

2. Martín del Barco Centenera, *La Argentina o la Conquista del Río de la Plata: Con otros acaecimientos de los reynos del Perú, Tucumán, y estado del Brasil* (Lisboa: Pedro Crasbeeck, 1602).

3. "The Revolution modeled Marianne's face as that of a young Greek goddess, with a straight nose, a high brow, and well-formed chin; her body tended to the fuller domestic form of a young mother. Sometimes Marianne appeared dressed in ancient flowing robes which clung to her breasts and thighs; sometimes the Revolution dressed her in contemporary clothes, but with her breasts bared. . . Marianne's generous, flowing, and productive female body first of all served to mark off the virtuous present from the evils of the *Ancien Regime*." R. Sennett, *Flesh and Stone: The Body and the City in Western Civilization* (New York: W. W. Norton, 1997). Juan de Mariana lived in Paris toward the end of the sixteenth century. Later his name and ideas were taken up by the revolutionaries of the eighteenth century.

4. For example, Marianne's profile is still visible today in the logos of the Argentine Federal Police and the Central Bank of the Argentine Republic.

Erika Doss

I Am Queen Mary, Copenhagen

We wanted to challenge the fact that 98% of the statues in public space in Copenhagen represent White males—so taking up a space with a huge sculpture of a Black woman, the first in Scandinavia, was a massive statement.
—La Vaughn Belle and Jeannette Ehlers, 2021

IN MARCH 2018, the temporary public sculpture *I Am Queen Mary* was unveiled at Copenhagen's Vestindisk Pakhus. A waterfront warehouse that once stored rum and sugar shipped from the Caribbean, the building now houses the Danish Royal Cast Collection, an art gallery featuring some two thousand plaster reproductions of statues charting the history of Western art from ancient Greece to Renaissance Italy. Installed outside, in front of the building, the twenty-three-foot polystyrene statue *I Am Queen Mary* depicted Mary Thomas, one of several women who led the 1878 "Fireburn" revolt against Danish colonial rule in the West Indies and, in particular, against horrific labor conditions on sugar plantations in St. Croix. Arrested and tried for arson and looting, Thomas and other female labor leaders were transferred to Denmark and sentenced to life in Copenhagen's Women's Prison at Christianshavn, about a mile from the warehouse.

Coated entirely in lustrous black paint, the statue of Mary showed her sitting in a rattan chair, barefoot, holding a flaming torch in one

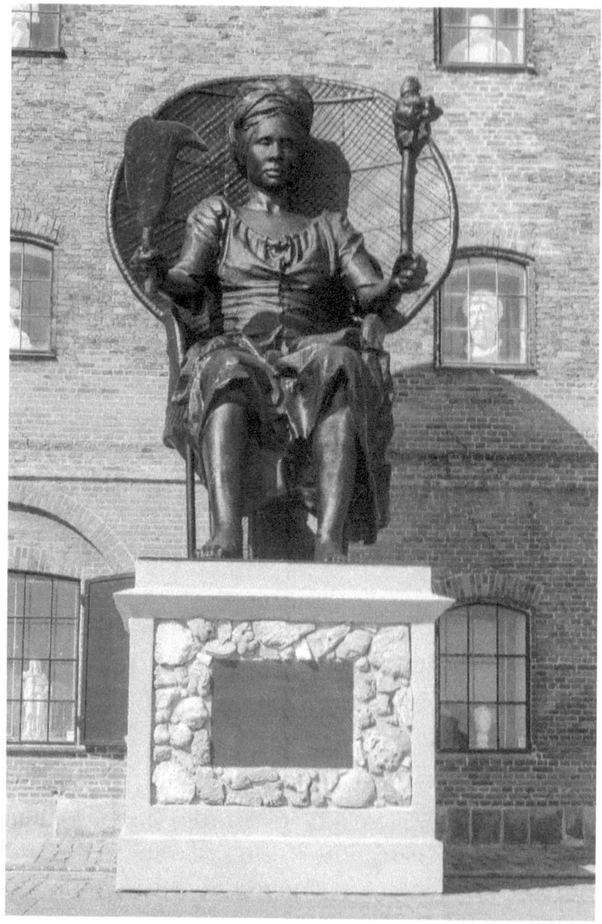

Figure 1. La Vaughn Belle and Jeannette Ehlers, *I Am Queen Mary*, 2018, Copenhagen. Photo 174047499/ Queen Mary © Oliver Forester/Dreamstime.

hand and a "cane bill"—a knife used to cut sugar cane—in the other. The monumental statue was set on a plinth containing 2.5 tons of coral stones cut from Caribbean waters, a material originally harvested by slaves and used in the foundations of colonial buildings. Mary's pose, her unshakable bearing, and straightforward gaze echoed the iconic 1967 photograph of Black Panther Party co-leader Huey Newton, an image of Black power and determination. Her dominating presence at the entrance to the former Danish West India Warehouse evoked the resistance movements that opposed Denmark's brutal colonial occupation of the Caribbean for more than two hundred years, and continue to challenge racist politics today.

Badly damaged by a winter storm in 2020, the statue of Mary was removed and supplemented with an AR (augmented reality) version visible with a smartphone. Overwhelming public response and support from the Danish minister of culture led to civic approval to erect a permanent statue at the site. In 2021, a $1 million crowdfunding campaign was organized to build twin *I Am Queen Mary* monuments in bronze in Copenhagen and St. Croix.

The brainchild of artists La Vaughn Belle of the U.S. Virgin Islands and Jeannette Ehlers, based in Copenhagen, *I Am Queen Mary* was originally conceived as an amendment to Denmark's mostly white male collection of statues, including a replica of Michelangelo's David in front of the warehouse. The centennial anniversary of Denmark's sale of the West Indies in 1917 to the United States prompted the artists to design a more ambitious, and permanent, public sculpture addressing Denmark's complicity in the slave trade and its colonial legacy. Mary is a popular heroine in the Virgin Islands but her story and Danish narratives about colonialism in the West Indies remain largely untold in Denmark. Their project, Belle remarks, was intended to "penetrate the collective consciousness and the Danish ego in terms of how they remember themselves."[1]

The public sculpture's title—*I Am Queen Mary*—invites audiences to think about how they might identify with this work of art and the history it represents. With roots in the abolitionist and civil rights movements, the phrase "I am" is an assertion of human agency and subjectivity. Identifying with this historical figure invites people to ask who she is, why they may not know this history, and to question the history they do know: to interrogate how history is made and to question its biases and absences. It's a feminist art strategy adopted from multimedia projects such as *The Dinner Party*: that icon of 1970s art organized by Judy Chicago that features table settings for 39 women, and floor tiles with the names of 999 more, with the goals of raising consciousness about women and art and subverting dominating masculinist historical narratives and assumptions. Housed today in the Brooklyn Museum, *The Dinner Party* is a powerful, emotionally engaging project that continues to provoke questions about art and history, and who counts in the stories we tell about ourselves.

Public statues of women are seen as important correctives to centuries of male-dominated stories. But just adding more statues of women does not necessarily prompt us to consider how male-dominated art and male-dominated historical narratives were created in the first place. Nor do they automatically reckon with the problems, in the past and in the present, of gender and racial bias and inequity. *I Am Queen Mary* speaks to both by interrogating Denmark's memory of transatlantic slavery: by visualizing a history of dissent and resistance led by Black women and by questioning Scandinavian colonial amnesia today.

Notes

1. La Vaughn Belle quoted in *Icons, Memory & Monuments: A Conversation about Memory Work*, YouTube video, September 27, 2021, https://www.youtube.com/watch?v=ESJdGjR1uAI.

Daniel Herwitz

Patience on a Monument: A History Painting

AGAINST AN ELONGATED background is a vast monument of stuff on top of which sits a Black woman, as if sculpted in bronze. She appears to be waiting (patiently). The red and gold background of the picture stretches in all directions as if toward infinity, which is exactly how the Highveldt around Johannesburg looks as it stretches out at two thousand meters above sea level under low-hanging clouds. Brown is tufted into the red and gold of the picture to resemble the roughness of the Veldt, where gold was first discovered. The sense of roughness is enhanced by the fact that the painting is done on board rather than canvas.

The year is 1988. The Apartheid state is collapsing, thanks to resistance in the townships, global economic boycotts, and three border wars in which the South African military was engaged since the 1970s. Penny Siopis's painting presages the end of Apartheid and its colonial roots just before that end came about (two years later, in 1990). It is a painting made in-hope or expectation-of a future-about-to-be. And from this perspective of the about-to-be, it reviews the past.

Where there is mining there is waste, and the mine dumps that ringed the emerging Johannesburg metropolis at the beginning of the twentieth century shed a fine dust of red—the residue of gold extracted

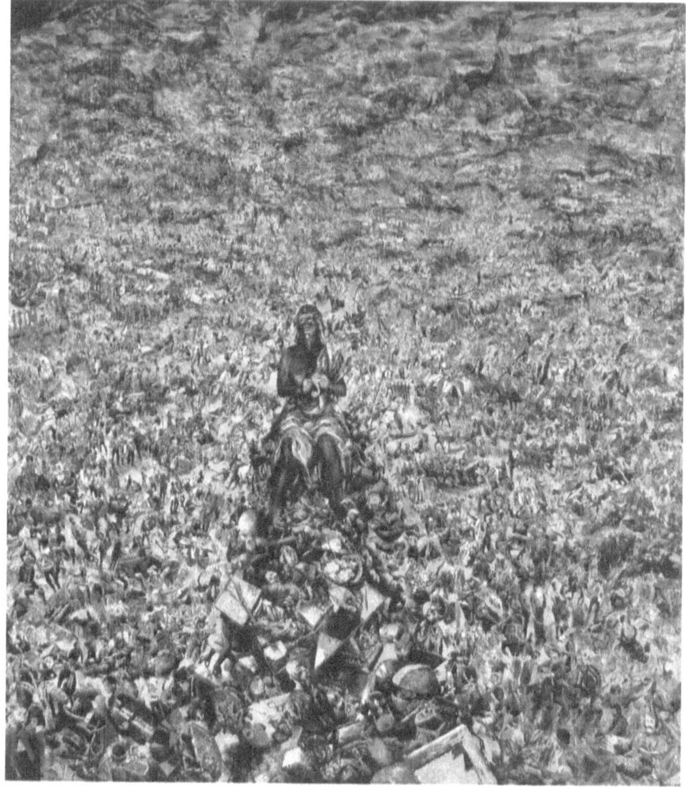

Figure 1. *Patience on a Monument: "A History Painting."* Penny Siopis, 1988, oil and collage on board. Courtesy of the artist.

from rock—which is said to have floated in the winds above the city, sending a filigree of dust over everything below. As a pile of junk, the monument has already collapsed. Yet qua monument it retains form. The monument contains the stuff that filled the great houses of the Randlords (the gold and diamond magnates of the turn of century), the contents of the European settler museums, the public artifacts of the cities, the culture of colonialism. All the things a woman like Patience would have slaved to clean, care for, polish, wash, and dry, without ownership or reward.

This accumulation of capital is finally a ruination: excessive, grotesque, ready to collapse of its own weight, like a dragon hoarding gold until drowned by it. It is what Marx called primitive accumulation. This pile is composed of "everything under the sun." But specifically gold, because gold has throughout history served as both commodity (precious objects made of gold) and *currency.* Insofar as gold was the standard against which coin and paper money were valued, collecting gold meant having something with *universal exchange value.* Accumulation of gold was *the prize* of the hoarding capitalist.

And here the question of heritage arises full blast. The modern form that national heritage took was modeled on banking. Heritage was understood to be a bankable currency of values, mores, traditions, wit, intelligence, and religion, of dress and manner, taste and leisure. It allowed one to belong.[1]

Patience sits on a pile. The word "pile" in British English refers to a building that is overdone and atrocious, as in "the man lives in an absolute nouveau riches pile!" But it also refers to a mass of junk (a pile of rubble). Is the pile on which Patience waits monument or waste? Is it mere rubble soon to be cleared away by the new democracy? What remains intact at the end of Apartheid/colonial history? What can be salvaged from European/Eurocentric heritage for the new democracy? What serves and is of use? This painting is about the fate of heritage for the future. Not simply about the accumulations of the past.

But the painting is about more than what is of use for the future. It is about reparation of the past. And this through oblique reference to the artist Paul Klee's *Angelus Novus,* a monoprint of 1920 owned and interpreted by Walter Benjamin in his "Theses on the Philosophy of History." In Benjamin's words:

> A Klee painting named "Angelus Novus" shows an angel looking as though he is about to move away from something he is fixedly contemplating. His eyes are staring, his mouth is open, his wings are spread. This is how one pictures the angel of history. His face is turned toward the past. Where we perceive a chain of events, he sees one single catastrophe which keeps piling wreckage upon wreckage and hurls it in front of his feet. . . . But a storm is blowing from Paradise; it has got caught in his wings with such violence that the angel can no longer close them. The storm irresistibly propels him into the future to which his back is turned, while the pile of debris before him grows skyward. This storm is what we call progress.[2]

I think the reference is indirect but meaningful. Patience faces the viewer, regarding us rather than being turned away from us, looking into the depth of the picture which spreads out behind her. One just might think of that depth as *time*: the future, from which she is turned away: toward the past. Which suggests the painting is not simply about what might remain of use for the future (democracy) but also about repairing the traumatic past. This need motivated the South African Truth and Reconciliation Commission: a public recounting of trauma by its victims, witnesses, and perpetrators, an address to the past in the name of bringing about a better, more integral, future.

Now we may ask: Why a woman? Penny Siopis is a feminist painter and it is important that the figure is female. There are various reasons for this, and let me end with a few.

First, a pictorial source is the Renaissance allegory of Patience, a memento mori for tombstones. In Vasari's exemplary painting, she faces a still life of an urn of precious metal. The urn is funereal. Coins circulated her image far and wide: an iconic copying lasting for centuries. The woman as a figure of death (rubble, humiliation, the end of time) is long-standing in European art.

Second, it has been the fate of women to remain patient with their lot in life, holding the family together, absorbing the abuse of the husband, earning a steady—if impoverished—income through "domestic work." Patience is the one who would be caretaker for all the stuff that comprises the monument.

Third, the association between women and passivity. She waits without agency (her agency consists in waiting).

Fourth, the person waiting is also waiting for the end of the brutal culture of monumentality, a culture that uses public art in the manner of assertion, telling the settler he is king, the native he doesn't count. Women are in gendered modern life less associated with monumentality than men. Monuments are gestures of solidarity under the banner of male agency. Whatever Patience will become will not likely be another version of monumentality. She is awaiting the end of the culture of the monument. And this is a good thing.

Notes

1. Cf. Daniel Herwitz, *Heritage, Culture and Politics in the Postcolony* (New York: Columbia University Press, 2012).

2. Walter Benjamin, "Theses on the Philosophy of History," in Hannah Arendt, ed., *Illuminations*, trans. Harry Zohn (New York: Schocken Books, 1968), 257–58.

CAROLINA AGUILERA teaches at the School of Sociology, Universidad Diego Portales in Chile, and is Associate Researcher of the Centre for Social Conflict and Cohesion Studies COES-Chile. Her main areas of research are focused on the sociology of memory and urban sociology. She has published in *Memory Studies, Kamchatka, Límite, AUS*, and *Bifurcaciones* and has written chapters in collective volumes including *Patrimonio: Contranarrativas Urbanas* (Universidad Alberto Hurtado, 2019), *Disputar la Ciudad* (Bifurcaciones, 2018), and *Golpes a la Memoria* (Tege, 2019).

MANUELA BADILLA RAJEVIC received her PhD (2019) and MA (2013) in sociology from the New School for Social Research. She is currently a postdoctoral researcher in the Sociology Department at the University of Valparaíso. She is also an adjunct researcher at the Centre for Social Conflict and Cohesion Studies COES-Chile. She has published her work in *Sociological Forum* (2019), *Mobilizations* (2019), *Space and Culture* (2020), and *Memory Studies* (2020, 2021).

DANIEL E. COSLETT is Assistant Professor of Architectural History at Drexel University. He is a scholar of colonial and postcolonial built environments whose work addresses intersections of architecture, heritage, archaeology, and tourism. He has published an edited volume, *Neocolonialism and Built Heritage: Echoes of Empire in Africa, Asia, and Europe* (Routledge, 2020), and two coedited volumes, *Rethinking Global Modernism: Architectural Historiography and the Postcolonial* (Routledge, with Vikramaditya Prakash and Maristella Casciato, 2022) and

Islamic Architecture Today and Tomorrow: (Re)defining the Field (Intellect, with Mohammad Gharipour, 2022).

ERIKA DOSS is Distinguished University Chair in the Edith O'Donnell Institute of Art History, University of Texas at Dallas. Her most recent books are *Spiritual Moderns: Twentieth-Century American Artists and Religion* (Chicago, 2023) and *American Art of the 20th–21st Centuries* (Oxford, 2017).

TANIA GUTIÉRREZ-MONROY is Assistant Professor at the University of British Columbia. She is the author of "Building Indigenous Resistance: The Casa de los Pueblos y Comunidades Indígenas, Yä nghü yä jhöy, Samir Flores Soberanes" and "Reframing Narratives: A Woman and Her Building at the Dawn of the Mexican Revolution," both published in the *Journal of Architectural Education*.

DANIEL HERWITZ lived and taught in South Africa during the moment of democratic transition and splits his time between Ann Arbor and Cape Town. He is Fredric Huetwell Professor of Comparative Literature, Philosophy and History of Art at the University of Michigan where from 2002 to 2012 he directed the Institute for the Humanities. He has written widely on contemporary art, culture, and politics in a cosmopolitan way, on philosophical aesthetics, and on transitional justice. His latest book is *The Political Power of Visual Art* (Bloomsbury Academic, 2021).

KATHERINE HITE is Professor of Political Science on the Frederick Ferris Thompson Chair at Vassar College in Poughkeepsie, New York. She is the author of *Politics and the Art of Commemoration: Memorials to Struggle in Latin America and Spain* (Routledge, 2012; Spanish translation Mandrágora, 2014) and *When the Romance Ended: Leaders of the Chilean Left, 1968–1998* (Columbia, 2000), as well as several publications on the politics of memory, memorials, and memorial museums across the Americas, including Texas, where she grew up. Hite is active in her Poughkeepsie, New York, community, including as cochair of "Celebrating the African Spirit."

LAUREN KROIZ is Associate Professor in the History of Art Department at the University of California, Berkeley. Kroiz is the author of

Cultivating Citizens: The Work of Art in the New Deal Era (University of California Press, 2018) and *Creative Composites: Modernism, Race, and the Stieglitz Circle* (University of California Press, 2012). She is currently at work on a project about whiteness and the visual culture of female suffrage.

ANA MARÍA LEÓN is Associate Professor of Architecture at the Harvard University Graduate School of Design. She is author of *Modernity for the Masses: Antonio Bonet's Dreams for Buenos Aires* (University of Texas Press, 2021) and *Bones of the Nation/A Ruin in Reverse* (ARQ, 2021).

FERNANDO LUIS MARTÍNEZ NESPRAL is Professor of Architectural History and researcher affiliated with the American Art and Aesthetic Studies Institute, both at the School of Architecture, Design, and Urbanism, Universidad de Buenos Aires. Currently, he is a member of several international associations, including the College Art Association, the Society of Architectural Historians, the Global Architectural History Teaching Collaborative, the European Architectural History Network, and Our North Is the South (cofounded with Ana María León).

PÍA MONTEALEGRE is Assistant Professor at the Instituto de Historia y Patrimonio, Universidad de Chile and member of the Gender, Space & Territory Studies Group. Her research focuses on urban and architectural history from a gender perspective.

SIERRA ROONEY is Assistant Professor of Art History at the University of Wisconsin-La Crosse, specializing in art of the United States, particularly commemorations of women and the politics of representation. She is joint editor with Jennifer Wingate and Harriet F. Senie of *Teachable Monuments: Using Public Art to Spark Dialogue and Confront Controversies* (Bloomsbury, 2021). Her writing has appeared in journals such as *Panorama*, *Public Art Dialogue*, *De Arte*, *Journal of Urban History*, and *Capitol Dome*, as well as the collections *Artists Reclaim the Commons* (University of Washington, 2013) and *Museums and Public Art?* (Cambridge Scholars, 2018).

VALENTINA ROZAS-KRAUSE is Assistant Professor in Design and Architecture at Universidad Adolfo Ibáñez in Chile and Harvard University Radcliffe Institute for Advanced Study Fellow (2023–24). She is the author of *Ni Tan Elefante, Ni Tan Blanco* (Ril, 2014) and the coedited volume *Disputar la Ciudad* (Bifurcaciones, 2018). These books join peer-reviewed articles in *History & Memory, e-flux, Latin American Perspectives, Memory Studies, Anos 90, ARQ, Revista 180, Cuadernos de Antropología Social,* and *Bifurcaciones* alongside chapters in *Golpes a la Memoria* (Tege, 2019) and *Neocolonialism and Built Heritage* (Routledge, 2020).

DANIELA SANDLER is Associate Professor of Architectural and Urban History at the School of Architecture and Planning at the University at Buffalo. She works on memory, preservation, grassroots urbanism, urban inequalities, and social inclusion. Her book *Counterpreservation: Architectural Decay in Berlin since 1989* (Cornell University Press, 2016) won the 2019 Antoinette Forrester Downing Book Award.

KIRK SAVAGE is the William S. Dietrich II Professor of History of Art and Architecture at the University of Pittsburgh. He is the author of *Standing Soldiers, Kneeling Slaves: Race, War, and Monument in Nineteenth-Century America* (Princeton, 2nd ed., 2018) and *Monument Wars: Washington, the National Mall, and the Transformation of the Memorial Landscape* (University of California Press, 2009).

ANDREW M. SHANKEN is Professor of Architectural History and the Director of American Studies at the University of California, Berkeley. He is the author of *194X: Architecture, Planning, and Consumer Culture on the American Homefront* (University of Minnesota Press, 2009) and *The Everyday Life of Memorials* (Zone Books, 2022).

SUSAN SLYOMOVICS is Distinguished Professor of Anthropology and Near Eastern Languages and Cultures at the University of California, Los Angeles. Her recent works involve coediting "L'inévitable prison/The Inevitable Prison" (*Année du Maghreb*, 2019) and editing "Historic Preservation in North Africa" (special issue of *Journal of North African Studies*, 2020). She is a Fellow at the Tangier American Legation in Morocco (TALIM) since 2020.

MARITA STURKEN is Professor in the Department of Media, Culture, and Communication at New York University, where she teaches courses in visual culture, cultural memory, and consumerism. She is the author of *Tangled Memories: The Vietnam War, the AIDS Epidemic, and the Politics of Remembering* (University of California Press, 1997), *Practices of Looking: An Introduction to Visual Culture*, with Lisa Cartwright (Oxford University Press, 3rd ed., 2018), *Tourists of History: Memory, Kitsch, and Consumerism from Oklahoma City to Ground Zero* (Duke University Press, 2007). Her most recent book is *Terrorism in American Memory: Memorials, Museums, and Architecture in the Post-9/11 Era* (New York University Press, 2022).

AMANDA SU is a PhD candidate in English at the University of California, Berkeley. Her dissertation explores how the cultural imaginary of Chinese womanhood served as an exemplum for both socialist and liberal feminisms during the Cold War. She also writes about memory activism and feminist interventions in the built environment. Her work has been published in the *Journal of Asian American Studies* and *ASAP/J.*

DELL UPTON is Distinguished Research Professor of Architectural History at the University of California, Los Angeles. His research focuses on architectural history, the Black cultural landscape, and statues and monuments since antiquity. He is the author, most recently, of *What Can and Can't Be Said: Race, Uplift, and Monument Building in the Contemporary South* (Yale, 2015) and *American Architecture: A Thematic History* (Oxford, 2019). Upton has been a Resident of the American Academy in Rome and Kress-Beinecke Professor at the Center for Advanced Study of the Visual Arts, National Gallery of Art.

NATHANIEL ROBERT WALKER is Associate Professor of Architectural History in the School of Architecture and Planning at the Catholic University of America. He recently published *Victorian Visions of Suburban Utopia: Abandoning Babylon* (Oxford, 2020) and coedited, with Elizabeth Darling, *Suffragette City: Women, Politics, and the Built Environment* (Routledge, 2019). He has also published essays in multiple journals, such as *Buildings and Landscapes, Utopian Studies, Arris,* and the *Journal of the Society of Architectural Historians.*

MECHTILD WIDRICH is Professor in the Art History, Theory and Criticism Department at the School of the Art Institute of Chicago. She researches and writes on art in public space, architecture, performative and participatory practices, and the theory of the public sphere. Her most recent book *Monumental Cares: Sites of History and Contemporary Art* (Manchester University Press, 2023) rethinks monument debates, site specificity, and art activism in light of challenges that strike us as monumental or overwhelming, such as war, migration, and the climate crisis. In 2022 she was guest professor at the University of Applied Arts Vienna, and 2022/23 Faculty Fellow at the Institute for Advanced Study at the University of Notre Dame.

.